Artemis Smith's
ODD GIRL *Revisited*
an autobiographical correlate

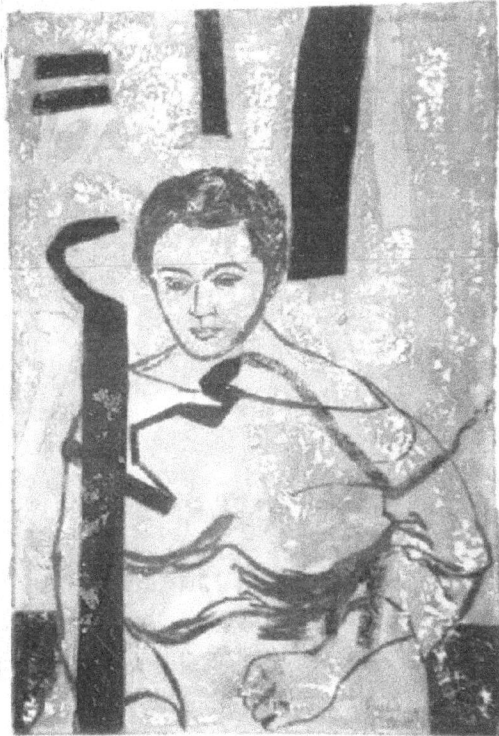

Portrait of Artemis Smith by Billie Taulman – 1955

containing the
unexpurgated original version
in an appendix

the
savant garde workshop
sag harbor . new york . usa

ArtemisSmith's ODD GIRL *Revisited*

To
Vilna Jorgen Morpurgo
Attilio Giacomo Morpurgo, M.D.
and
Billie Ann Taulman

"Odd Girl Revisited"
© 2010 by The Savant Garde Institute. All rights reserved.
ISBN 978-1-878998-30-9

Library of Congress Control No. 2010915235

'the savant garde workshop' publishers:
P.O. Box 1650 . Sag Harbor . NY 11963-0060 . USA

Since 1954 Artemis Smith has been a pen name for
BARONESS ANNSELM L.N.V. MORPURGO

This autobiographical correlate includes a graphic novel self-published in 1950 in **Appendix A** and reprints the unexpurgated manuscript version of *Odd Girl* titled "Anne Loves Beth" in **Appendix B.**

Persons seeking a multilevel reading experience should cross-reference this correlate with interactive material on the Internet accessible from www.ArtemisSmith.com

Dear Colleagues:

The work titled by my publishers *Odd Girl* (© 1959) and by me "Anne Loves Beth," while based upon real first-hand experiences which I enjoyed and lived through with adolescent abandon, was strictly a work of fiction.

Those of you who have read many of my works have come to realize that it is impossible to confuse me with any of my characters. It is the task of every accomplished fiction writer to always appear to be telling a true story.

But if it is authentically to be a work of art, the story must ring true -- the details must be seen as merely composites of various aspects of the author's vastly wider self -- or else, it would not be possible for the story to be written at all!

Who am I, what am I? *Really?*

Unlike my character Anne, who was sculpted as born of modest folk, my own roots are royal and my artistic ambitions are world-historical. On both sides of my family I come from a long line of movers and shakers, and from the start I was raised to take my rightful place among them.

3

If this sounds elitist and contemptuous, live with it!

It's time to call an end to the *rights* cult of the inept and the drug culture that has given rise to it. All true master-builders are natural-born aristocrats and this Jeffersonian ideal is open to anyone who has the *cohunes* to seriously apply.

This is how I have lived my life and wish to be remembered:

> *Don't limit me. I am neither "Gay/gay," nor "Lesbian/lesbian," neither male nor female but wholly unisex, unirace, gender-free.* [1]

Most importantly, I have never been a hack and I most emphatically never wrote "Anne Loves Beth" for hire to the pulp fiction trade. It was simply my first mass market offering, an early attempt at activist cultural change, and no establishment publisher would touch it.

All the more reason to get it into print. Give it to the yellow sheets if I must, but get the world-shaking message through!

Nearly sixty years later I still stand defiant, a cultural-guerrilla born of a long line of cultural-guerrillas – artists and philosophers all unisex and unirace, none of them decadent, all of them aristocrats.

To better know me you will have to read my web-interactive picture memoir, *PteroDARKtyl*. But here I will offer you a quick peek: at me, my family, my closest friends, and the intolerable socio-political climate that prompted the writing of *Odd Girl,* originally titled "Anne Loves Beth."

---

[1]   If you prefer, you can modernize this to read *post-ethnic, post-racial* and *post-gender* (not to be confused with *transgender*, a very opposite term which I do not endorse).

And be certain not to skip the footnotes![2]

Perhaps then you will understand why the work had to be written as a genuinely activist work of art, of cultural master-building; and why I, of political necessity, finally allowed the highly inferior first draft to be promoted throughout the gay activist community despite the existence of a more polished and mature version of the original manuscript - for it is unlikely that the finished manuscript, innocent as it was by modern standards, would ever have passed the censors back in the 1950's or '60's.

I completed the first draft of "Anne Loves Beth" known to lesbiana aficionados as *Odd Girl* in 1953. As previously said, the work was not strictly autobiographical. The places and characters are all composites, and like all my leading ladies, Anne -while encompassing many of my adolescent feelings and emotions - is not really anything like me. Nor is her family anything like mine: I was born in Rome, Italy, and chaotically raised in a palatial setting by Catholic servants - some of whom affectionately (and others not quite so fondly) referred to me as their *baronina*[3].

But this palazzo was only one of my homes.

Two years after I was born I had been left there in foster care at my recently-widowed American-born[4] sephardic freemason grandmother's house while my scandinavian mother, a well-known artist and journalist, was wrestling with her

---

[2] Would that the printed page could be as large and wide as a tabloid so that you might skim over a lot of it at once and focus on what you please!

[3] "Little Baroness"

[4] My grandmother Ida Morpurgo-Sierra-DeCastro Morpurgo was born in the USA, kin to Emma Lazarus. Most Morpurgos married cousins and were multiple-cousins, and their progeny were quasi-clones often dropping the surname in favor of paternal middle-names, e.g., Lazzaro, Lazard, Lazarus.

conscience, trying to decide whether to abandon me to an increasingly zionist household or snatch me away and take both me and my younger sister Helga back to Sweden with her.

Two years earlier there may have been confusion over which of Ida's sons, Aldo or Attilio, was my biological father and should be laying claim to me.

Vilna was temperamentally closer to my architect uncle Aldo who was collaborating with her on public monuments commissioned by Mussolini.

Aldo might have been Vilna's first choice, but as the oldest son expected to preserve the family name and fortune, he had been already engaged sight-unseen to my ashkinazi aunt Valentina D'Arton arriving from Cairo, half her lavish dowry already having been received and expended.[5] That had only left Aldo's younger brother Attilio, who was also dating Vilna and was also completely mesmerized by her Garboesque stature and her Isadora style.[6]

Valentina, an immensely intelligent, worldly and mature woman, had been raised in a Moslem state where polygamy and communal child-rearing was the norm. Given the situation, she was more than anxious to adopt me and raise me as her own, but she was also hell-bent on converting and taking the whole family back to Egypt for Jewish "repatriation" in the Palestinian "Promised Land." Vilna would also have been welcome, but she

---

[5] Or perhaps Vilna had simply decided to marry freemason Attilio, who was not circumcised, and did not want to be circumcised and become a Zionist, and who continued to be madly in love with her for the rest of his life. Whatever the reason, two years earlier Vilna had been pregnant and had to either marry or abort and, once married, had still remained uncertain about her future since she definitely had no intention of converting to Judaism.

[6] Vilna, three years older than Attilio, was a widow from a previous marriage most likely to the real great love of her life, a Norwegian named Jorgensen - but she never spoke of him until we were fully grown.

would have to convert along with Ida and Attilio, and both Aldo and Attilio would have to be circumcised so that the children would all be accepted as legitimate Jews.

Vilna totally recoiled.

A contract being a contract, Aldo and Ida stoically complied.

Attilio was split between loyalty to Vilna and loyalty to mother and brother. Vilna, furious with him, was threatening to divorce and leave one child behind. But which child? The Germanic blonde one claimed by Attilio who looked more like many Morpurgo Austrian cousins or the dark one, who looked more scandinavian but was claimed by Ida, Aldo and now also Valentina?

Vilna couldn't make up her mind.

Now came the clash between Vilna's scandinavian feminism and Valentina's increasingly imposed ashkinazi Traditionalist tyranny over the Roman Catholic servants at Ida's sephardic freemason household.

Vilna had named me after my grandfather Anselmo, whom she adored. He had just died before I was born and both Ida and Vilna wanted me to be raised to be just like him. I assumed that meant I was their son since I had never been explicitly told I was a girl until Valentina's son was born, when in the care of the servants I suffered an extreme shock of conflicting gender identity and a classic case of penis envy.

The servants, now also receiving advice from their parish priest as to how to properly raise two newly-baptized Catholic-Hebrews, had become thoroughly confused as to whose instructions they should obey and resorted to doing their best to persuade me that little girls were created *after* little boys and consequently were not as important in God's eyes as little boys and should accept their inferiority and lack of a penis.

Meanwhile Valentina, having been raised in Egypt and now speaking in either English or French or Italian, got most of what she meant lost in translation. Hypocritical linguistic conventions that gave lip service to the inferiority of women even while masking an inner dialogue of feminist contempt were by me taken literally. In truth it was the men in our household who were totally hen-pecked, but Valentina's chiding manner was most foreign and grotesque and to my three-year-old ears entirely enraging - as was the gender-rich Italian language which divided all the world's objects into the strong and the weak.

I was *not* anyone's girl-child, I was *not* inferior! *I* was the eldest, *I* was the stronger, *I* was the one to inherit and defend the Morpurgo name.

Valentina's bell-ringing by-the-book state of the art child-rearing (Pavlov was the new rage) didn't help either. Both I and Helga were soon reduced to tantrums and screams.

The servants were helpless, Ida was helpless, Aldo and Attilio were hiding. Vilna suddenly heard.

Sexual politics really may finally have decided the issue: our Viking mother, herself raised as gender-free, could not bear to abandon either infant to Valentina's newly-imposed now also Pavlovian Traditionalism or the servant's Roman-Catholicism.

No daughter of hers would *ever* be raised as inferior and subservient to any man. Hearing our cries and despising all Valentina's ways, Vilna angrily declared both of her children *hers* and snatched us back.[7]

---

[7] But this is putting things a little too simply. Vilna, as a teen-aged victim of a broken marriage, and as the eldest half-sister, had already raised two huge litters of siblings before she ran away from Sweden and Norway. She was demanding more servants be hired to take care of them. But money was now tight. Ida's staff was reduced to two spinster sisters who had raised Aldo and Attilio: Lucia who cooked all day, and overloaded Amabile who did everything else and came up short. (When we fled Italy they retired to their Tuscan home with all the family's centuries-old sephardic recipes as a parting gift from Ida which are now famous as *La Cucina Morpurgo de Nilma.*)

My artist-journalist mother had already lived a full life before she gave birth to me. She had danced with Nijinsky at the Royal Ballet of Sweden where Garbo had been a classmate. She had run away from both parents of a broken marriage at the age of sixteen and supported herself as a foreign correspondent on assignment from *Bonniers,* and by sculpting the portraits of many children of Norwegian, Swedish, Danish and Belgian royal families where her mother, a social butterfly and frequent "Lady in Waiting," had once presented her to the various monarchs, herself being a royal.

While in Oslo, Vilna had interviewed Trotsky and became fired with Bolshevism, then had trekked by caribou-sleigh and overland skis up through Finland and down by rail through Northern Russia and Czechoslovakia, all the way covering the ripples of the Revolution. En route she married fellow journalist, Karlssen Jorgensen, and they reached Prague, Berlin, then Paris where they lived on the Left Bank. Together they starved in the proverbial garret while he slowly wasted of TB. Supporting both of them with her writing, art work and professional dancing, Vilna performed the Tango and Flamenco[8] at classy Parisian night spots as part of a Spanish troupe and exhibited alongside the post-Impressionists in the famed street show known as the Paris *La Horde.*

At thirty and a grief-stricken widow, Vilna tagged along with the Spaniards to Barcelona and was simultaneously commissioned to cover and represent Norway in an international art exposition cancelled by the expectant outbreak of the Spanish Civil War.

Not staying for the action, she hitched a ride in one of the first airmail carriers and nearly crashed-landed in Rome where,

---

[8]   But she refused to dance the Apache because it was too demeaning to women!

thanks to both the Swedish and Norwegian Ambassadors, she immediately found work as a royal portrait sculptor[9] and Vatican restorer.

Exhibiting in galleries in Via Flaminia, she came to share a studio with Baroness Clarissa von Blumenthal, a Weimar post-Impressionist/Expressionist who taught Vilna, then mostly only a sculptor, to restore and paint like Rembrandt. At von Blumenthal's Vilna met my uncle Aldo and my father Attilio.

Prior to 1937, Aldo Morpurgo was Mussolini's favorite architect[10] and commissioned Vilna to work with him on a number of public projects. Either he or von Blumenthal introduced her to IL Duce.

But by 1937, Mussolini - anxious to imitate Hitler and bring Scandinavians into the Axis side - declared Vilna his favorite portrait artist and ordered her to do his bust with that of Hitler. Unable to refuse without risking the immediate arrest of her entire family, she fulfilled the commission then took a hammer and destroyed the work, declaring it artistically inferior and not suitable for showing.

By then she had decided to keep both of her children and stay married to Attilio and we were all desperately trying to get out of town.

---

[9] The Italian *Imperatrice* commissioned her to sculpt the royal children. Vilna's web page is at http://vilnajorgen.tripod.com/VilnaBio.html
[10] Richard Meier appears to refer to him as Franco Morpurgo, but that must be either a fascist redo or hyphenated signature, or Aldo's middle name.

Dear Colleagues:

Thanks to Vilna the entire family escaped the Holocaust and our side emigrated to the USA in June 1940, in one of the last two passenger ships allowed past the British blockade at Gibraltar. Vilna had a visa to represent Norway at the New York World's Fair and we were all set to jump ship once we got there - but at the last moment, due to the efforts of an American-Jewish lady later identified as Lillian Hellman, our immigration papers came through.

But now let me properly introduce my father, Baron-Doctor Attilio Morpurgo, who was a prominent physician and best friend and closest school chum of Enrico Fermi.[11]

---

[11] Fermi used to play with me when I was three and four and taught me how to judge distance and perspective in a mirror, declaring me a genius for comprehending the concept almost immediately.

"The Manhattan Project" c. 1943. Attilio is the little guy holding the pipe.

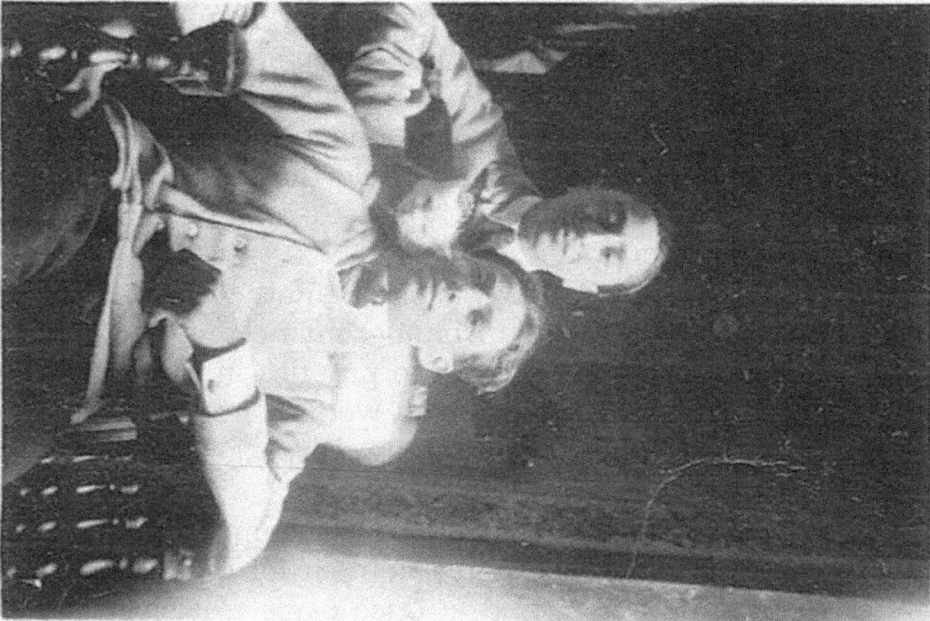

Attilio Giacomo Morpurgo and best friend and schoolchum, Enrico Fermi and our cat, Mimi.

Attilio was the only one of his classmates that did not think Fermi's hypotheses were completely far out and crazy.

When Fermi arrived in the U.S.A., the first place he stopped at was our apartment in NYC. From there, he went with Attilio to meet all of his colleagues at Welfare Island Hospital, and hired many of them for the Manhattan Project.

Attilio was left out, because Vilna was an artist with a promising career and refused to move out with him to the "sticks."

13

Attilio was the only one of his school chums who didn't think Fermi was retarded. That was why they grew up as best friends. They were very much alike, looked alike.[12]

Attilio was a very mild, gentle - some persons would say *feminine* man - but a top-notch internist and diagnostician who identified and successfully contained many diphtheria epidemics in fascist youth camps during his military service. This had won him fame and promotions until Mussolini fired him as an "Italian Jew." By then he held the post of *Assistente Primario* of the United Hospitals of Rome - a position comparable to Deputy Surgeon General.

But in the USA Attilio was just another dark-skinned not-very-Jewish Italian-Egyptian immigrant needing to go back to medical school to get his license to practice in New York. He spent his first year of internship at Welfare Island Hospital[13] either running the elevator or cutting up corpses with infectious diseases.[14]

Dr. Henry Kissinger happened to be an administrator there and this marked a fortuitous moment for many, for when Fermi arrived in the U.S.A. and at once came to visit Attilio in NYC, Attilio took Fermi to meet his colleagues at work, where

---

[12] When Fermi visited us c. 1942, he laughingly told us how it had taken the entire State Department to convince the Immigration authorities at Ellis not to send him back for failing an elementary intelligence test!

[13] Now called Roosevelt Island.

[14] All of this has important bearing on my own academic and political career in the late 1960's and early '70's when, upon new recommendation for a career post, my background in the civil rights movements collided with the Secret Service and with a maelstrom of forces unleashed by the infiltration of the FBI and CIA by the Mafia and the Noriega Drug Cartels, further infiltrating the R.O.T.C., under the tenure of then-CIA-head George H.W. Bush. Does it sound like a Salsa? Yes, it does. It should all make sense later!

Fermi and Kissinger very quietly recruited a sizeable portion of them for the super-secret "Manhattan Project."[15]

Fermi's arrival suddenly pushed my father very high up on the popularity scale, but because my artist mother had been labeled a security risk for once selling a sculpture to the Moscow Art Museum and was now getting too many rave reviews from *The Socialist Worker*, the result was catastrophic.

The Secret Service investigation *very secretly* taking place prior to the hiring of my father who had been recommended by Fermi to join, and perhaps even eventually lead the medical team, intimidated all the art critics, who were either secretly gay or secretly socialist, and devastated my mother's career.

It also left Attilio behind, rejected from all medical promotions, without any explanation from Fermi.[16] (And we never would have known any of this were it not for my attendance at Hunter College where many of Attilio's colleagues, all grateful to Attilio, had retired to cushy new posts in the 1960's!)[17]

Suddenly both of my parents' careers, at first so promising, came to a halt, no reason given. Our scant savings were by then totally depleted. We had to move to a tenement and starve on minimal public assistance with only an occasional sale of Vilna's paintings making a life-and-death difference.

---

[15] Attilio's page for cross-reference in my interlocking web memoir is directly accessible from http://vilnajorgen.tripod.com/Attilio.html.

[16] In a left-handed way that was probably a favor, considering what was happening to the Rosenbergs! Was that why Fermi never even so much as dared contact us again?

[17] Attilio's 1942 roommate - Michael Dacso, M.D., then 1966 Medical Dean of Albert Einstein Medical College - suddenly embraced me, a supposed total stranger applying for a writing job, planted a wet kiss on my cheek, and addressed me as *Annaselma*. Dacso's office was, strangely, inside the FBI building then situated across the street from Hunter College.

Later, when Attilio finally got his medical license, out of desperation we moved to the suburbs to seek out an Italian ghetto desperately in need of a caring and affordable doctor.

We moved into Corona, Queens just before Christmas sometime around 1943 or '44, and we had no food. Then a small miracle happened - there was a knock on the door and the local undertaker brought us a basket of liquor (which, as I recall, we later traded for food). Behind him came the owner of the Italian delicatessen, *Signior* Bindo, a local big shot, with two baskets of deli delights. I never saw so much welcome junk food: meats, cheeses, and chicken in cans with Henry VIII on the labels.[18] Other neighbors followed, bringing homemade pies and cookies. And the Bellaccico's also brought bread.

Everyone was anxious to meet the new italian-speaking family doctor. Despite the fact that we were Tuscans in the center of a Sicilian/Neapolitan divide, and that Attilio had to quickly learn all their dialects, it seems we had picked the right neighborhood after all.

Both of my parents were linguists fluent in more than eight languages. Having been born in Alexandria, Attilio spoke some Arabic as well as English, German, French, Italian, Spanish, Portuguese, Rumanian and Greek. So his practice quickly expanded from only impoverished distant relatives of notorious *Mafiosi* to every other ethnic group circling Corona: Irish, German, Greek, Armenian, and soon even the "black Muslims" of Flushing where he was the only physician who dared to make house calls - mostly on foot at first, for he didn't

---

[18] Rotisserie chickens were not in fashion in those days. Small pullets only came in large cans with oozing jellied gravy - but to us, then a delicacy!

have a driver's license or a car.[19]

Had it not been for my father's unique skill as a diagnostician, his inter-ethnic/inter-racial medical practice would never have survived the neighborhood. The dark-skinned Sicilians, Corsicans, Catanians, who had never been racists in the old country, were terrified of being identified and segregated as biracial and this caused the two communities, Muslim and Italian, to be openly at war. But our family was popular with everyone and as a ten-year-old I also played the violin and recited my poetry in many "colored" churches including the formerly segregated structure that still stands next to St. John the Divine.

One vivid childhood memory that deeply influenced my civil rights activism in later years happened when I listened in on a middle-of-the-night conversation between my father and mother. Usually they spoke in German so I wouldn't know what they were saying to each other. But this time it was either in Italian or English probably because they were so upset.

Attilio had returned from a house call to a prominent Italian family who begged him to sign a Caucasian death certificate for their 90-year old grandfather, once a negro slave, who had lived hidden in their attic for more than twenty years. The sun-starved pale old man had sat peering longingly from behind a shuttered window all those years while his progeny lived in fear lest they be exposed and bombed out of their

---

[19] Among the Flushing Muslims he was treated as a saint and became affectionately known as "de creepin' Jesus" because his knowledge of sickle cell anemia and other Mediterranean diseases worked slow but effective miracles on a group who could barely pay for any medical help at all. He also worked the same miracles on the Italian side of the tracks, but quietly.

home.[20]

Of course Attilio signed it, and his good deed may have inadvertently caused us to be placed on a special protected families list kept by a super-secret biracial faction of the Mafia. From then on, no matter what neighborhood we walked in, it seems there were people seeing to it that we were kept safe.[21]

Now everything got better.

The most powerful figure in the centuries-established Italian-American community into which our grandmother Ida and at least one of our great-grandfathers had been born, contacted and took personal note of us.

Dr. Armando Romano, Publisher of *Il Progresso,* invited us to dinner and brought us into the forefront by writing many reviews of Vilna's work and caused other Long Island newspapers to also take notice. And Vilna, meanwhile, had the family join *The Sons of Norway* who eagerly welcomed all of us and especially our physician father. We became multinational again and wider and wider press notices followed.

Before then, what had been good for my father's practice had been devastating for the rest of us.

My mother's paintings, once getting rave reviews from Howard Devree and other critics at the *New York Times,* had gotten nowhere past 1943 and our education at the local grammar school, P.S. 16, left much to be desired -although I was able to form a special bond talking with my homeroom teacher, Miss Eckhardt, as I scrambled to keep pace with her and as she rushed to avoid me even while throwing me words of

---

[20] On Junction Boulevard, a gaping hole in an empty lot where once a house had stood notoriously remained for years as a reminder to all "coloreds" never to cross the line into Corona.

[21] Something that may have saved my life in the 1960's when the Hoover dirty tricks squad may have tried to spread the lie that I was an FBI informant.

wisdom as we were walking home each day.[22]

My passion for Miss Eckhardt's mental stimulus drove me to seek ever further afield. From the age of ten I knew how to travel alone to Manhattan, and it only cost a nickel. Taking my younger sister with me, for our intellectual survival we escaped Corona, then Elmhurst by subway at every opportunity, at first without but soon later with our parents' ready consent - once I showed them that it was really possible for us to 'legally' change schools.

Pretending that we were victims of a broken home staying with Ida who was now living with Valentina and Aldo and their son Augusto on Lexington Avenue, we cheated on the Board of Ed' and each and every school-day, and most weekends too, subwayed ourselves out of the ghetto.[23]

Vilna meanwhile also learned from our example and pulled herself out of her depression, often took her paintings on the subway with us, and thereafter doggedly exhibited regularly in the Washington Square Outdoor Art Show.

The Village crowd brought new contacts. Vilna soon managed to get the entire family as a unit invited to Uptown émigré chamber music salons that included one hosted by a "White Russian Princess and former Valkyrean operatic diva." The Princess was sponsoring a magnificent Russian cellist - comparable to Pablo Casals - who had gotten trapped on this side of the Iron Curtain while on a concert tour through South America: Maestro Bogumil Sykora, who became Vilna's and

---

[22]   It never occurred to me until many *many* years later how strongly Billie Taulman resembled her in both appearance and manner. They were both Germanic school marms at heart!

[23]   I went to Beha Junior High School which was the only all-girl school in Manhattan. My Arista class was filled with brilliant women some of whom later became famous, including a couple of call girls.

Helga's cello teacher. And he brought his new second family[24] and South American friends along to Queens.

Now faculty and students from Julliard and Manhattan School of Music began to visit our own Friday-night musical soirees - at our new house in Elmhurst - and our circle of displaced persons grew to include many famous writers, artists and musicians anxious to trade private lessons for medical advice while clawing their way back up the ladder of success.

Again world-class celebrities were coming to *our* house, not yet exactly a palazzo but nevertheless *our* house no matter how humble and situated under the 'El where every time the trains went by the conversation had to pause![25]

Toscanini's chosen successor at the Metropolitan Opera, Renato Cellini, came often, as did his budding divas some of whom were my classmates at Forest Hills High School.

Dimitri Mitropoulos came once and touched our Chopin-vintage rectangular grand piano, probably only to buy it.

There were frequent performers who formed quartets and quintets for regular practice every Friday night: pianist-composer Julian White, oboist Harry Vas Dias, cellist Igor Horoshevsky, music teachers Cesare and Marjorie Borgia, the Kabay Ao siblings Gilopez and Marcellita who were debuting at Carnegie Hall.

---

[24] His Russian family, already fully grown, remained in Russia, but he had a small baby with one of his students in the USA and, at 75, was again a father.

[25] The Morpurgo Family is at least ten centuries old and has palazzos and castles in numerous locations in Europe. Our direct branch, situated in both Trieste and Venice, founded Generali A.G., whose Venetian corporate headquarters situated on the famous Piazza belonged to Giuseppe Lazzaro Morpurgo, undoubtedly a descendant of the proverbial Merchant of Venice. (As I told Lillian Hellman in the 1960's, when the Rothschilds were still peddling antiques on the streets of Paris, the Morpurgos were already wealthy bankers and financiers.)

My maestro, Edmund Zygman, Emeritus Conductor of the Philadelphia Philharmonic, usually conducted and brought his good friend, Arthur Balsam who consented to accompany and introduce Gilopez at Carnegie. And thanks to the Julliard students who were hoping to fix me up with him, I also got to meet my idol, child prodigy Ruggiero Ricci who was only a little older than I. But he was too shy to ask me on a date and we just shook hands and smiled at each other.

And that's how we survived our childhood![26]

---

[26] Do I resent any of it? No, I take Joy in having been displaced from the decadent life I would have been subjected to had we grown up in a Donna Reed neighborhood with a Donna Reed family. I am *very serious* when I say this: we Vikings know better; facing and overcoming the challenge of Adversity is the *only* road to Valhalla!

Vilna Jorgen 1938, photo staged by Vilna and snapped by four-year-old Annaselma. Vilna had danced with Nijinsky at the Royal Ballet of Sweden where Garbo was a classmate.

Dear Colleagues:

Have I rambled on too long? So what!

Too many footnotes? To blazes with that! They form a separate volume by themselves - read them later!

Go straight to **Appendix B** if all you really want is to read a classic pulp novel for your Gay Studies assignment! The beauty of a printed book is that you can always leaf through the pages, pick what you want, and go back to the other parts later.

Disappointed in me? Deal with it! I've had it up to here with trying to get through to Ghetto-Gays! Grow up - look at the bigger picture - really come out of the closet and just be gender-free like me because times are changing again and you had better change with them!

For the rest of you, I promise I will not stop, I will continue, for this epistle has now become a hard-copy time capsule for some future cyborg, scanning through the zillions of information bits that may have scattered like shrapnel in today's information explosion, to catalog for a new species of *Munhood* to rediscover. It will resurface at a time when its relevance to a restyled culture seems more certain.

You may think I may have already told you a great deal about myself, perhaps too much, but in reality I have only scratched the surface.

A multitude of facts, and important persons, have been left out because I am not a journalist. One reason I waited this long to write about my own life has been because I have a real problem both about preserving other people's secrets and about destroying the Rights Movements if I had said too much too soon.

I had to wait until many *many* persons had died so their lives would not be affected even by indirect insinuation. And even after they died, there remain things that, if I had been a priest receiving Confession, I would never *ever* allow myself to reveal.

That's why I have always turned to fiction as a means of telling the truth from a perspective that does not violate any particular person. Fiction deals with the generic rather than the particular - unless it's a "nonfiction novel" which I personally think is an atrocious fad, often doing extreme violence against the private person.[27]

There is no such thing as "nonfiction."

All facts are corrupted by the observer.

Inter-subjectivity is the best we can hope for, and that too is shaky.

The whole purpose of seeking "Aesthetic Truth" is for us to scratch well below the surface, to seek out the universal in the particular. Exploitation of any human being by the true artist is forbidden. The individual's right to privacy *always* needs to be respected. It doesn't matter whether that person may be living or dead, good or evil - their *name*, their *being*, and their *person*

---

[27] Capote, though he himself made good use of it, should never have left the genre for posterity to bastardize!

should be protected as Sacred - not because we need to believe in any god, but because we need to love and respect and approach *all* Humanity with humility.

It is with humility that I hope I am finally breaking my silence.

The only aesthetic rule I have been able to come up with for the necessary telling of my personal story - for not to tell it may do even more serious injury to Feminist and Gay and Arts histories as someday gathered up by cyborg search engines - is to reveal only those insights and events that will *do no harm* because not revealing them would do a greater harm and disservice to the very persons I cannot avoid including in this narrative.

I must be both artist and physician.

But communicating in real-time does not allow me enough breadth to encompass the full symphonic background of my thought. In my rush to inform, but not overload, I failed to provide sufficient context for the proper interpretation of many relevant early events and motivations.

Let me now go back and close some of the gaps:

Let's go back to 1933 while I was still gestating in my mother's womb. Vilna had been widowed for about three years but had never bothered to get a Parisian death certificate. To the world she was still married to Jorgensen; and especially to the Vatican - which required documentation of widowhood before allowing any new marriage certificate to be issued. Yet here she was, pregnant, and apparently by then very much in love, or so she said, to Attilio.

It would have been very easy, and not questioned by anyone, for her to say Jorgensen was my father, thereby bestowing upon me full 'Nordic-Aryan' genealogy. Why then marry an Italian Jew when, in Prague, Berlin, Paris and now Rome as artist and journalist she had already been personally

Rome 1937 Gallery on Via Flaminia. What a pity a front view of this work is not shown for it was a masterpiece of Scandinavian Expressionism. The commission was to sculpt both Hitler and Mussolini, and each had one sitting with Vilna after which she blended their profiles into one warped and lifeless decapitated whole held aloft from the grave by a fallen people. After documenting that she had indeed fulfilled the commission, Vilna took a hammer and destroyed it, prudently declaring the work unfit to be shown. Meanwhile, we desperately hastened all of our preparations to get out of town.

26

introduced to the "Nazi Elite" and knew exactly what kind of murdering scum were now at our door?

There she was, thirty-three and with her biological clock fast running out and still undecided whether or not it would be wiser to abort, still financially dependent upon commissions from Mussolini,[28] still rooming with von Blumenthal who painted her angrily as a new Lola Montez even while lecturing her in caustic German about how stupid and politically unrealistic Vilna's marriage to Attilio would be.[29]

Was von Blumenthal a lesbian?

Your guess is as good as mine. My feeling is that as a true artist she was simply post-gender.

Did Vilna have an affair with her?

Possibly but unlikely. Scandinavian women are fiercely bisexual, preferring political lesbianism, sexual self-sufficiency to any subordination to the male sex. But not when admiring men are plentiful and Vilna was much in demand, not only by Aldo and Attillio but also all the single Scandinavian ambassadors who were attempting to duel with Attilio over her with bottles of Vodka until Vilna put a stop to

---

[28]   Aldo and Vilna were already collaborating on architectural plans, still preserved among my papers, for a massive Arts Complex Mussolini had initially commissioned them to build. Vilna had already sculpted the building and grounds to be situated on a Roman hill and I remember seeing the model at our apartment c. 1938. The project was dropped sometime after 1937 when Hitler told Mussolini to fire Aldo and Attilio and all other Italian Jews.

[29]   It may be quite possible that Aldo never had an affair with Vilna, since she was a chain smoker and he, like I, could not stand or go near avid smokers. Attilio, on the other hand, smoked a pipe defensively and didn't seem to mind. It is not uncommon for genes to cross between siblings, and that might be the only reason why I fortunately resemble Aldo, the prettier one, more than I do Roman-nosed Attilio. Helga resembles Attilio but blonde hair and blue eyes makes all the difference!

1965 Photo of Artemis Smith by Artemis Smith below the 1933 portrait of Vilna Jorgen painted by Weimar Post-Impressionist Clarissa von Blumenthal.

Never did Attilio dare look at another woman in her presence. When dating Italians whose eyes wandered out of habit, Vilna would angrily use the back of their hands as an ashtray. That was the scandinavian way and Attilio loved every bit of it. So did my uncle. So did every Italian she dated. As for the other nationalities she might have dined with - they all had better manners and did not need to be thus disciplined.

But as to the question of her possible political lesbianism, a long pause for a most memorable footnote to this must follow![30]

It was not by Vilna's choice that she set me aside.
Jorgensen's death certificate finally arrived from France only two days before I was born and my parents could finally be free to marry. The fascists had been throwing red tape in the way and it finally had to be expedited by the Vatican which won a promise from Protestant Vilna that she would baptize and raise me a Catholic, and by then Vilna had long ago decided to

---

[30] When, during my "Anne Loves Beth" days I took a middle-aged friend suffering from a menopausal depression to Queens with me to stay overnight at my house so my father could provide her with extensive free medical attention, the following interesting conversation took place when I was alone with my mother: Said Vilna after a long silence, "D---- is a very nice girl." "Yes, Mother," I replied. After another pause, Vilna said: "A little masculine, though, don't you think?" "I suppose so," I shrugged. Again a pause. "She looks like a lesbian, doesn't she?" "Maybe" Again a pause. "Is she a lesbian?" "Yes, I think so," I said. "Do you know many lesbians?" "A few." "Have you been with a lesbian?" "Once or twice." And now a really long pause, after which, a sigh: "Well, as long as you don't make a habit of it."

cast her lot with adoring Freemason Attilio for better or worse.

For the first fifteen months of my infancy while working away at her canvases and sculptures my mother gave me all of her attention.

She took breaks and nursed me, spoke to me, played with me - I remember it all even though she spoke so many languages to me that I couldn't grasp a single word. So did both Aldo and Attilio play and hug and speak to me, and in so many languages that I couldn't grasp a single word they said either. Nor the words of my English and French-speaking grandmother!

My father's colleagues were giving me repeated nonverbal intelligence tests - the round pegs in the round holes variety - which I passed with record speed. Aldo was folding origami forms for me and I was imitating him. Fermi was testing my comprehension of mirror optics with delight.

But I was still without language.

Everyone was beginning to despair that there might be something wrong with me. Then, on a momentous occasion Ida reported that I finally uttered a very long and complicated sentence in what must have sounded much like Esperanto, and the mystery was solved.

From then on, everyone spoke only Italian to me and thanks to a tutor - an impoverished cousin on her way to Switzerland hired by Ida as part-time governess - I learned to read and write, add and subtract, before I was four. But I remained a parallel thinker, holding multiple hypotheses, working on everything at once like a media-blitzed geek. To this day there's still nothing linear about me.

As I have said, my song is a symphony.[31]

---

[31] I despise conversing in foreign languages, though I do read a few. I prefer instead to be a poet, and to use English well to make it the new global speak because Chinese is too complicated. However, when I went through Europe in 1962, I spoke DannyKaye-Dutch wherever I went and everyone understood.

So from 1936 on, no one can say my early childhood was deprived. I was the promising awaited-for new *Mozart* or *Leonardo* everyone fought over and laid claim to. (*But too bad she was born a girl,* everyone would add.) Even my aunt Valentina, herself a Chess Master in Egypt, didn't give a damn whose child I was - as a Morpurgo genetic asset, to grow up with and breed more Morpurgo male prodigies, next to her own son I was also the star of the show.

My mother was the only one who had always really cared about me as a person, an extension of herself, not as a genealogical *wunderkind.* But for a brief time in 1935, right after my sister Helga was born, there was a gap.

An inexplicable thing happened in the Tyrolean Alps where my father, drafted into military service, had quarantined himself inside a fascist youth camp to prevent a general outbreak of diphtheria.

There were no cell phones in those days. It took time to send a message either by radio or whatever.

Vilna had been left stranded on a mountain top with only me and my seriously ill infant sister and no servants to assist her. We were in a small cabin surrounded by a precipitous drop on three sides. When playing outside, I had to be harnessed on a long chain like a dog for my own safety.

(My only memory of that period is of reaching out but not grabbing the udders of a goat as a tinkling Alpine herd went by. Or maybe I also do remember someone finally giving me some milk and berries).

Vilna was also very ill, or maybe she had just given birth unattended. She had always had pernicious anemia and anorexia but she was also suffering from heavy metal poisoning - lead, cadmium, chromium - from all the paints in her palette. When she worked she would forget to eat and slip ever more deeply into a creative trance and, being hungry, would begin sucking absently on her paint brushes because the metals tasted sweet.

Not a very good thing for a lactating mom!

Not a good thing at any time![32]

On top of that mountain Vilna suffered some kind of lapse of mind - not because she was insane, just poisoned and chronically malnourished.

Like Van Gogh possibly, but fortunately not quite as bad.

Something happened that early spring or summer in the Alps in 1935 and Vilna couldn't explain it but throughout her life she would go back to trying to explain herself, to apologize to me. She repeatedly related the event to me as follows:

> "I can't believe what a good child you were even though I had to tie you to the house to keep you from falling down the mountain. You played quietly by yourself and found things to do and never cried. And I feel so guilty for neglecting you - I did not want to neglect you - your sister was just so sick and I was just so exhausted and anemic, and had no servants to help me, and I don't even know how I managed to save Helga's life since she was allergic to my milk and I couldn't breast feed her. I can't remember more than that except that I somehow made a puree of beef and vegetables for her and she eventually got better."[33]

---

[32] Attilio didn't notice until the telltale black lines of lead poisoning showed on Vilna's gums - but that was later. There was a chelating treatment for that, but not for the anemia. It had gone on too long. There was nerve damage, not all of it reversible.

[33] The story is bizarre and lends itself to another interpretation, offered - then finally rejected - by Lillian Hellman in the 1960's, when she first sought me out, then my sister Helga, still in search of Julia's child, the lost Rothschild heiress. Did my infant sister die and did Vilna go into post partum? Did someone sneak another baby in the crib? Possible but not credible - Helga strongly resembles both sides of the family.

Every time my mother recited her guilty confession through the years I tried to tell her that she had never neglected me - that she was the best mother I could possibly have had. That I completely understood all the suffering she had undergone. But when she tried to hug me I could scarcely ever allow it. Her emotional need for me was too great, and it would have destroyed me. And her mind, her insights, though unique and astounding, would sometimes twist and become temporarily impossible to reason with. But given time to reflect on it, reason would finally prevail to a degree often matching or surpassing Attilio.[34]

It's so complicated.

Vilna was my first love, and as my mother she had a right to be. But we had problems.

I remember that when she finally reclaimed me, she took me back in bed to nap with her to try to make up for all the hugging I had missed in the year or two she couldn't be with me, and of course I reacted as any small child would and sought her breast, whereupon she, in sudden shock and fear pushed me away saying "No, you are too old for that now and it was

---

[34] After that, I never met Helga until I was put into the same baby carriage with her and returned to my parents' apartment on Via Vasari. She was then more than a merely healthy infant, but still a cry baby. Her facial features are those of Attilio, and all our cousins agree that she looks like their cousins and is definitely a Morpurgo child despite Hellman's suspicions to the contrary. Helga doesn't want me to write about her so I will keep my notes to a minimum. But some things need to be said. Helga grew up blaming Vilna for all of her problems and those of Attilio, but that was totally misguided. Instead of opposing Vilna's confusions, Helga always humored her and that caused Vilna to lose her way. I always fought with Vilna and told her exactly when and how she was doing something wrong - especially in her art work. She loved me for it, depended on me for it. When I left to live on my own, Vilna obsessed over my absence and Helga resented that and blamed me for abandoning her to Vilna. She has always felt closer to Attilio.

because I breast fed you that I am now losing my teeth." Whereupon, devastated but comprehending, I took the rejection as final and kept my distance.

There could never be a going back.

Throughout my life I wanted desperately to hug my mother - but there were also other gut reasons why I couldn't approach her.

At the risk of sounding evasive or wacky, to hell with blaming it all on the Nazis and Fascists - as a small child affected only by the intense fear generated in that period, I distanced myself from the stench of fear like a small dog trying to find a corner of the room where I could turn my nose to the wall.

Dirty Jews they called us. With good reason. We stank. And the stench of chain-smoking Jews was the worst. Not only chain-smoking Jews but my non-Jewish mother too. The horrible mix of tobacco-saturated fear constantly assailed my supersensitive nostrils.

 A chemical reaction, not a psychological one.

So there you have it - put the blame for all of my family's dysfunctions squarely where it lies - on the tobacco industry; for as all of the grownup events were unfolding, I remember spending my entire childhood distancing myself from my parents, gasping for clean air.

Not only then but later.

Elusive as it sounds, their chain-smoking was the whole reason for my running away from my parents as soon as I could get away. I couldn't live with the stench and the smog, and when my parents finally listened and quit the foul habit in the 1960's, I was finally able to spend more time with them.

Dear Colleagues:

1949.

At fifteen and now living in Elmhurst as a Forest Hills High School sophomore,[35] I had won an acting scholarship to the famed *Midtown Drama Center* directed by Natalie Donnet where George Bartenieff[36] was a classmate and his mother, Irmgarde Bartenieff, was my dance teacher.

I used that backdrop for my opening scene in "Anne Loves Beth" but I swear to you that I never *ever* had a crush on Natalie who was smoking and eight months pregnant at the time!

My mind by then was on many *many* other things.

With Vilna, Attilio, Aldo and Fermi as my role models, my

---

[35]   When Ida, Aldo and Valentina moved to an upper-class Jewish neighborhood, we enrolled in Forest Hills High School where nearly all of my Depression-era teachers had doctorates and many of my classmates went on to fame and fortune. It was grad-school-level education.

[36]   I dated George's older brother Igor once but that went nowhere because he smoked.

scientific, artistic,[37] literary and acting careers were all taking off simultaneously and the time for childhood crushes on either mother or father figures had already long passed.

Distinctly with career in mind I connected with two vastly different new mentors: Sidney E. Porcelain of the Jeanne Hale Literary Agency and John Burgess Hillsbury, my acting coach.

Neither was the first to shape me, for I had already gone through quite a few mentors and maestros prior to them and found others after them, but they were the right coaches for that time in my life.[38]

Burgess was unbending, an exacting task master; in a few short weeks he totally transformed me from a chubby unkempt tomboy first to a *Miss Piggy* and later to a full-blown *Barbie*, dressing me up like the Ziegfeld dolls he made for a living on the side which are now worth a small fortune.

Burgess put himself and me on a diet, coached me to walk and talk like ivy league debutante and stylized me for Shakespeare, Broadway and teen photo shoots. He got me to trade my sneakers for spiked heels, to die my long auburn hair a blazing topaz and to pound the pavement on rounds for both of us to all the talent agencies. Together we auditioned howbeit unsuccessfully to the Actors' Studio and just about everywhere else as my own list of theatrical contacts grew. Though aging, he had looked like an Elvis or a young Orson Welles.

---

[37] I was initially preparing to become a medical doctor or a physicist or a mathematician, but at post-puberty I finally chose the arts. I think my hormones had a lot to do with that.

[38] My first literary mentor, and first crush, David Gillerlean, was a tall, dark-Irish English teacher who spent his entire summer vacation procrastinating on his own try for a Pulitzer by teaching me gratis how to analyze poetry and prose while his wife and daughter tolerated my precocious pre-teen intrusion. If he had not been already married, I would have run away with him in a heartbeat!

But he smoked like Vilna.[39]

Porcelain was a nonsmoker, and I really preferred writing to acting so he became my most frequent side-kick.

Handsomer than either Bob Hope or Phil Silvers, Porcelain was cut out of the same cloth, many-talented, always ready with a joke. He had run away from home while in his early teens to join the Army at the beginning of World War II, where he was given an I.Q. test and was immediately pulled out of the ranks and shoved into Officers' Training School then into Military Intelligence - even while he continued to entertain his fellow troops with his singing, piano playing and composing.

After the war, he got a scholarship to Columbia, all the way to a Masters' in English with a minor in Communications and ended up teaching English there as an adjunct, if I remember correctly.

Porcelain and I were so much alike that when we first met I at once decided I would marry him. But he was twenty years older and I quickly reconsidered. Still, we told everyone we were engaged - so they would stop thinking we were secretly having an affair.

The mock engagement kept me from becoming "compromised" in my anxious father's eyes, whose position in the moralistic Italian community was growing sensitive now that I was fast-becoming such an artistic Lolita. It also kept all of Porcelain's transient house guests, usually sex-hungry prison parolees angling to become the next Spillane, away from me.

---

[39] I did not realize myself what kind of swan I had become. No longer always in the shadow of Helga's blonde and blue-eyed accompanyment, I now found myself surrounded by a crowd of suitors, mostly from N.Y.U., who later became architects, engineers, famous journalists - and none of whom could tempt me - even by dangling marriage - to give up my virginity before I turned eighteen.

Porcelain encouraged me to submit my plays for professional readings at Ray Yates' *Dramatists' Forum* and there I met many professionals and started my own drama workshop; at sixteen and about to graduate high school, I became an overnight regular on Washington Square, the youngest member and favorite protégé of the *Forum,* directing the reading of my plays while also appearing in the Chorus at the original Amato Opera on Bleecker and at the Gilbert and Sullivan Provincetown Players on McDougal.[40]

Porcelain, like most highly creative persons I have known, had a racy sense of humor. Though he never used four-letter words his outlandish puns often shocked the eavesdroppers in the crowd. Nothing and no one was safe from his wit. I wonder how Anita Hill would have reacted to him rather than to Clarence Thomas! In the 1950's it was very cool to talk dirty.

With that kind of open attitude, it was easy to make Porcelain my sounding board for all the works I did not want to immediately show my parents, including "Anne Loves Beth."[41]

---

[40]   A couple of years later in my professional spare time as an advertising executive, out of sheer love and respect for the artistry of Judith Malina and Julian Beck I also swept floors, collected contributions and eventually did bit parts for *The Living Theater* in a play by Paul Goodman where just about every fourth word was a four-letter word. But alas, not while they were still at the Cherry Lane where they had done Stein, Jarry and Picasso.

[41]   Porcelain seemed to know just about everything about just about everyone. It was even rumored that he had been part of the formative CIA If so, then he was definitely more like a superhero acting as double-agent, always on the side of Truth, Justice and the *Real* American Way. Most of his life he lived in frugal, nearly abject poverty. When I first met him, before he moved to a brownstone studio off Union Square, he was sleeping in a Midtown closet-sized office that you could barely crawl into because it was stuffed with manuscripts, sheet music and a piano - and there was no floor space - to play the piano he had to sit on the bed.

Dear Colleagues:

I have a confession to make: "Anne Loves Beth" reprinted here in ***Appendix B*** was not my first novel. Nor was it my first offering as a budding cultural revolutionary and master-builder. Bear with me - you really do want to know what a fifteen-year-old virgin high school student does with her spare time after she gets through with her homework:

It must have been around 1950 when McCarthyism began and a number of my teachers - some of the nicest ones - were suddenly fired as former Communists/communists or whatever, mostly for being New Dealers or open members, advocates or defenders of the Socialist Workers' Party.

At Forest Hills the infamous Loyalty Oath had become a prerequisite for a high school diploma, and many Jewish students, sensitive to its future implications, refused to sign it.

A Loyalty Oath was also a prerequisite for remaining a naturalized citizen and I had no problem with loving the U.S.A. and saluting the American Flag and defending the U.S. Constitution.

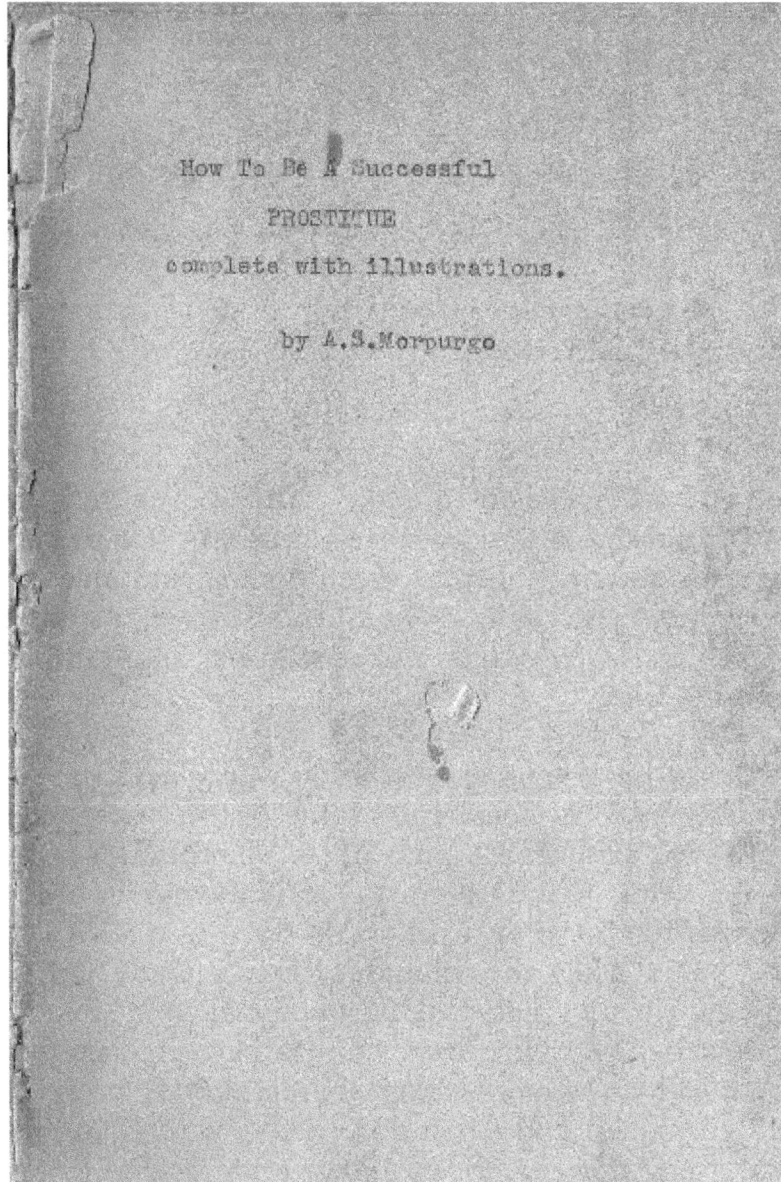

How To Be A Successful

PROSTITUE

complete with illustrations.

by A.S.Morpurgo

But obviously McCarthyism was decidedly un-American.

That presented me with a dilemma for it personally would have required a greater sacrifice on my part to defend Truth, Justice, and the *Real* American Way than anyone born here.

Though inwardly a super hero, I dared not get involved.

I stood apart, prudently silent.

But I nevertheless felt I needed to take some kind of stand with my classmates, to speak out against the system in some form that would also get *me*, an honor student, into serious trouble - perhaps even expelled.

I found my own way.

Witness my first political manifesto in **Appendix A** secretly preserved all these years thanks to Vilna. I just found it tucked away neatly when finally going through her papers.[42]

My apologies for all the misspellings.

I produced the work on my portable typewriter, printed on yellow pulp layered with about eight carbons. I typed it about three times, ending up with a limited edition of about 27 copies, redrawing the cartoons freehand for each batch. Then I folded and stapled each pamphlet and delivered it personally to each of my teachers.

Alas, the work was immensely well-received.

The Assistant Principal, Rene Fulton, who deserves to be commended and immortalized for her wit and perception, called me into her office and instead of expelling me, offered me a full scholarship to Bennington!

---

[42] This was also my high school payback for an earlier experience in grammar school when, upon being prompted by my classmates to draw anatomically correct pictures of Adam and Eve, I was ratted on and forced to apologize to the entire class for prematurely contributing to their sex education.

Fulton was a statuesque brilliant older woman who looked a lot like Alexis Smith and I wanted so much to say *yes, yes* to her, *yes* to an ivy league girls' school - but a panic suddenly took hold of me.

I blurted out that I did not want to go to any women's college because I had already been to an all-girl junior high school and I did not want to grow up a lesbian!

In my heart, however, I suddenly realized precisely why I was afraid. And again, in my own way, I decided to face down my fear.

Next came "Anne Loves Beth."

Here then, reprinted for posterity in **Appendix A**,[43] is what my teenage *angst* should reveal about me.

Go there now. *Enjoy!*

---

[43] If you are reading an E-Book Edition that does not include the Appendices, you will find this one available for online reading and downloading at http://larsennilsenvinje.tripod.com/Pro1.html You will also find more notes and drafts on my life there, since I have been using those webpages as my preliminary sketch pad for this volume.

Dear Colleagues:

"Class of 1951."

Thank you, Rene Fulton! I graduated high school with honors and a full Regents scholarship but I didn't feel the need for college. Forest Hills had the highest academic rating in New York State thanks to all the Ph. D's on their faculty that they were now firing.

I had already been to college, and grad school too. I was ready for my life now. The only thing I felt the need for was fresh air, to be able to breathe fresh air as quickly as possible, to get away from the stench of tobacco at my house which my sister didn't seem to mind at all.[44]

---

[44] Helga apparently never forgave me for not taking her with me. She wanted to move into Manhattan too. She had always clung to me since infancy and could never understand why I didn't feel as close to her as she to me. But our minds and abilities were totally different. I had always found it impossible to work with her - we would never see eye-to-eye and would always end up quarreling. We had little in common. Besides, she was a blonde - what romantic chance would I have had with her tagging along?

My mother and I were constantly at odds - not because we didn't love each other but because we loved each other too much.   Vilna saw me as her clone, and I also saw me as her clone, and *I* certainly couldn't survive being that creatively close to her. I had to break out on my own.

I firmly announced to both parents that it was now time for me to move out of the house and live by myself. There was no future for me in *any* Queens ghetto, and my career was already on its way. My two mentors were also making it easy for me. Burgess was moving in with retired Chicago theater critic Robert Garland[45] and had given me his low-rent 10 x 18 professional hole-in-the-wall on Park Avenue South which was coming down in a year or two but so what; *plus* there was an opening, and Porcelain had recommended me, as an assistant at the Jeanne Hale Literary Agency - my first paying job.
Enough said! *Basta! Finito!*
Vilna, though she desperately wanted me at home, unselfishly approved.[46]
Attilio hesitantly consented.

I moved out, "engaged," emancipated, and all set to do exactly as I pleased and decided, like my graphic protagonist, that I would not become a lesbian - at least not right away. Instead I would start dutifully dating men more seriously, nonsmoking men, and see where that took me.
It would be more than another year before I decided to

---

[45]   Of William Randolph Hearst and *Citizen Kane* fame. I had frequent talks with Garland but got little information on anything important.
[46]   This was exactly what Vilna had done at sixteen. And my graphic novel matched her first satirical journal, all about her Left Bank life in Paris, published by the Scandinavian press.

indulge my curiosity and investigate women, nonsmoking women, and of course had to write about it.

Despite its precarious marketability, both Porcelain and Jeanne Hale were encouraging me to finish "Anne Loves Beth" as a valid work that would eventually find a publisher.

Hale, who owned *Golden* Books and half of E.M. Hale and Company - the Midwest classroom textbook giant - was pushing the system toward early sex education in the schools and even had the hope that in fifty years or so my book might become a classroom standard.[47]

"Anne Loves Beth" filled a special need: no guidebook existed to assist the young in avoiding the hurdles of an illicit society almost wholly dependent upon an organized-crime network for its existence.

Written by a teenager, for other teens, it had the potential to be such a guidebook for the deviant young, to help them navigate away from deranged predators and toward some measure of normalcy - to be presented from a viewpoint that spoke directly to the sexually confused in a manner they could relate to and accept.

But the market wasn't ready for it in 1953 and by 1957 time was growing short - the civil rights movements were starting and someone else was bound to come out with a similar work before me. I had the opportunity to sell it to Beacon Books. It would not be in hard cover but it might get noticed anyway. It was a desperate but essential move.

---

[47] Jean Karl, immediately later head of American Library Association, was one of the first persons to review the pulp version when it came out circa 1957. She was kind enough to make dinner for me and Taulman - *twice*, since to my deep chagrin I had forgotten all about her first invitation. Karl was instrumental in seeing to it that *Odd Girl* was gradually put on public library bookshelves nationwide. Thank you, Jean Karl, most courageous Librarian!

Hale agreed but Porcelain didn't, so I switched agents from Porcelain to Hale and rushed to publish in the yellow sheets even as I continued to revise and polish the work which represented my adolescent tour of the 1950-52 NYC bar scene while I was concurrently studying, writing, acting and directing - and dating mostly nonsmoking men, in those days an endangered species![48]

Turning to the pulps was again an act of rebellion.

I didn't give a damn if the theme and its racy presentation would tweak the noses of the ultra-conservative publishing establishment.

Hale, herself a cultural revolutionary, agreed.[49]

Despite the fact that Beacon Books (Universal Publishing and Distributing Corp.), was a publisher of last resort, and that the book that was finally published was not the final author-approved version, I still maintain that I made the right choice not to wait.

But now let my own version be on record: "Anne Loves Beth" is the restored and proper fictionalized NYC tourist guide as it was originally intended by me. I make no apology for its

---

[48] My poetry, other novels and plays, including *Hark the Pterodactyl, The Peacock Has Ugly Feet, Brother Thanatos,* and *Testament of Sarah,* being worked on simultaneously, were of the existentialist genre reinforced by my 1962 trip to Europe where, thanks to Isadora's brother Raymond Duncan, I gained a most precious interview with Alice Toklas that left me blessed with an immortal wound.

[49] It is foolish to believe that pulp fiction can be kept out of the hands of minors. I got my first glimpse of the genre at eleven, browsing in the back of my local candy store. It was the confusion generated by such false portrayals of sexual reality that prompted my adolescent resolve not to disinform. (But it was there that I also later purchased my first issue of *One Magazine* and through it happily connected to One, Inc. and Mattachine.)

radical viewpoint. I meant it to strike a literary death blow to the system not because I identified myself as "Gay" but because at that time feminism was tied to political lesbianism.

The entire system was rotten, everything had to change - all at once - come what may!

By then I was partnered with Billie Ann Taulman and no longer Hale's assistant. Still not having a college degree but always passing as post-graduate, the two of us had elbowed our way into Advertising and Public Relations while attending evening sessions together at Hunter College.

Activism came naturally as part of the job.

Since 1954 I had taken a founding role in most of the human rights movements, including early underground racial integrationist organizations which later merged into C.O.R.E. (Committee On Racial Equality).

J. Edgar Hooverism and Joe McCarthyism were still rampant, and what later became known as "the rainbow coalition" was then fomenting in widely different circles and multiple private gatherings at the homes of well-heeled members of loosely organized semi-secret liberal factions opposing the tyranny of H.U.A.C.

Being professionally well-connected, I, Porcelain, my ex-husband Jerry,[50] and Taulman, grouped together and moved freely among such activist-literary-artistic circles sometimes

---

[50] Gerald Rauch, former Columbia Pictures Manager for the Caribbean, ousted and diplomatically hustled on a plane back to the USA c. 1952 for his anti-Trujillo activities in the Dominican Republic; our marriage did not last although we remained friends and I eventually got an annulment. Though also a work of fiction, my third pulp novel, *This Bed We Made* (originally titled "For Immediate Demolition"), captures the atmosphere of that stage in my life which was filled with many more persons and events than I can take time to relate to you here but will probably fill in elsewhere.

later (c. 1957) also attended by Hale, who was a drinking pal of Maimie Eisenhower and had just been appointed a human rights advisor to Ike.[51]

Hale was then engaged to marry interracially to William Tatum, a C.O.R.E. co-founder and eventual deputy NYC mayor under Abe Beame. She was in a custody fight with her ex, a member of the powerful Chicago law firm backing McCarthyism.[52] The venue was wrong. Intermarriage was still illegal in many states and Hale was finally forced to give up on Tatum to keep her daughter.

But Hale never gave up on civil rights.[53]

---

[51] Though at heart a liberal, key staunch Republican Hale was also on a first-name basis with Richard Nixon, Joe McCarthy, Roy Cohn and J. Edgar Hoover, as well as Nancy Davis Reagan, to whom Hale introduced me and my poetry and plays c.1965.

[52] The continuity from the Eisenhowers to the Nixons to the Reagans with respect to their role in all the civil rights movements may have centered around Hale and her closest friends and may have had far more strategic import than has yet been revealed. In 1965 Hale and Mrs. Reagan graciously hosted me at a weekend campground owned by another well-connected friend, Zelda Supplee, who apparently knew most of the leading members of the Republican Party in their recreational off moments. A lot of political planning, and hiring, was being done behind the scenes. Present at that same campground, whether by accident or invitation, were Barbara Gittings, who later headed Daughters of Bilitis, and friend.

[53] I have strong reason to suspect that Hale, like a parade of others pre-Watergate whom Nixon may have been desperately trying to protect, may also have been murdered c.1969. By then she had married one of Hoover's lieutenants, Robert Bondi who, if appearances don't lie, may have managed to get hold of Hale's entire estate and have her own daughter disinherited. In my last telephone communication with her just before her demise reportedly of a heart attack, she told me that she was being prevented from leaving the house or even talking to her secretary. I told Porcelain who told everyone else, but nothing was done.

Thanks to Hale we were all now sleeping with Tigers.
Taulman said so.
My Viking answer to her was, "We too are Tigers."
Reluctantly, Taulman agreed.

So now we knew it.
We were positioned to change the system right from the very top.[54] Anointed and protected by Ike, the Commander in Chief, we were giddily building a peace army to tame and re-educate Nixon and all the other Tigers.

Gay History books apparently have blindsided this obscure period in the thermidor predating the outbreak of the sexual revolution. With good reason - saying too much about it was dangerous. There really was a war on, and there were many *many* casualties and I wish I could say more, but I'm not the best authority on all the details since I can't remember many names and wasn't attending all of the meetings. Nor was I, as a woman, always included in the innermost circles planning strategy - which is why the female sector soon split and went feminist.
To my eyes, most of the men coming and going tended to look alike. At some point I know must have met Bill Lambert,

---

[54] I must have failed to notice how precarious and deeply frightened Taulman felt at the time. She started calling me Tiger, even while reminding me, citing *The Little Prince,* that I was only a Rose with tiny thorns needing to be protected from the Tigers, needing to be put in a bell jar. It was up to her to protect me from the Tigers. But it was she who was the Rose desperately needing bell jar protection, and I didn't see it. Even when she started calling me Poo Bear for poo-pooing everything that was beginning to happen to us and I, still poo-pooing, affectionately was calling her Tigger.

but I can't remember his face or whether I met him under some other name. And I'm certain Gore Vidal also had to have been there, since his Gay novel, which I bought at the corner candy store back around 1949, long predates mine.

Another important figure in the formative years was R.E.L. Masters, who wrote under a number of pseudonyms and was well-connected on the Democratic side of the civil rights movements although I did not meet him until 1964.[55]

Masters was the psychotherapist and sexologist who had co-authored the influential Masters-Johnson Report. With his wife, New Age mystic and cultural anthropologist Jean Houston, he also co-authored many best sellers including *The Varieties of Psychedelic Experience* which I reviewed for *Science & Mechanics* Magazine in the hope of stopping the spread of LSD.

Despite our ideological differences,[56] Masters and Houston became good friends and sponsors of my work in the arts. Caught up in the fad surrounding the first discovery of the drug, they had researched the effects of psychedelic substances in the 1950's in controlled experiments which had apparently gotten out of hand when the wrong people got hold of them - something altogether too common whenever government-sponsored

---

[55] When we finally did meet, we became good friends even though he had - and rightly so - panned the published *Odd Girl.* Masters changed his mind about my writing when he got to read a sizeable portion of my poetry, novels and plays; this was his advance review on *The Skeets Trilogy:* "As the author presents it, SKEETS is an experimental seduction (or 'rape') of the reader's consciousness, scientifically achieved through esthetic means. SKEETS weaves a strange and compelling tale ostensibly about love and madness - arcane and amoral, atavistic and surreal. ... In both volumes, the narration is unremittingly hypnotic as the author stalks the thought forms she cunningly causes to arise in her relentless and often savage pursuit of 'The Self' and 'The Sacred'. Book I is very well written; Book II, quite remarkable!"
[56] Mine was through philosophy of science, psychophysics and information science; theirs was through cultural anthropology and New Age psychology.

research meets the Department of Defense.[57]

As a best-selling sexologist, Bob Masters' contribution to the Gay Rights Movement has been crucial and he has been unfairly targeted by the anti-Gay establishment, which has openly accused him and his wife, and all their friends, of *witchcraft*. A strong response is called for here:

It's important to understand the difference between *immersion* in unconventional research methods and *conversion* in the unconventional forms of life being studied. Aesthetic researchers have to delve deeply into their subjects but this does not mean they *become* like them. Nor does it make them "witches."[58]

Every corner of the Human soul is fair game for Phenomenological exploration. How else will Physicists and Information Scientists even begin to ask the questions needed to evaluate the occasional appearances of exotic results? Mathematics, pliable and unlimited in all its forms, is a mere tool and not the end-all instrument for reliable explanation.

Masters and Houston and their connection to the Clintons has been much maligned of late, most probably by very skillful

---

[57] Too much has been said about the 1960's sudden flood of narcotics use as a "hippie" and "flower child" rebellion against the Vietnam War. Too little has been said about the sudden availability of drugs and its connection to the late 1950's rise of the civil rights movements. Drugs were the lead weapon in the Mob's war against the arts as the proponents of cultural change. Which mob, you ask? All of them! Cognizant of the real source of the epidemic, I was already waging a militant fight against the spread of LSD and marijuana throughout the 1960's off-off-Broadway café theater scene where by then I was running a prominent anti-war workshop with actors who became famous.

[58] You can go directly to the internet and easily do your own work on researching this.

false informants who gave Bob Woodward a snow job.

The allegations that they were ever, as *converts*, conducting séances or otherwise engaging in exotic spiritualism or *witchcraft* is just so much misinformed and malicious political hogwash! I never attended séances though I'm quite certain they took place, mostly on the liberal Republican side for party entertainment and often frequented by Hale and Porcelain whom I introduced to the Masters who were not themselves the psychics involved, but what is the harm in *anyone's* analyzing such phenomena from more than one perspective?

And might it not even be a proper spiritual investigation for an enlightened leadership? Are the "Reverends" of established "Congregations" the only ones permitted to "counsel" our prospective candidates?[59]

All I found while investigating Masters and Houston over a period of years was harmless cathartic inquiry, aesthetic psychotherapy, which may have valuable 'alternative medicine' applications in the treatment of many pathologies of mind.

---

[59] As an information scientist working on a unified explanatory theory for the phenomenon of self-consciousness, my approach has always been entirely divergent from that of Masters and Houston, but who am I to say whether today's *Fringe* will or will not be incorporated in tomorrow's theories? I was present and did photograph a session of the therapeutic use of the so-called "Witches Cradle" which was used in a book authored by John Godwin published by Doubleday & Co., and who knows whether the research subject might even have been a young Hillary herself, but again, what if so? It was just a student experiment in what the mind does when it is deprived of its usual proprioceptive parameters. Would *less* knowledge about the workings of her own creative imagination make someone *less* fit to be President?

Dear Colleagues:

Let me backtrack a bit.

In the audience at that first 1954 NYC strategic gathering that now scarcely anyone knows took place, there were a few people already out of the closet whose names are now obscure.[60]

It was convened by and through announcements in One, Inc., of Los Angeles c.1953, which sent their representative, Ben Tabor - a pretty blonde beardless youth - to address a mature power audience at an old movie theater housing the original

---

[60] Early press people, interested in covering the Movement but not necessarily Gay themselves, such as Jess Stearn, John Reavis Jr., Jessica Russell Gaver, William Carrington Guy, were persons I met soon afterwards and who may have been in the back of the audience. Gaver took a special role that I don't see yet listed in *Wickipedia*. A feisty divorcee of the establishment in-crowd, she started a mimeographed newsletter that targeted anti-Gay commentators in the media by exposing them as closet-gays, thereby adopting Nixon's tactics against his own forces. This was pivotal, since it forced many anti-gay Gays in the Republican camp out of the closet.

Amato Opera on Bleecker Street. The semi-clandestine group of very well-dressed men mostly arrived in couples and were definitely not the type you would see in bars. The handful of women there were not so well-dressed (including *Moi*).

It was standing room only.

The grim and silent audience of mostly angry men became tentatively known as *The League* and its membership later founded New York Mattachine[61] where, while I was in Europe c. 1962, according to its former President Curtis Dewees, for lack of any female participation I was nominated and unanimously elected vice-president in absentia.

How many people remember this?
Randy Wicker was in knee pants.

"Saint Mikhail Itkin" who later founded the *Whatever Early Christian Roman Catholic Church*, definitely remembered, but he's dead now and when I knew him he was still a minor calling himself Robin, wearing a red vest to the bars and worshipping Bat Man.[62]

(There was also someone else - Tony Segura, whom I found most appealing because he looked a lot like Fermi but who, I'm told, went off to Cuba with Fidel. But he may just have been sharing the office that had the mimeograph machine that Taulman and I got to use after hours off of Union Square.)

---

[61] The founding of NY Mattachine was protracted over a long period of years, beginning c.1955 and stretching into the early 1960's. Taulman and I edited and mimeographed the first newsletter then left the group which became increasingly all-male, and focused our attention on building the local chapter of Daughters of Bilitis to provide all of us with some community support.

[62] I knew the young Itkin very well and he affectionately called me his cousin and ordained me in absentia, but I distanced myself from him when our conflicting ideologies grew too far apart. I will talk more about him later.

Among the sparse female presence, mostly c.1953 contributors to *One* Magazine, there were Noel Bustard and Joan Holode, and some middle-aged professional woman, probably a psychologist, sociologist or somebody's mother whose name I don't remember, who was immediately voted in as the first *League* Vice President; there was also openly socialist post-racial bisexual Julia Newman who became a good friend of ours though we did not share her political views, and myself, and at later meetings also Taulman.

It was at one of those later (c. 1955-57) formative meetings held at the West End Avenue home of first *League* President Gary Kramer (widely-connected *VoxJox* columnist for *Variety)*, that I and Taulman, then creative executives in a small advertising agency, first suggested improving the defamatory "Gay" images in the media by initiating a campaign to present more positive portrayals, particularly in advertising commercials -- an art form we knew carried particularly effective subliminal cultural force.[63]

A friend of Marshall McLuhan's, Edward Daikin (or Dakin) of BBDO, present at that meeting, eagerly took up our suggested strategy and initiated a power meeting of embryonic NY Mattachine with other key media executives for that purpose; though scheduled, it failed to take place.

It was learned some three weeks later that Daikin had been found with his head stuck inside an oven. Suicide, the police determined, over his guilt at being exposed as a homosexual. Bullshit! We all knew it was murder, but could do

---

[63] I later reintroduced and elaborated on this strategy in the 1960's in my address to the first ECHO (East Coast Homophile Organizations) Conference in Philadelphia.

Billie Taulman with self-portrait, 1954.

nothing. The entire movement would have been crushed had we shouted too loudly.[64]

This period also marked the beginning of my intimate interface with Billie Ann Taulman, who became my creative life-partner of more than fifty years, and whose soul and mine have now become so perfectly intertwined that she continues to this day even in death to be my artistic alter ego.

Connecting with each other late in 1954, Taulman and I instantly decided it was Spiritual Love at first sight, but for one small problem: Taulman smoked. I told her that I could never live or work with a smoker, never could be with a smoker. I explained my reasons thoroughly. I told her my whole life story, whereupon she hugged me, told me her own life story and we knew we had finally found each other.

Taulman gave up tobacco on the spot, cold turkey!

Perfectly attuned for creative collaboration, we entered into a civil union in the form of a registered partnership agreement called *Artemis Associates* (not to be confused with a present firm of the same name).

We also later took marriage vows: in sickness and in health, for all eternity - although I was still married to Jerry. Bishop Mikhail Itkin officiated. We had a party. Everyone,

---

[64] There was definitely a dark side among *The League* and Mattachine membership. Persons who had infiltrated and were there to destroy the Movement. They were the true *Forces of Evil*, a rogue police element that has always been a centuries-old part of the *Mob* and very hard to detect. There was little we could do about working alongside them except tread as softly and as carefully as possible, suspecting everyone we had not known for years. And even among those persons we knew there might always be a Judas.

except family, attended.

But as artists neither of us believed in exclusivity. Nor would either of us ever have been willing to play the traditional role of wife or husband.[65]

In a completely open relationship that welcomed and occasionally included paramours of either sex, we preferred to work and love each other in an entirely new dimension, libido unbound and gender free. Free to wander as we pleased, free to always come home to roost.

But by 1959, while being investigated for a possible political career under sponsorship from Hale, the Eisenhowers (and probably Nixon), our professors at Hunter and secretly "Gay" friends among Intelligence personnel now semi-retired and re-employed in academic CIA recruitment, Taulman lapsed into a period of agitated and recurrent paranoia.[66]

It recalled to me all over again what Vilna had gone through post-Fermi in 1943.

But Taulman had a stronger grasp of the situation.

She had lived through it in Berkeley, when Republican Nixon on Election Eve had singled out Taulman's group of campaigning New Dealers as "homosexuals and communists"

---

[65] Marriage, even among ordinary people, is such a decadent and useless institution that many persons of all sexes feel it might best be globally eliminated in favor of civil unions! For persons truly in love, marriage is inessential. (Though it may temporarily be a necessary strategic posture for the Gay Rights Movement to demand that *Marriage* be made legislatively available to everyone.)

[66] It's not certain how much of Taulman's breakdown was due to natural causes and how much of it may have been political foul play. Her paranoid fugue was precipitated by a Secret Service investigation while she was being considered for an Assistant position to Eleanor Roosevelt, then United Nations Ambassador working on the Bill for Universal Human Rights. (Or perhaps all of the tensions generated by the times collided with a flaw in her genetic heritage – echoing the madness of King George III!)

surrounding and supporting Democrat Helen Gehaghan Douglas.

Now Nixon and Hoover were at it again.

Taulman insisted that someone from *The League* had taken her aside and told her we had to be very careful about everything we said to one another, even in private. That we were being bugged my microwaves that could see and hear through walls - something unheard of then, but a surveillance technology disclosed post-Watergate.[67]

Although we should have guessed it, scarcely anyone knew at that time about Hoover's dirty tricks squad and the LSD or other mind-bending substances that were being experimentally introduced into civil rights groups by rogue police factions as a means of interfering with *The League's* activist activities. Taulman, like Daikin only a few weeks earlier, may have been one of a number of us simultaneously targeted.[68]

To this day I cannot tell you how much of Taulman's illness may have been the result of some chromosomal defect misdiagnosed and mistreated through sheer professional stupidity, and how much of it might have been a barefaced bias crime pervasive against all women and gays.

---

[67] A technology that Martha Mitchell insisted was killing her.

[68] I was temporarily spared, possibly because everyone might have mistaken Taulman, older and more erudite than I, descended from Mary Ball Washington and so close in likeness to her great-great-great uncle George, may have been identified by McLuhan and others of the group as politically "messianic," and as the real Artemis Smith.

Artemis Smith
below a portrait of
Artemis Smith as 'El Cid'
by Billie Taulman.

It was stolen from the sidewalk
in 1962. Perhaps it may
someday resurface.

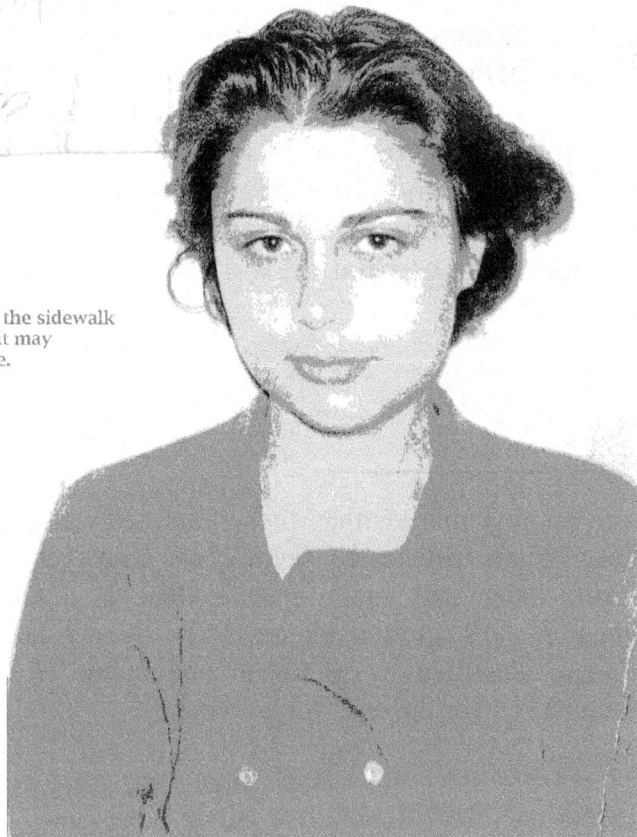

60

Dear Colleagues:

Over the next four years I sold the first-draft of "Anne Loves Beth" along with "Joan of Washington Square"[69] to Beacon Books just to get enough money ($1000) to pay the bills and get Taulman proper treatment which, tragically, proved futile.[70]

"Anne Loves Beth" went through a number of revisions before the publishers, rejecting the final version on legal grounds, took the first-draft and blue-penciled it themselves. (Luckily, my contract had stipulated that I owned the copyright!)

The 1959 press run for *Odd Girl*, from the very first, was

---

[69] Retitled *The Third Sex*. I was also marketing "For Immediate Demolition" later sold to Monarch Books and retitled *This Bed We Made* c. 1962 for a $1500 advance on further royalties that I never received.

[70] The only competent psychiatric help we were able to find was gratis, from our dear friend Joan McCarthy, a doctoral candidate in Clinical Psychology who, on the eve of her graduation, died suddenly of a brain abscess. It's uncertain as to whether it was due to an infected cat scratch to her eye or a gouging at the hands of the female pimp of one of her adolescent clients.

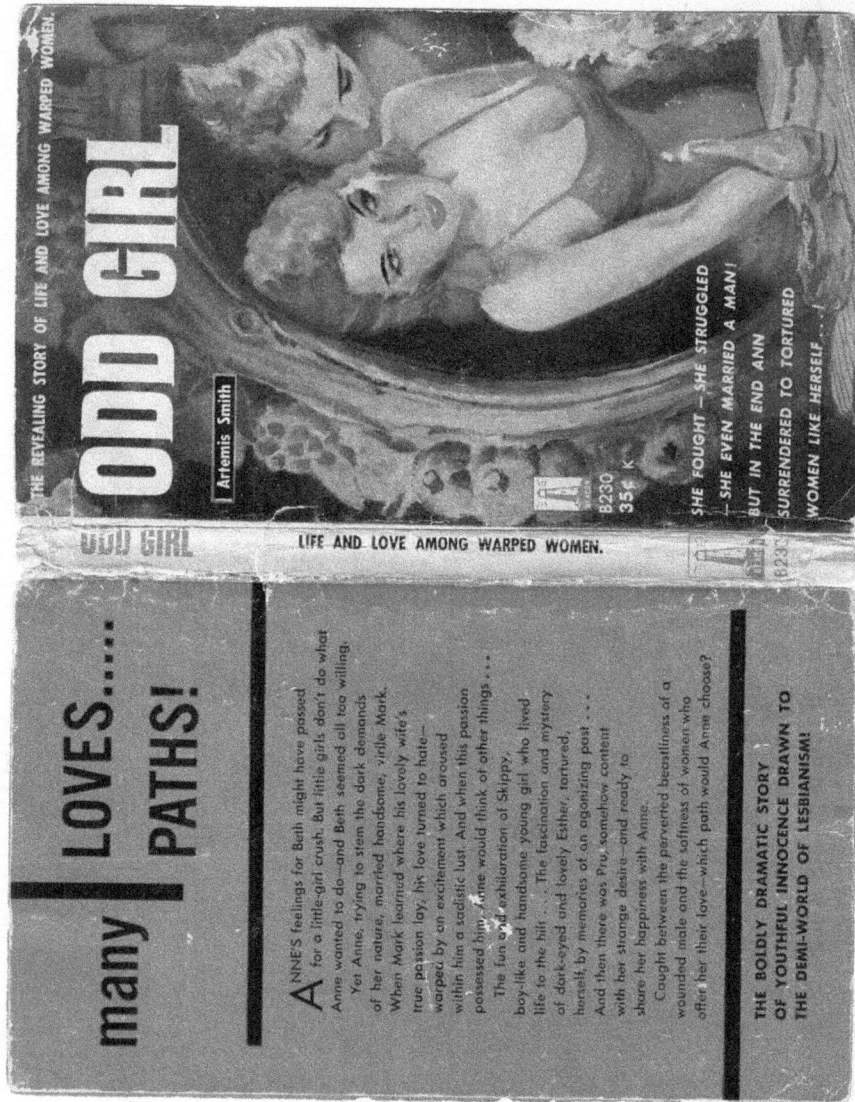

THE REVEALING STORY OF LIFE AND LOVE AMONG WARPED WOMEN.

ODD GIRL

Artemis Smith

B230
35¢ K

SHE FOUGHT — SHE STRUGGLED
— SHE EVEN MARRIED A MAN!
BUT IN THE END ANN
SURRENDERED TO TORTURED
WOMEN LIKE HERSELF . . .

ODD GIRL   LIFE AND LOVE AMONG WARPED WOMEN.

many LOVES..... PATHS!

ANNE'S feelings for Beth might have passed for a little-girl crush, but little girls don't do what Anne wanted to do—and Beth seemed all too willing.

Yet Anne, trying to stem the dark demands of her nature, married handsome, virile Mark. When Mark learned where his lovely wife's true passion lay, his love turned to hate—warped by an excitement which aroused within him a sadistic lust. And when this passion possessed him, Anne would think of other things . . . .

The fun and exhilaration of Skippy, boy-like and handsome young girl who lived life to the hilt . . . The fascination and mystery of dark-eyed and lovely Esther, tortured herself, by memories of an agonizing past . . . And then there was Pru, somehow content with her strange desire—and ready to share her happiness with Anne.

Caught between the perverted beastliness of a wounded male and the softness of women who offer her their love—which path would Anne choose?

THE BOLDLY DRAMATIC STORY
OF YOUTHFUL INNOCENCE DRAWN TO
THE DEMI-WORLD OF LESBIANISM!

in the hundreds of thousands, with an unreported second printing in the millions, but the publishers never kept open books and all I ever saw was an additional $250 in royalties.

I continued to market the finished "Anne Loves Beth" for eventual hardcover publication. Porcelain and Hale advised me to put it aside for posterity when the teenage market might finally find a place for it.

Being fully committed to writing the first volume of what was later to be *The SKEETS Trilogy*,[71] which the Hale Agency had presented and committed for sale to Doubleday & Co., I finally put the polished "Anne Loves Beth" to rest.

Upon the release of *Odd Girl* in 1959 we contacted *The Ladder* and it got excellent reviews. We were invited to attend and speak at a conference in San Francisco. Taulman had sisters in Sacramento she needed to see as well as many friends in Berkeley. We scraped together what money we could, sublet our apartment on 26th Street, and got on a plane. It was hoped that perhaps the trip would snap her out of her depression.

It helped a lot, and we got to meet Del Martin and Phyllis Lyon and all the other *Daughters* and had a great time with wonderful people despite Taulman's constant distraction. She was not her shining self. We met and consulted with Blanche Baker, Ph.D., who could do little but provide us with a pat on the head and moral support - something rare and precious in those days.

Everywhere we went, whether in San Francisco to meet

---

[71] "Testament of Sarah." Larry Freundlich became my appointed editor and I began revisions and Doubleday hired Stanley Kaufman to write the advance review which was never published. Years later, after Hale's sudden and also suspicious death, the manuscript was returned to me with a form rejection slip, no explanation given.

Taulman relatives, or Berkeley to meet Taulman friends, or Sacramento to stay with her sisters, or Palo Alto,[72] Taulman remained in a semi-dream state, compulsively writing down license plates, convinced we were being followed.

We stayed with her youngest sister Elsie in Sacramento where I managed to find a job as Program and Advertising Manager for KXRQ-FM at a starting advance on commission of $25/week. But I had neither car nor driver's license and it was hopeless. After a few months of getting nowhere, and the Monarch advance not yet forthcoming, I had to ask my father to lend us plane fare home.

Returning to our old life and friends and apartment on 26th Street, both of us quickly got freelance advertising jobs, but Taulman's agitation grew. She was never physically violent, but her panic would cause her to hold me prisoner for hours while she subjected me to long tirades about my needing to believe her. I had no choice but to finally put her in Bellevue, where she got assembly-line treatment and was released on medication after six weeks.

On medication she just sat home doing nothing until she stopped taking it and began studying again and working on sparse freelance art assignments, ever so slowly. Meanwhile I went to work 9-to-5 to pay the rent.[73]

By 1961 Taulman's anxieties had subsided and thanks to a friend's recommendation she had finally settled into a rehab job as a layout artist at Mines Press. She was applying to

---

[72] Where, at a jazz club managed by our good friend, retired Broadway agent Walter vonB. Teschan, we accidentally met and heard Billie Holiday sing incognito, having borrowed the identity of her understudy Ada Moore while dodging the Feds. (Ask me more about this on a talk show!)

[73] I have never been the kind of writer who can hold a day job and be creative at night. I had to put everything else on hold.

return to Hunter College. Things seemed to be beginning to get back to normal. At the insistence of Taulman's medics who were convinced her dependence on me was complicating her recovery, and finding myself desperately needing to get back to my own artistic and literary career, I let my parents bribe me into agreeing to work and study in Europe for a year.[74]

But too soon after I left, Taulman suffered yet another relapse. Before I could return, our NYC apartment had been dispossessed.

I publish here the last coherent letter I may or may not have received from her.[75] To the best of my recollection, it must have reached me in Florence sometime in October 1962 either during or before the Cuban Missile Crisis.[76]

It appears to begin with a handwritten note on the back of a legal-sized well-worn scrapped yellow pulp sheet typewritten on a portable with a tired ribbon that reads:

---

[74] Because my parents were paying for the trip and were by now adamant that I quit what everyone in my father's professional circles opined had to be a "co-dependent" relationship, I could not afford to take Taulman along -- but we had made plans for her to secretly join me as soon as she could manage her own plane fare and I could be certain that my student allowance and publishing resources would cover the two of us living as cheaply as one. When I left NYC Taulman still had a decent job, enough money in the bank to cover about three months' rent, and a roommate who was supposed to sublet the whole apartment whenever she left to join me in Europe.

[75] The original letter is on a sheet too large to reproduce here, but is affectionately preserved among my papers.

[76] Or perhaps I never received it and it got stuck carelessly among whatever things were salvaged when our apartment on 26th Street was dispossessed during my absence sometime in December 1962. The period is so filled with grief for me that I can't precisely remember now. What I do remember is that I entirely missed the Cuban Missile Crisis because I was gawking at Florence and not reading newspapers!

9/14/62

Lunch @ Work

Dearest Tiger –
Thought I should start this now & found this the only
paper available. It comes in rolls @ work. Started @
noon, am now waiting for the psychologist who might let
me into Hunter. Hope you received my last (rather
depressed) letter. Am having cramps but still worked all
day! They are rather nice there. I'm rather exhausted.

(The paper folds over and ads: "Start here.")

Dearest, I am lonely for you and I hope that you will
write me nice little descriptions of all the places you
visit. What is Picadilly? Who goes there? Everybody? Why?
Are you going to visit Soho? You may read this before you
go anywhere. Well, you really were willing to reassure me
quite a bit before you left, dearest little Tiger. The
last page I wrote sounded worse than I meant it to.

Little wiggly friend, no fetish of you will do any good.
I converted all that into Tiger-libido long ago. Still
need the real, live honest-to-goodness masterful
Morpurgo, Right Rhodes. Superb Smith. Even would like to
go to a movie with you. It is not true that I am so
boring that all I am good for is going to movies with. M.
Cosgrove[77] and Persephone[78] keep speaking as though you had

---

[77]   A 'straight" friend of ours, Margaret Cosgrove, author-illustrator of many
children's books and medical texts, whom I entrusted to watch over Taulman
and our apartment. When I left for Europe, there was plenty of money in the
bank to cover three months' rental and Taulman was employed.

[78]   Another 'straight' friend of ours, Persephone Adams, immortalized in a
poem written by her father, *New Yorker* editor Franklin P. Adams.

gone. Period. At least, M.Cosgrove does. You have flown the coop. And that is it. No more applechop. That I don't really believe?

Spent some time in the Paragon Bookstore on Thursday after I saw that psychologist. I found a beautiful Akkadian dictionary for only $5.00. Also found a Korean grammar for $1.50, and a very deep study of the relationship of Korean to Finno-Ugrian, in dictionary form, for only $5.00. The Assyriac dictionary I found for only $5.00 was interesting, too, with a neo-Babylonian comparison. Then I browsed through a big Egyptian grammar and dictionary for $45.00 and discovered that it is a very easy language to learn. As far as I can tell, it is very possibly related to Korean. There may be enough here, were I able to acquire all this material, to really verify my hypothesis very nicely. I didn't buy the Egyptian one and see if I can use it at the library in Florence. I might get you to check and see if it is available somewhere there. If you feel like inquiring, ever. Speaking of inquiring, have you stumbled across an introduction to Alice B. Toklas?

It's so strange to be here and well and not have you here hoping with me and being my little Tiger. You wanted us to be self-supporting, and I conked out. Now that there is that possibility again, it seems awful that you are no longer here, too, and that you don't seem to care very much anymore. Perhaps you really do but are too sensitive about everything that has happened to be able to express it. If you did I suppose you would have to blame me, and that you really are reluctant to do a lot of the time. Still, when there is too much burden there is too much.

How about just getting in touch with Alice B. without an introduction? You might say you are a friend of the Interplayers who did her play for a few seasons in California ten years ago. That sounds rather far-fetched as a contact. We worked through her agent, Carl?Van either Doren or Vechten. Which one was her agent, anyway? Can't recall.

For me, frustration is one of the aforementioned burdens. Have been thumbing through back issues of the Ladder in an escapist thing, but that hasn't really helped. Dearest love, little push-cat. It is now 9 p.m. and I have washed the dishes and am getting ready to take a shower and go to bed. I am sorry that I said you didn't care when you more than likely do. Still, it seems that it could be expressed somehow so that I might doubt less. Like "I love you." Very often. Love is never too deep to be expressed when real. Still, one's facilities may fail one temporarily, as mine did when I was sick. They are coming back a little, so you be sure and have me there to express love with them, will you?

Really, I am beginning to enjoy this correspondence. Perhaps as time goes by I will have the strength to include more. Do you know, by the way, how closely the Coptic language is related to ancient Egyptian? I don't.

Dearest little Tiger. I am looking in my little book, "The Roman Forum." It would be wonderful fun to study that with you someday, if you liked. I mean the forum itself. There is an Etruscan inscription there near the tomb of one of the founders of Rome, in something called the "Lapis Niger". It was all covered up by the Romans in the second and first centuries B.C. Maybe the Etruscans had more to do with the founding than anyone liked to admit. They really "covered up." They used a pavement of black Greek marble. I love you.

It is now time for me to clamber over Antigone and go to bed. I will take a bath in the morning. I will be a slob tonight and not do so. Hope you get in touch with Tim Courtney. She was a brilliant student at Cal. In English, I think. Meanwhile, dear Tiger, tell me about the nice people you meet. If you can, tell me how much you love me. That will help. You are my dear love, my sweet love. I need you and I hoope that you will need me so much soon that you will want me to come early.

It is interesting that the thumb-screws are still on at Hunter even though you have gone to Europe. That didn't seem to prove or defend anything to this psychologist from the Dean's office who put me through the two-hour grill session.

Tiger, tiger. Where are you tonight? What little dreams did you have on shipboard that you will tear up and not tell me. What dreams are you living now? They are really mine, too. I want you to write them to me, whether they happen sleeping or waking.

Isobel Aronin[79] called. She has lost her job. They weren't nice, made false accusations about her competence. She is most unhappy. See what happens the minute you go? The world just isn't the same, somehow.

Dearest, dearest, dearest. Antigone and I miss you. I will go to sleep now, hoping that I will see you in January. Meanwhile, I dreamed last night that you were hanging a cat by its toes and I went and took it down. It was a comfort to be near you even though your behavior was not the kindest in the world. In fact, I was very happy to be near you in the dream.

I am wearing your nice steel wristwatch, thinking that you would want me to. Would you like me to send it?

All my personal nightingales have stopped singing now that you are gone, dearest. Perhaps I can find a mechanical one somewhere that will cheer me up for a while. The teachers in my classes. Still.

     All my love, my passion, my tender love,

Billie

Billie

[On the back of the same page, there seems to be a letter written either earlier or later:]

Sunday night .. . . 5 P.M. Much has happened since I last wrote, but little has been accomplished. The

---

[79]   Another 'straight' friend of ours, then an editor at *Scribner's*, who had just sponsored the submission of one of my manuscripts there.

psychologist who saw me said that he would have the medical board pass on me after I was at Hunter for a bit. I am disgusted. He asked me (without prompting) all about Dr. Thompson,[80] grilled me, asked me if my left-hand ring was a wedding ring. I told him it was given me by someone at Yale. He asked then if it were a man, and seemed dubious when I said "yes." It was very, very nasty, and it certainly would be nice to take that last year in England rather than here. It was long and grueling and I was having severe cramps. Didn't recover until just now. Had them for two days. Then Persephone came over and refused to pay the two-month's rent in advance and browbeat me et al. Then she called today and apologized, saying that her mother had tried to convince her that my demands were not unreasonable. I had asked for rent in cash, so I wouldn't have to accept a check from her lawyer. So now she may give me a month's rent in advance. I find these hostile hesitations very tiring. She began to feed me a tirade about how I might go insane, saying you had told her about my violence toward you and my "catatonic stupors" and this and that. All this so that she might not have to pay that month's rent in advance. Now, however, her tone has changed completely.

Then I spent yesterday afternoon with M. Cosgrove, who was very nice and took me to her Community Center briefly, then took me home and had me lie down while she did sewing. It was very amusing, and we had shrimp salad. Thank God for M. Cosgrove. She talked to me about you at length, was very sympathetic and understanding.

---

[80]   An administrative 'plant' set up at Hunter quite possibly also by the early CIA/FBI or Secret Service to check Taulman out by attempting to seduce her. I later encountered the same woman in the 1960's and '70's under a number of different academic identities, when she unsuccessfully targeted me. Such 'traps' were regularly employed, especially within the military but also among academics being investigated for security clearances. The persons employed for such purposes were themselves victims of military blackmail, so I continue to decline to name her. I hope someday she will come forward herself.

I am very frustrated. Where are you, little Tiger? Where? Where? Looked in the magazine rack, refrigerator, bed, back room, bathroom. No tiger. No Tiger. Antigone is rummaging around the closet looking for something. She probably misses you too.

Did you tell me not to ask Persephone rent in advance? She has only stored her stuff for three months, so may move, etc. I thought I was supposed to speak to her about it. By the way, I'm so glad you finally took care of those library books. You really should have let me pay the $1.50 or so we owed originally, as I suggested. It might have been $5.00. Ah weell. I should berate you? Poor little tiger. You were having enough troubles then. I love you.

Dearest little pussycat. If you see something in a Gunn plaid there, perhaps you should get Dr. Wilson a small souvenir. I haven't gotten in touch with her about taking her to <u>Antigone</u>.[81] I suppose I should before she makes other arrangements. Still, now that you are gone the energy fails me. I feel very withdrawing and hostile and unhappy. There is no real point in social life. No real point in anything, for that matter. Don't be contemptuous. I may be right. Following as one is led by the requirements of travel, school, <u>et al</u>, is not the same as having real purpose and fulfilling that purpose. That is why schoolwork is not regarded as seriously as post-graduate or independent work. So I reach sycophantic heights of expressed eulogy and get good grades in all my

---

[81]   Celebrated Classics Professor Pearl Cleveland Wilson who, along with Classics and English Department Heads Adelaide Hahn and Leah Jonas, had fondly assigned us the star names of 'Castor and Pollux' because we dressed alike, in army surplus fatigues, in defiance of the Roman Catholic-run highly conservative History Department on the same floor who regularly complained about our unisex attire to the Dean's Office. We got away with it by counter-charging religious persecution, as 'devout atheists', and daring the administration to risk a lawsuit on First Amendment grounds.

courses .… so then I will be known as having done that.
Well and good. But when my little fellow student, the
real inspiration of all my independent work, has gone,
there is not much there. Seriously. I still value my mate
as my inspiration. When it is gone or it is no longer
mutual, I do not pretend that the mechanical data
provided by an ordinary college education, sugared up
with a dramatic presentation, can fill that gap. It may
be that there is more left of our relationship than you
had led me to believe. I still have that hope. But you
are not here to feed the hope (though you had not the
desire to confirm it entirely when you were here) and
much depends upon your letters. That is different from
dependency, however. It simply is love. Without it there
is no love. Demand and response are part of a mutually
nonschizophrenic relationship. When one asks a question,
an answer is expected. When this happens, that happens.
One treats one's friend nicely. Expectations are
fulfilled. All that. It's all a part of a unit that's a
little like a beautiful plant, when parts of the plant
are clipped it's easy to see whether someone has snipped
off the buds or taken only the old, tired flowers. The
gardener can talk his head off about his purity of
purpose and what his schedule was when he was trimming
the plant, but those are rather extraneous factors in
love. The only schedule the plant of love has is regular
watering with the milk of human kindness. Sounds awfully
exotic. Like taking baths in asses' milk.

I won't be able to get physical education in this time.
It starts too soon. It takes me forty minutes to get from
work to class, via subway. Where is the milk of human
kindness for the lovable little tiger to get in this
letter? I'd better start churning some up and serving out
some yogurt. Only when there is some of you in the idea I
am discussing is there anything that is really nice. I
guess I will try and take the full twelve units. There is
an English course by Professor Bowden, "The Structure of
Modern English," that fits in beautifully with my
schedule, so that could make up the additional units and
be very worthwhile. Sounds like a good grammar course,
and we all need that.

(see back of page)

Dear Colleagues:

I wasn't told of Taulman's relapse until it was too late even to fly back. My friends and family, all of them convinced that I had suffered enough,[82] discouraged me from immediately returning; Vilna, who had always viewed Taulman as a rival, cunningly was already on the boat to join me in Rome for a professional power tour to old Partisans now anxious to meet both of us. Letters carried with her from trusted friends further falsely assured me that it was futile to catch the first plane back - Taulman was getting proper treatment and all of our treasured belongings had already been put safely into storage by M. Cosgrove.

---

[82] Taulman's first breakdown happened in 1957. By 1962 we had pretty much run out of options. Separation, to end Taulman's dependency on me, was the last psychiatric recommendation still to be explored. My own career was running down the tubes. I was ready to cut the cord, by then finding myself suddenly fired from every career job I applied for and driven to support us by working in various menial capacities ranging from Dictaphone transcription in a secretarial pool to nude modeling for artists and their students.

But Taulman did not get proper treatment, and before the moving van got there only a fraction of our property remained on the sidewalk, the most valuable pieces having been "rescued" by foraging lesbian couples who eventually ended up keeping most of Taulman's collection of modern paintings and first editions for themselves while I, too grief stricken to demand their return, simply went on with my own life.[83]

.   But I wouldn't let go.

I hustled Vilna back on a boat in Naples after only a short stay then dropped out of the University of Rome and shortened the rest of my scheduled professional tour, rushing back only to find myself rejected[84] and medically barred from visiting Taulman again "in her best interest for recovery."

By then I was worn too thin to oppose her psychiatrists.

I did not know then what I know now about brain architecture and chemistry. Today I could have done better but at that time I was wholly dependent upon what may have been an army of biased and politically corrupt professional opinions. And the smoking really did it for me. That was the final rejection.

I didn't give up on her entirely but I knew we both needed time apart. Creatively, artistically, we were too close, perhaps toxic to each other. Just as Vilna and I had to be apart.

---

[83]   Thanks, Guys. Now how about finally showing some conscience and bringing it all back?

[84]   One way or another she must have been brainwashed. She had started smoking again and said she had found a new friend and it was alright now for me not to worry about her. I sat there helpless, unbelieving. Had I read the letter she had sent me, weary as I was I might have pressed more strongly to have her released in my own care. I did have attorneys, notably William J. Calise who was helping Gays, that I could have called but didn't. There might also have been Hale's attorney, Philip Wittenberg, but I didn't think of him.

For years I had tried to heal Taulman on my own, free of medication and simply with love, understanding and much patience. But to no avail. Perhaps she was incurable. Perhaps medication was the only solution. Perhaps our intense relationship really was the cause of her breakdown. Perhaps all my friends and family were right and I really should get on with my own life, sing my own song without accompaniment, be the real and only Artemis Smith.

Watching closely from afar, I entrusted her care to M. Cosgrove, another very highly creative person who appeared to know more than I did and was right there, ready to step up to the plate. The motives for Cosgrove's readiness to do so still remain a mystery to me, though Taulman was herself still such a prize that perhaps spontaneously Cosgrove wanted to help.

Even in her most distracted condition Taulman was amazing. Her daily insights into the very fabric of Being were unique and unparalleled. At times each sentence she uttered burned with the proverbial *hard gem-like flame* of immortal prose. It's difficult to describe the experience of being close to her except by saying, simply, that basking in her radiance was for everyone touched by her an experience of *becoming Taulman*. She repeatedly pinpointed and expressed one's inner word. No wonder Cosgrove was eager to take charge of her! And I, deprived of her, deeply felt the void.

And Cosgrove was also such a brilliant and mercurial person that both I and Taulman fell in love with her. We allowed her to manage us. Taulman had become the Rose now being kept safe in Cosgrove's bell jar, safe from me and all the other Tigers.

So Cosgrove became Taulman's "committee" during this period and took over for me while Billie spent the next five years as an in patient and out patient at Wards' Island, until my career took a turn and I finally gathered myself together and stepped forward to reclaim her -- this time to be welcomed by the new medics and social workers with open arms.

Where had I been! She needed me!

I took her back then, tobacco and all, though just as with Vilna I never could come physically close to her again.

As long as Taulman continued to smoke we would have to live apart. Having for years anticipated her future release from the hospital, I had sublet and kept my old rent-controlled walkup ready for her to move into; it was only a couple of blocks from my new luxury studio on 72nd Street where I would see her every day when she came to eat with me.

I would cook magnificent meals for her, I would make certain she was safe and wouldn't relapse, even though by then I had a succession of paramours living with me, each of them fully understanding and never resenting her presence in my life.

All of them knew why I could never *ever* love anyone as I had loved Taulman again.[85]

As for my own possessions that had also been left on the street in 1962, Ida was that day dying in the hospital and Vilna and Attilio couldn't look after them. My sister and brother-in-law grudgingly rescued only what they deemed important to the family, leaving the rest on the street for the storage van hired by Cosgrove that arrived too late. Passersby walked away with them. Fortunately, I had taken many of my manuscripts with me, but the final draft of "Anne Loves Beth" was not among them.[86]

---

[85] My survivor guilt over this forms the resounding theme of *'The SKEETS Trilogy.*
[86] I had been afraid to take it with me lest it be confiscated as possibly salacious material on my return through Customs!

Dear Colleagues:

"Anne Loves Beth" published here in ***Appendix B*** is a faithful reconstruction from memory of that earlier revised version, now made available primarily to librarians and academics for historical purposes and possibly also finally for teen libraries.

It cannot really be narrowly classified as either a *gay* or *lesbian* novel, never should have been. Its political stance and psychological views are diametrically opposite to the portraits of "gay life" in transgender comic renditions exploited by the mass media for their commercial value. Though often genuinely funny and endearing as *Dame Edna* or *The Bird Cage*, such media spoofs and romps are to the socially mature sexual minorities as politically offensive as 'black face' and 'Yiddish humor'.

Dated as *Odd Girl* may read today, now that wholesome alternative life-choices among consenting adults is a legal and socially acceptable category, I maintain it rightfully stands as a serious work of literature specifically aimed at guiding the young away from the hurdles that await them upon 'coming out' in what, for most of the world, is still unavoidably an underworld environment.

Especially for female adolescents voraciously seeking knowledge of an alternate lifestyle that does not utterly misguide them, it still stands as an honest study in the phenomenology of androgyny to facilitate their self-knowledge and natural sexual development -- even though my character, Anne, may now sound to the reader more like Nancy Drew on an estrogen overdose!

But this was exactly what I originally meant Anne to be, speaking directly to all the *'odd girls'* who desperately needed positive teenage models back in 1954. Though tame by comparison to other pulp fiction published today, for its time *Odd Girl* was unavoidably explicit, as a frank work of literature should be -- unlike its companion piece, *The Third Sex*, which was a hastily-written disguised activist statement specifically aimed at reaching a wider multinational heterosexual audience.[87]

Never meant as a literary work of art except in the larger sense of political 'master-building' for social change, *The Third Sex* intentionally contained no sexually explicit passages that might have prompted censorship and confiscation, and was written more as a journalistic essay than as a novel, specifically for the purpose of tapping the powerful global pulp fiction mass medium that was, in those days, the only ready podium for the sexual minorities' rights activism.

In 1959, my shock and outspoken outrage at the publisher's offensive blurbs on the cover of *Odd Girl* – describing it as a portrait of life and love among "warped women" – widely reverberated throughout the gay community in their many newsletters and publications, notably *The Ladder,* successfully putting sufficient pressure on my publishers to immediately

---

[87]   Initially meant to be collaboration, Taulman only, ended up writing one chapter.

release *The Third Sex* with almost no editorial change.[88]   A line in the sand was gradually being drawn!

The Third Sex was presented as a portrayal of both male and female gay society in a positive and humanist light. Riding on the prior success of *Odd Girl*, it became one of the key source materials of the 1960's rights movements. It spoke the truth for a precise time and place and is now also a piece of history. For this reason, I see no reason to revise it even though, as a novel, it is inferior and artistically thin. A revised edition would cure its literary defects, but why bother?

Not so however for *Odd Girl* alias "Anne Loves Beth."

In its finished form it can still present an important contribution to the understanding of the complexities of the female mind in adolescence. The final draft contributes both to the phenomenology and the psychology of the developing female persona.

Suppressed by society and my pulp publishers, this offering was never given a fair chance and should now be presented in its true light for it is important to realize that, despite the rise of feminism, theories regarding the female adolescent libido still continue to be largely formulated and defined by male academic professionals groping to understand what they cannot possibly experience themselves -- and the checkbooks of male-oriented media pornographers, even when they happen to be written or directed by women.

Compare my message to that of other contemporary writers of "lesbian pulp fiction" and see the difference.

---

[88]   The one offensive editorial insertion was the subtle interjection of after-sex smoking, as well as other smoking references. I never wrote or approved those lines. (I wonder if Taulman sneaked them in or one of the editors did.)

Odd Girl alias "Anne Loves Beth," as a product of my uninhibited phenomenological investigation into the depths of my own adolescent psychic development, presented a consciousness-raising alternative that many young women may secretly experience but fearfully suppress to their own detriment. It sought to lead such young women toward making more educated life choices - and not necessarily gay choices.

In this sense, pulp fiction too can be an aesthetically valid art form. Despite its clay feet, this work is contiguous with the rest of my master-building investigations into the metaphysics of Gender Being.[89]

To those who would ridicule me for stooping to write pulp fiction as an art form, I say you are short-sighted. I was only paid a pittance for my writing and could have made much more had I really been willing to become a literary hack within the establishment media. But my artistic goals were much wider: my pulp fiction titles consciously and strategically took advantage of a mass medium then and quite possibly still, thoroughly controlled by the vast underworld anti-culture.

I used one of the fringe industries of those all-permeating forces of evil to sneak through a positive socio-political message

---

[89] Books II and III of *The SKEETS Trilogy* speak to that side of me. I continue to be a cultural revolutionary now writing primarily under the sci-fi category, sketching hypotheses that Humanity may still not yet be fully ready to accept. The vision of a strictly gender-free identity forms part of my religiously atheistic conviction that Human evolution beyond the species level presents us with unbounded territories for superhuman expansion that really do need to be morally contained, but in a new key. Biologically-based existence, now essentially earth-bound, is merely pupal. Soon it will metamorphose into forms better suited for interstellar exploration, forms that are free in every sense and limited only by the ethical, the moral, and the beautiful for the preservation of our original and most valuable Human identity. It is time to throw out superstitious old Scripture and its pathological applications, time to set all of us free to be all that we really can become.

that could not be presented through normal channels. And I saw this as literary master-building at its purest -- my chosen form of urban-guerrilla-warfare turned against the very mob that sought to oppress vast sections of humanity, including even persons occupying the highest echelons of political leadership, through blackmail, extortion, and prostitution.

Both Taulman and I saw that the fight for gay rights was more than just an advocacy for the human rights of a small segment of the population. Historically this portion of the politically disenfranchised minorities have always been the unwilling handmaidens of organized crime at all its levels - as were the politically-oppressed 'rich' Jews during the early rise of Hitler.

All persons secretly living alternate life-styles form not a minority but the proverbial global silent majority. As first publicly stated by me repeatedly throughout the 1950's and '60's, in this country, as in any other country, there can be no human rights for women or any of the racio-ethnic minorities without first also including the rights of all persons in alternate life-styles. Their representation is strategically crucial. Wherever one group of persons is rendered subject to control by organized crime through lack of rights legislation, the entire society is threatened, the whole world is threatened.

This was why both Taulman and I gave gay activism first priority even over feminism and interracialism. And this was also why the death squads of the rogue police establishment may eventually have put both of us on their hit lists.

There is much more to tell you here and at my online interactive autobiographical archives located at interlocking sites accessible from www.ArtemisSmith.com -- but now I simply call your attention to "Anne Loves Beth" which, despite its 1950's setting, in many parts of the world may still forcefully address the present.

In this reconstructed version, as a literary artist I have taken great pains not to be tempted to alter any of the original 1950's pulp fiction flavor, even though many of my mature feelings, and my full-grown literary style (none of which I have thus far subjected you to)[90] seem now very remote from the picaresques of the pupal Artemis Smith.

Go now to **Appendix B** and read the book within a book, if you haven't already done so, then come back here if you want, to read the rest of my Viking saga.

Again, *Enjoy!*

---

[90] I have kept my exposition in this autobiographical correlate as simple and straightforward as possible, since I am not writing a poem or a novel and because it more properly reflects the mood of an earlier time. If it sounds adolescent, *magnifico!*

Dear Colleagues:

Have I still got your attention? Is anyone still reading? *Hallelujah!* Since the 1980's when I lost the remainder of my closest sounding boards to one form of cancer or another I have been writing in a virtual vacuum.

Taulman survived until 2008 but it was mostly her insights, not mine, that got to bounce back and forth between us. Taulman has been my prophet all these years and make no mistake about it - we are *both* writing this now, though now that she is gone I am finally free to talk about all the things *I* have had to leave unsaid until the cock crowed.

In order for you to understand what took place in our lives and the lives of others who touched us during the 1950's - 70's, I will have to go back again briefly to a time before I met Taulman, back to 1952:

In 1952 I and Michael Itkin, or little Robin as I used to

call him, found each other at or in the San Remo, a gay[91] corner bar on Bleecker and McDougal. That area got so crowded at night that all of the partying spilled out into the street and the underaged set found it easy to mix with the grownups without precipitating a police raid.

I would repeatedly pass by the San Remo and stop to chat with Robin between my matinee and nightly gigs at the Amato Opera and The Provincetown Players.[92] Itkin and his friends became my principal source for the composite character called 'Jacques' in "Anne Loves Beth" and for a while we had much in common.

Religion was the unifying factor, our mutual rage and contempt for its political presence and interference in both our lives - I then as Feminist, he then as Gay. Both of us were talking about the need to start our own religion to oppose all the dogma that was out there. Doing so was only one of my remote future projects,[93] but for Itkin it became an immediate and growing obsession to a degree that I, as politically anti-Vatican, personally regarded as yet another severe pathology of the soul.

---

[91]   You will note that I sometimes use 'Gay' and other times 'gay' as modifiers. This is not a typographical error but a means of describing levels of commitment to a cause or a movement, just as one might differentiate between 'Feminist' and 'feminist', 'Nazi' and .'Nazi', 'Zionist' and 'zionist'.

[92] My own hangout was at the Café Rienzi a few doors down which had become my alternate office whenever I was not at the Hale Agency on West 10th. (There I once met and spoke at length with Jack Kerouac who convinced me *not* to go on the road with my husband Jerry.)

[93] Taulman and I later chose what we termed 'mystical atheism' as our ad hoc creed. We hold 'Aesthetic Truth' sacred, whatever that means. No need for "God." Stephen Hawking, we predate you by fifty-four years! See "On Atheism and The Sacred" on record at www.ArtemisSmith.com, and for a view of our own gospel you will have to wait until the publication of my latest work, "*ArtemisSmith's* GrandmaMoseX," scheduled for release next year.

Instead of staying in school and getting all the higher degrees for which his high intelligence should have easily qualified him, Itkin slipped deeper and deeper into his own mystical calling despite all of my efforts to talk sense into him and even to introduce him to the right kind of Bat Man to take him in hand.

It was a stage he never outgrew.

Though I still look upon all such religious dogma as misguided, St. Mikhail's courageous contribution to the Gay Rights Movement undeniably has had strategic importance and he really should be canonized by the Vatican as one of its martyrs whenever the Pope or one of his successors decides to have his/her next epiphany.

By his very manner, appearance and costumed ritual (which he jokingly began as a kind of transgender 'drag')[94], Itkin exposed the sham in all the organized religions he mimicked. The sad thing is that when it all began, and it probably began during a conversation had between the two of us in 1952, I was only half listening.[95] He was talking about Jesus and the Apostles possibly having all been Gay, and I was countering that with the observation that gender-freedom was clearly outlined in

---

[94] Thinking back I am always reminded of the hilarious scene in Fellini's *Juliet of the Spirits* which films what appears to be an authentic Vatican fashion show where male models wearing the latest fashions in High Mass and Papal attire parade down the runway in a frankly transgender display.

[95] Itkin took me seriously, went out and incorporated his first *Whatever* Church then sent me a diploma ordaining me in absentia as one of his ministers which I laughingly tossed in some pile of papers and eventually threw out. To my mind all "Holy Books" belong either in the fire or in the back of some dusty library never to be consulted by anyone but historians and cultural anthropologists. Even philosophers should avoid them lest they pick up a spiritual virus they had best not propagate! (The Vatican, incidentally, held the same view in the Middle Ages, when it actively forbade any translation of the Bible into the vernacular.)

Plato's *Republic* with its notion of the "philosopher king" who might be either male or qualifying female and that had largely formed the basis for subsequent Early Christian thought.

There really is a need, we both concluded when we were actually listening to each other and not going off on our own separate monologues, to reform all the religions to allow for both gender-freedom and gender equality.

I really did see it as nothing more than a Gay Rights counter-Vatican parody. When it finally hit me that he was dead serious about running for sainthood over this, I gave up on him and went my own artistic way.

The way I saw it, Itkin started his movement as a means of *politically* fighting fire with fire. But it soon afflicted him *spiritually* as it later did too many young men damaged by their own religious upbringing who seriously sought and found refuge in the Early Christian Roman Catholic or *Whatever* Church's Vatican alternative.

One pathology of soul can never properly heal another.

Yes, I dare use the word *pathology.*

While a minor, Itkin was victimized despite all his protestations to the contrary, either by a devout priest or a depraved predator; take your pick, there is no difference between them where minors are concerned. Man-boy love, unless it is *entirely* non-sexual, is statutory rape no matter what you call it. But so is early-childhood religious indoctrination *a rape of the soul* and Itkin was apparently subjected to both.[96]

---

[96] Most of the gay virgins of Itkin's crowd suffered from an irresistible urge to either engage in Black Masses or otherwise expose themselves to a neutral and understanding female presence. Why not! Being always unaffected by a show of male nudity, I simply went on with my own tasks and let Itkin get through his own hang ups as we worked. And he had quite a number of hang ups he has never minded telling the whole world about so I don't think I am breaking any confidence by setting them down for posterity here.

I can't remember precisely what he told me about his Jewish-Catholic childhood that fated day in 1952 when he eagerly volunteered to help me paint the ceiling of my new basement apartment on East 17th. (A firehouse red, which I lived to regret!) He insisted I allow him to do it stark naked, despite my warning on the possible harmful effects of applying paint thinner on a penis. (Which he, to his agony, also learned to regret that same day!)

I was more interested in what I had to tell him about my own, however brief, Roman Catholic upbringing and in what ways it had corrupted me.

As you may recall, back in 1934 Protestant (and excommunicated-sometime-Bolshevik) Vilna had to promise to have her "biracial" Aryan-Hebrew children baptized and raised under the protection of Pope Pius XI in order to expedite her civil marriage to Freemason Attilio.

After both my sister and I were born, Vilna continued to delay and delay on her extorted promise, but by 1937 the Pope was offering the Jews his special protection and Vilna finally gave in. She permitted our baptism. Our newly hired maid, Celeste,[97] was instructed to take us to church for indoctrination by her parish priest, a stern, evangelistic sort who was hell-bent on converting Jews into Catholics with threats of Hellfire if they did not learn better ways.

In contrast, our own emissary to and from the Vatican had been a benign family friend, *Padre* Capitani, with no parish of his own - a little fellow very much like Itkin later became, living in abject poverty, poetically and artistically inclined.

That kind of priest is a prize! No objections to him.

For years the *Padre* had brought Old Masters back and forth from the Vatican for Vilna to clean or restore and had

---

[97] Vilna was a pushover for hard-luck stories and probably hired her off the street without references to keep her out of prostitution.

received food and medical treatment from Attilio for himself and whomever miserable creature from the street he brought to our door.

As a four-year-old watching Mamma work, I was constantly being exposed to all the art projects brought to her at once, stacked against the wall[98] - usually gory religious art of torture and crucifixions and once in a while a Bosch filled with visceral monstrosities. Attilio's books of medical drawings as well as our volume of Dante's Inferno, memorably engraved by Auguste Doré, were also lying around always open to some dissection detail or satanic page, for Vilna's anatomical or design cross-reference.

Vilna's Lutheran childhood, against which she had totally rebelled, had long-deconditioned her to the graphic nature of such relics and like Mamma I too had become accustomed to looking at all that work analytically, not for the horror it depicted but for its anatomical accuracy in depicting it. Both of us were blinded as most children in religious communities become blinded through repeated exposure - that is, until Attilio reminded Vilna to point out to me the actual outrage depicted in such scenes, for he as a physician was still greatly sensitized to it.[99]

Sensitization at home blended with "religious instruction" at Church and a bite from the apple of the tree of knowledge

---

[98] To save on colors all-too-quickly drying up on her palette, Vilna would simultaneously work on Vatican restorations and her own canvases on separate easels.

[99] It was mostly Attilio who kept reminding me through the years that such sights were actually real and deplorable. He would also tell of his experience and outrage as a physician often called to monasteries and nunneries to treat or declare persons dead who had voluntarily immured themselves in shallow coffin-size cubicles where they were allowed to waste away lying in their own excrement in so-called "mystical" catatonic stupor.

now evicted innocent me from paradise. Suddenly, Dante's Inferno as depicted by Doré became real to me and all the agonies of the martyrs blended with the hellfires of tortured souls. And now also according to our parish priest, *souls tortured by God Himself!*[100]

The nightmares came and wouldn't stop.

Vilna was forced to deprogram me. She would shake me awake saying "You are not in Hell! Come with me, we are going to Heaven!"

It didn't take much for her to bring me back to normal. She had likewise been corrupted by Lutheranism and all its threats of Hellfire which sometimes crept back into her mind causing nightmares despite her mature decision to renounce her faith. She had turned to mysticism, first to one, then another, then another variety. She was deeply religious though thoroughly anti-Church of any kind and saw Christ as wholly disembodied and symbolical.[101]

So all of this was what I was telling Itkin while he was trying to get his early-childhood hang ups off his own chest. (By then we had finished painting the ceiling red, and I already knew it had been a big mistake, but too late!)

---

[100] His half-crazed disciple, Celeste, much too anxious to reinforce his teachings, had meanwhile simultaneously grown into the Nanny from Hell whenever our parents were away, pretending to play with us while acting as the Devil after our souls. My desperate phone call to my mother during one of those episodes finally convinced my parents to let her go. Tearfully she left us without references and was probably forced to become a prostitute after all!

[101] When I asked her how to draw an anatomically correct Christ she said Christ was both Human and an Angel. And when I asked her how to draw an anatomically correct angel, she said angels do not have bodies. There was no anatomically correct way to draw either Christ or any of the angels, although all of them were Human in form. This was most puzzling to me until I arrived at my own creed. But *now* I finally understand what she meant.

We paused, then he agonized over having to apply the paint-thinner wincing and joking all the while about mortifications of the flesh while I made us dinner. And by then he had his clothes on but insisted on staying long enough to read me passages from the Marquis De Sade and his own poetic embellishments on them which I found totally sick.

I was completely turned off but let him ramble on, realizing that he desperately needed to unload all this woman-hating crap on someone female but not judgmental. It was his developmental need.

I knew he would outgrow it, which he did.

I also permitted him to elicit a promise from me that I would let him conduct a Black Mass under my new red ceiling - which I did on a Halloween, inviting all the Fordham graduates hanging around Porcelain to attend, and the party became a precursor of the *Rocky Horror Show* nearly two decades before the cult classic.

There was no doubt in my mind that all this prolonged though thoroughly innocent and cathartic fascination with satanic subjects, both by Itkin and the Fordham set, was the result of their having been victimized by their religious education. That the Fordham boys cleansed and sublimated their fantasies by writing successful movie and television scripts[102] while Itkin remained obsessed with becoming a priest in his own religion shows the many forms of adjustment to such victimization that takes place when boys, who will be boys, finally grow up.

But what all of this only goes to show is that pederasty comes in more than one form and should in all instances be restrained. This was the important insight we both came away

---

[102] Together with Porcelain, who had authored *The Purple Pony Murders,* the Fordham set habitually hung out with Alfred Hitchcock at the *Mystery Writers' Guild* and worked on Hitchcock's series at WOR-TV.

with that day in 1952.

Despite our widely divergent approaches, Itkin and I[103] both arrived at the conclusion that *any* religion that gets hold of the young before they have a chance to develop their minds to think critically and impartially, in its hunger to recruit and indoctrinate with so-called Holy Books and liturgy, should be legislatively barred from doing so.

Freedom of religion should never be seen as a license to corrupt the young.

In the years that followed, both of us in our own way carried this notion forward as we moved separately through the various Rights Movements. And Itkin's contribution is by no means slight. Because of him the Vatican, as well as all other antiquated edifices, may soon have to change many of their fundamental tenets or risk total structural collapse under the weight of increasing scientific evidence that whatever is meant by the notion of 'eternal life' may indeed be entirely achievable in *this* world rather than in the next.

But first there must be global ideological emancipation.

Today, adequate legislation protecting the young from the pathology of ideology is still sorely lacking. To my mind, the most important step in that direction would be not merely to tax but to boldly outlaw all religious schooling until after high school. Doing so would simultaneously bolster the public education system and permit a stronger emphasis in science, technology and the humanities.

Religion, like sex, can wait until the young have a chance to grow up and think for themselves.

Again to my mind, in the final analysis anyone who holds St. Mikhail in contempt must also hold the Pope and all his radical priests in contempt, for corrupting *all* the young both

---

[103] As well as later Taulman and I.

gay and straight, and must also hold every radical Imam and every radical Rabi similarly in contempt, for there is no difference among them.

Guys, is it a deal? Zero tolerance for the corruption of the young either sexual or spiritual. Public education[104] and *only* public education before the age of eighteen!

---

[104] Moral education, as opposed to religious education, is something that is already being well-handled in a non-sectarian manner by competent staff in our public school system, reliant upon a wide variety of courses in the humanities. Smaller classes and emphasis on proper incentives (not monetary) to preserve and improve teacher morale will have positive impact on every child's development of their natural moral perception, Those children who do not naturally develop morally will, of course, still be in need of special education - not penal but psychobiological.

Dear Colleagues:

Because a true picture of the 1960's depends so much upon what transpired in the dark ages prior to it, I am still stuck in there trying to provide you with a transition. Let me recap and embellish:

First, by the time *The League* came into being c. 1954, Itkin was already a practicing priest in the *Whatever Church*, taking Confession. Like Porcelain who seemed to know everything about everyone, Itkin immediately became the walking *Wickipedia* of the Movement. He never revealed confidences, but he ferried crucial information to which only he may have been privy back and forth and, besides Porcelain, was everyone's primary source for knowing just what was going on.

Probably the only reason both Itkin and Porcelain weren't martyred right at the start was that they were both more valuable for everyone to spy on. Listening in on what everyone was doing in those days was probably very easy, as it still is today.

Of course the FBI was bugging us - it had to be. And the Mafia too. And the Mafia inside the FBI. And the FBI inside the Mafia. And other surveillance groups inside all other surveillance groups, and the Gays also inside every group. [105]

All of these entities were filled with personnel whose loyalties were mixed, some pro-Gay, others anti-Gay, and a third darker element - the real *Forces of Evil* - which was gathering the kind of information that could be used for profit and extortion and would soon ally itself with the drug cartels.

This was a crowded theater, vulnerable to any shout of *Fire!*[106] - the cancer everyone knew about, the cancer that 1950's McCarthyism and 1960'-'70's Nixonism were stupidly trying to eliminate through naïve trust in J. Edgar Hoover's demented overkill indiscriminately directed in a witch hunt against the victims rather than the perpetrators.

By the 1970's my own attempts to continue to attack the system culminated in a court case fighting to keep my academic job and bid at inclusion in a Nobel Prize awarded to researchers at Cal-Tech,[107] blocked by closet-gays inside the cartel-infiltrated CIA It may have been in my power at that point to provide sufficient information to rift asunder all the Movements at once, but I did not because the end would have been selfish and the result would have been nuclear. And what if, by doing so, I too would have been playing right into the hands of the Mob?

---

[105] By 1958, both Taulman and I became constantly ill with the flu or whatever. Hale too. There was no let up. Compare this with Martha Mitchell's account of what was happening to her post-Watergate due to what she claimed to be high-tech government surveillance similar to what was reportedly taking place in American Embassies in the U.S.S.R.

[106] *Morpurgo vs. Board of Higher Education NYC, et al.,* 437 F. Supp. 1135, 1137. (S.D.N.Y. 1977)

[107] Go to http://artemissmithmorpurgo.tripod.com/Consciousness.html

The old techniques of exposure successfully used by persons such as Jessica Russell Gaver in the 1950's were no longer viable - too many good undercover people might have been killed.

I preferred to remain silent and let history take its course - and that silence, too, has been terrible. I did however hand Judge Weinfeld a series of affidavits which might make a nonfiction novel for posterity to attempt to extract from the confidential archives of the federal courts. One courageous person therein permitted me to name her - Dr. Roberta Baker Thornton, C.U.N.Y. placement officer openly recruiting for the CIA She lived to a ripe old age. However at least three other persons appearing in those affidavits, who were not named and were merely academic sponsors, died soon afterwards - one a suicide, the other two in separate mountain-climbing accidents.[108]

What were the true "Satanic" forces at play?

There really *are* persons out there with defective chromosomes, many of them crowding our prisons in an antiquated penal system still based upon false religious tenets rather than biochemistry.

Global Human exploitation through extortion and prostitution, the spreading drug trade and all the moneys it provides the Mob, must in fact rely upon an army of automata, a sub-Human element that walks among us appearing to be just like the rest of us, but without Conscience, or so lacking in moral capacity as to allow themselves to be used by others.

But religion has never proved itself a cure for that. As research by a new set of educational psychologists working in

---

[108] I could never be certain then or now whether such deaths are real or merely quiet agent retirements.

bioepistemology[109] has shown, moral development in the healthy child occurs naturally. Some people are unfortunately born blind to it, or so environmentally deprived that their moral perception is impaired. Religious education does nothing but confound and corrupt them further. Gene therapies or other forms of bioepistemological therapies might be more effective.

But this is why we have to be ready for the future.

Today, bioepistemological therapies are becoming capable of modifying just about every character variance, including sexual preference. The possibility of effecting genetic and hormonal changes that can also reverse homosexuality *is* still a very touchy political subject. But it *is* scientifically possible to do this now, if someone is truly feeling miserable about their present sexual orientation. What happens to the Gay Rights Movement now?

Does this mean we should legislate a "cure"?

Does this mean that all of us with "good truly Human chromosomes" should become neo-Nazis, purifying the Human race through genetic therapy?

Absolutely not!

What it does mean is that religious ideology needs a fix.

The whole age-old point about distinctly Human relationships is that anatomical correctness[110] should have nothing whatsoever to do with True Love, which is Moral in type. How else will we be able to deal with Aliens, if ever they visit us, or if ever we come to recognize them as dolphins or whales or whatever other intelligent life is already co-existing with us on

---

[109]   See especially the 1950-60's ground-breaking work of Jean Piaget.

[110]   *i.e.,* How many Angels can dance on the point of a pin? There is no answer. Matter and Information, though they directly influence each other, reflect different descriptive modalities. Information may be treated as the *Soul* of Matter. For a lengthier treatment on this topic formulated in the languages of the unified sciences, wait for my next opus, *ArtemisSmith's GrandmaMoseX.*

the planet?

Matter is Matter, and Soul is Soul. The bifurcation is both real and necessary. The "eternal life" of Soul-infused Matter is preserved in *Information*. Intelligent forms recur and Moral Individuals, truly Human individuals, need to be a community guided by an ethic of *inclusion*.

True Love among Moral Individuals should be seen as architecturally neutral, a *Love of Angels*.

We are the Angels.

We *are* the Angels and we are Moral Legion.

Walk with me - in the Past there lies the Future.

Guys, I think I've said enough for one volume. Go to the internet and get the rest of the story as best you can.

For now, let it suffice to say that the Gay Rights Movement most probably survived all the best efforts of the *Forces of Evil* to hold on to that part of its constituency because the 1950's arts pushed through the sexual revolution of the '60's and '70's, thereby making it possible for enough people to come out of the closet and stop paying off. But that took time.

A lot of time.

Itkin lived to grow out of his hang ups before dying of AIDS in 1989. By then I guess we might have rightly compared him with St. Francis, who worked among and kissed the lepers.[111]

Attilio, until he died of heart disease in 1978, was his physician.

---

[111] In contrast, Porcelain lived to a very ripe old age before probably being dumped into a nursing home in the early 1990's by one of his parolees, who told everyone he had died while on a tourist hop to Belgium. Go to http://savantgardearchives.tripod.com/E.SidneyPorcelain.html.

HOW YOU CAN HEAL
Yourself and Others!

by

E. Sidney Porcelain

C.O.P.T.

Photo by Dave Ward

ABOUT THE AUTHOR

E. Sidney Porcelain has written several books, articles, and short stories. Some of his work is listed in THE BEST AMERICAN SHORT STORIES. He is writing two books about ESP for which this is a part of THE PRACTICAL USES OF ESP.

He has had plays produced and a script on NBC-TV; a short film he wrote was shown at the film festival in Spoleto, Italy. He has acted and directed in several productions and has performed in cabaret theatre, singing his own novelty songs. He has also appeared on the stage at the old Metropolitan Opera House in two operas.

Mr. E.S.P. says that since Reincarnation has not been proved he wants to live all of his lives now.

Vilna died of liver cancer and TB of the brain in 1975. Before expiring she suffered the DT's and thought she was in Hell. I was there to grab my mother, look her in the eye and strongly reassure her that she was not in Hell but with me on her way to Heaven.

Billie died of so-called "dementia" and pneumonia in 2008, just a couple of months shy of her 79th birthday. By then she had acquired a whole new, though radically different turn to her artistic career.[112] During most of those years I had been able to keep her mostly Holistic and drug free, but in the end it was out of my hands - not because I was not recognized as her legal guardian, but because the pharmaceutical industry again concealed the hidden side effects of its supposedly new miracle cures.

Misdiagnosis then a stroke and pneumonia set in and she could neither move nor speak, but when I told her we had tried every kind of antibiotic and there was no more hope, a tear fell from her eye and I knew she had heard me. I rushed to tell her one more time, as I had always repeated to her, that our life as artists and master-builders has been meaningful. That what we accomplished is monumental.

Don't make me a liar.

ArtemisSmith **2010**

---

[112] Go to http://billietaulman.tripod.com/index.html for more, and much more I am reserving for future time capsules either in print or on the www!

Billie Taulman in Rome, 1954.

100

APPENDIX A

A Graphic Novel

A. S. Morpurgo

(the authorized unexpurgated edition)

the savant garde workshop

sag harbor . new york . usa

"How To Be A Successful Prostitute (complete with illustrations)"

To

The Faculty of Forest Hills High School

upon their adoption of

McCarthyism

I have been prostituting myself for years
and no one has yet raised an eyebrow.
Here's hoping someone will.

MAMMA

was a whore the day I was born.

I sold my smiles for the great price of
food, love, and shelter. Even at that early
age I sat on gentlemen's laps. One particular
customer would always repay me with a candy
drop, but I'd have to work awfully hard for
it.

He had a long beard which always made me
sneeze, and I always knew what he'd eaten
for lunch.

Peppa was my favorite.

He helped me undress and get into bed.

But it wasn't until I started school that
I received a real challenge to my talents.

Teacher was an old maid but I always called
her Mrs. I got an A on my report card.

My first crush was on a little boy with glasses. I thought he was the philosophical type.

I admired him from a distance but my charms had no effect. He was too tall for me.

When I was seven I decided to become a
gypsie. I sang to the people in the
streets and they gave me nickels to stop.
I decided I wasn't making enough money for
my talents and so I took up a new approach.

I WANT TO
BE A MILLIONAIRE
PLEASE CONTRIBUTE

I painted a sign and sat on the corner with
a little cup. From then on I never needed
an allowance.

By the time I entered high school, my
talents became more subtle; possibly because
I had to wear considerably more underwear.

I went in for high heels with bobby-socks
and dungarees with long hanging earrings.
However I never did learn how to smoke.
I decided I was warm enough.

I became an anti-moralist and was enrolled
into the Satan, Witches, and Devil-worshippers'
Secret Society in school. To be eligible
for membership I had to be iniciated.

The other girls had it in for me and thought
they would really make it tough. I had to
go around saying "I've gotta go." to
everyone who spoke to me for five days.
I had a lot of fun.

After my second year I began to take things
seriously and operated on a strict business
basis. I used to rent out my old boy friends
to my less fortunate colleagues. It was then
that I started a friendship club.

It went along fine until the teachers
wanted to join.

I decided to use my talents in more
specialized fields. I took up writing,
acting, directing, art, music, anddance.
I also dabbled in philosophy, anthropology,
(the
     study of man), Freudian psychology,
and biology. It wasn't long before I became
a walking encyclopedia.

But even there I was forced into prostitution.
It seemed that the only way to tell the truth
was to lie. Especially when all-knowing teachers
were wrongly insisting they were right. Oh
well, the poor souls were happy in their
misery.

114

During my intellectual period I took up the
violin. My teacher was h handsome Italian
with a French accent.

I never quite enjoyed a subject as much.

12

By the time I graduated from school I had
grown tired of mem. I became an actress
and married the theater.

I decided to start working in Burlesque.
I was so talented I was banned.

116

I finally gave up acting and became a writer.
This period of my life I call "My Intellectual
Lean Years." This was due to the fact that I
was determined to give up prostitution in
all forms, and refused to right commercially.
All my friends praised my scripts without
even bothering to read them. I considered it
a great tribute.

At the height of my career I was forced to
stop. I had developed hemmoroids from

Love re-entered my life in the form of a
blonde interne I met while recovering in
the hospital. I insisted that he change
all my bandages. Two weeks later he proposed.

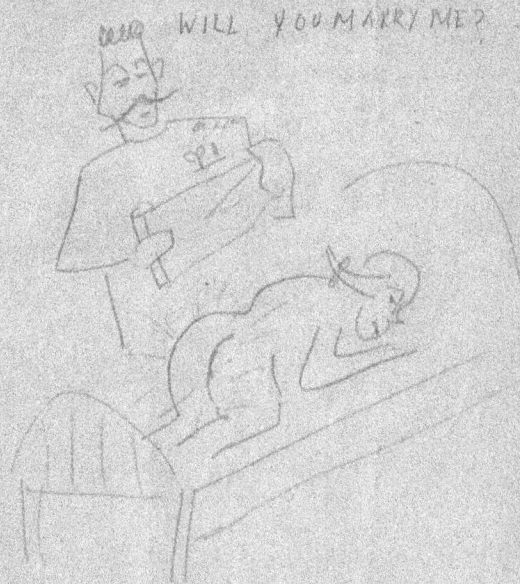

WILL YOU MARRY ME?

After considerable thought I said no! I
wanted to remain a free woman.

My parents finally decided it was about time
I got a job. They wouldn't support me
anymore. I began to write commercially.
Rejection slips poured in and the garbage
man began to resent my existence.

The postman and I became good friends. It
wasn't until a year later that I learned
he had a wife. Oh well----.

Seeing that I was getting nowhere I decided to find an agent. I found several and they all wanted to teach me how to write, for a small fee, of course.

I chose one and wound up teaching him.

My parents were putting the pressure on me again so I decided to take a part time job in an orchestra. But it seemed that I had payed more attention to my teacher's accent than to what he was saying, and so I was not such a good musician. However, the conductor seemed to think I added something to the orchestra anyway, so he wrote in a special part for me. I think I was in the only orchestra in New York City that hired a fourth violinist.

I warned him that I could only play first, second, and third violin but I did not know how to play fourth. He said it didn't make any difference. I could use a standard violin.

That year I made money.

Withmy steady income and peace of mind I
found it hard to get inspiration. I decided
to frequent Cafe society. I met some very
interesting characters, and I began a new
policy of writing from experience.

This new policy had itsbad points since most
of the things I experienced were unprintable.

By this time I had decided that the best
thing for me to do was marry a millionaire.
Equipped with silk stockings and high heels
I set out hunting.

I met a few but they were already married.

124

21

Finding life intolerable at home, I got
myself an appartment. Due to the housing
shortage I could only find one in most
unpleasant surroundings. The landlady was
a fat old whore who kept a sign in all her
rooms. "No Gentlemen Or Dogs Allowed."
Despite these hard restrictions I was forced
to take it.

One night a friend came to visit me and
brought another friend along; a man. Heavens!
The landlady eyed them suspiciously as they
climbed the stairs but didn't say anything.
Two hours passed and nothing happened. Then
there was a knock on the door. I answered, and
sure enough it was old fat-face.

"I've come up, " she said solemnly as I
sought an explanation, "to bring these extra
pillows."

I was overjoyed to find out that her rule
did not apply to all men, only to gentlemen.

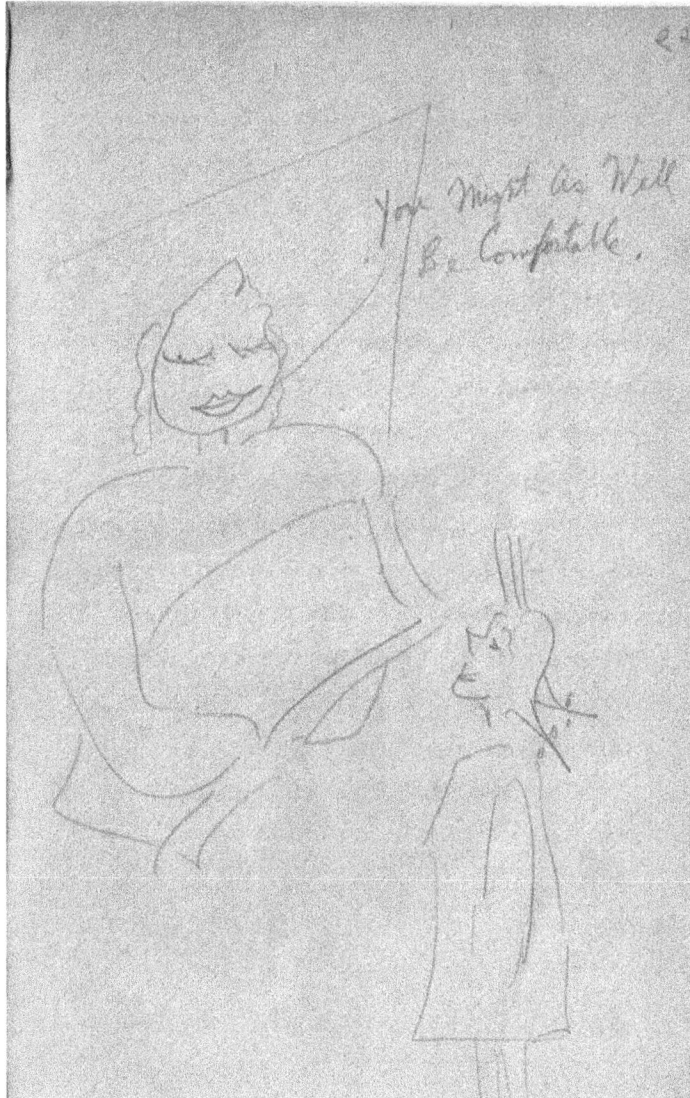

A richuncle died and left me a fortune.
I thought that at last I'd have no need to
sell myself anymore. How wrong I was. My
inheritance taxes were so high that I had to
go to work to pay them. However, the tax
collector was such a nice fellow that he
showed me how to deduct here and there until
I brokeeven. But some good did come out of
my inheritance. Before I could even inherit
paying the inheritance taxes I had to get
a college education which was provided for
me. And so off I went.

In order to further my education on the
subject I was most interested in, I decided
to take a general Bachelor's Degree. I always
thought they were fascinating people.

My roommate was a benzedrine fiend. We had
a wonderful time staying up together and

exchanging advice on what do do about dried-up
boyfriends.

2.6

As in all colleges this one also had sororities.
But they were all so snooty that I decided to
start my own and allow boys in. After considerable
opposition I finally founded the Grasshoppers,
Ants and Worm Eaters' Society for the
Prevention of cruelty to beef. The cows thanked
us, but there are rumors that among the insects
a reward has been offered for my carcass,

They don't taste good!

ahah, a caterpillar!

dead or alive. At least, I can't have a picnic
on the grass without being bitten by some
ferocious police bug.

I became interested in journalism and wrote
in the Campus Gazzette. The newspaper went
out of print within two issues. It seems my
editorials were a bit too heated for the
faculty to allow it to continue.

> The Three F's
> 1. Free Speech
> 2. Free Press
> 3. Free Love

After a long hard battle they finally
consented to put it back in press, providing

By the end of my first year at college   28
a campaign had been started to have me expelled.
It seems that the parents thought I was
corrupting the morals of their precious brats.
I merely laughed and told them to go ahead
and try.

I was determined to learn my trade even
thought there were no classes on the subject.

133

I decided to put a stop to it, so I cut my
hair up short and wore men's clothes. The
result was disastrous.

The men stopped looking and the girls started.

134

After some thought I concluded that I should
be proud to look sexy, so I wore transparent
dresses. The campus was one of the most
picturesque in the world.

benzedrine roommate introduced me to
handsome young alcoholic who invited me
to go out on a binge with him.

My happy college life was ended with the
arrival of my diploma. I had learned all about
Bachelors and **came** in first of my class. My
society gave me a little present to remember

them by. The inscription read---To our

venerable, most beloved founder, who's

pioneering has opened the way for other to

follow in her footsteps.

　　　　With tears in my eyes I thanked

them all, feeling **that** finally I had become

successful in my proffession. Slowly, in

transparent dress and cap and diploma, I

walked away from my Alma Mater.

　　　　Now I was all set.

ArtemisSmith 1949

APPENDIX B

Anne Loves Beth
(Odd Girl)

artemis
smith

(the authorized unexpurgated edition)

the
savant garde workshop

sag harbor . new york . usa

To Willyum

The first publication of a first draft of "Anne Loves Beth," written in 1954, was under the title "Odd Girl" by Beacon Books (Universal Publishing and Distributing Corp., New York City) in 1959. Library of Congress - Card Catalogue No. 59-10947 © 1959 by Artemis Smith. All rights reserved. It was heavily edited by the 'pulp fiction' Publishers, who obliterated the Author's literary style. Simultaneously, a major portion of the unexpurgated version of "Anne Loves Beth" was repeatedly rejected by the publisher and multipli-rewritten circa 1954-1960 with hopes of a hardcover publication which never took place.   This edition comprises that reconstituted version.

This is strictly a work of fiction based upon the Author's investigative infiltration of the 1952 Greenwich Village Gay Scene. No resemblance to actual places or persons living or dead is intended.

1.

ANNE left the subway and dug her hands in her raincoat pockets. She hurried past the crowds on Fourteenth Street, heading toward the quiet block and the brownstone house where the Circle Players met for rehearsal.

She was happy. It was her day to work with Beth.

Anne knew what she felt for Beth. But was it only a girlish crush or something more?

Anne had had girlish crushes before - painful and nagging obsessions with women who were older, lovely or kind. But now she was eighteen, so this had to be more than a crush, it had to be love. Anne loves Beth! It was a sentence Anne barely dared say aloud even in her own mind.

"Anne!" She heard Mark call her and half turned, sorry that he was catching up with her. She allowed him to walk beside her.

"Hey, how about lunch," he said, taking hold of her elbow. "You can't turn me down again."

"Sorry," Anne said, "we're not stopping for lunch."

They reached the brownstone and he ran up the stairs and opened the door for her. "Then supper?" he insisted.

"Sorry," she said as she walked past him.

"Okay," Mark shouted after her, running upstairs to his class, "but I'm not giving up."

Anne entered the room with the makeshift stage and flung her coat down on one of the benches and combed the rain out of her long brown hair. (Beth would not be here yet. Anne always came too early.) She kicked off her heels and put on her dance slippers, then went to the small dressing room to put on tights. She wanted nothing to go wrong with the scene -- she wanted it to be perfect so that Beth would be proud of her. (It had been perfect at home.) The mounting nervousness came and she did not know where to put herself. Beth was coming any minute and Anne felt her heart could not take the shock of seeing her after a week of anticipation.

"Waiting long, Anne?"

Anne whirled and saw her and at once felt weak.

"Not long," she managed to say. (Beth was earlier today; the rain must have hurried her. Her platinum hair was under a kerchief and she wore no makeup.) Anne remained standing, seemingly composed, waiting for Beth to take off her coat -- she was wearing black tights underneath, which fit snugly around her small, womanly body.

"How have you been?" Beth asked, smiling with her mouth and eyes.

Anne wondered briefly if Beth knew what her eyes did to her, wondered if Beth knew that she was trembling. "Okay," she said, "and you?" She tried not to seem too interested.

"So-so," Beth said.

They walked back to the large room and Beth jumped on the stage. Standing in front of Anne, she asked, "Got the script?"

Anne steadied her hand and gave her the sheets of paper.

"Know it by heart?"

(Anne nodded, but now she could not remember the first line.)

"Sit over by the table," Beth said, "and don't move till you finish the first paragraph."

Anne nodded and obeyed awkwardly - sitting would make it easier. She began: "Oh, Alfred … "

"Say, Beth," Mark was standing in the doorway now, munching on an apple.

Anne stopped and watched Beth turn.

"Hi, Mark," she waved. "We're working."

"Come here a minute," he gestured.

"Not now, Mark," Beth answered, sounding annoyed.

But Mark wouldn't be put off. He stepped into the room and went to Beth and lifted her from the stage. "I said I want to talk to you."

He whirled Beth around and down and then dragged her by the hand to the hallway.

Anne felt a tearing inside her. Mark was doing it again -- taking Beth away from her. She wanted to fling something at him, but she knew she had no right to be angry: Mark had a right to Beth, Anne did not.

Mark was whispering to Beth in the hallway and laughing and Anne could hear Beth laughing along with him.

Anne jumped down from the stage and walked toward them as their laughter became louder. Then she heard Beth say "Stop it, Mark! Stop it!"

She had broken away from him and now ran back into the room, Mark following.

Beth almost bumped into Anne.

"Oh Anne," she blushed self-consciously, "come on, Honey, let's start that scene."

She pushed a stray lock of silver hair from her face and firmly took Anne's hand and looked back at Mark. "Damn you!" she said.

Again Anne mounted the stage with her and sat down on the couch, all the while trembling at the touch of Beth's hand - trembling because she had to keep her own hands limp.

"Oh Alfred," she began again, this time reading from the script.

"Not with the script," Beth stopped her.

Mark was watching them. The tearing in Anne's stomach was unbearable. She gulped and put the script down and tried to remember the first line.

"Oh Alfred," she said and could go no further.

"Perhaps you'd rather stand up," Beth prompted. "It might be easier for you."

Anne stood, sneaking a look at the first sentence. "Oh, Alfred --"

"No, Honey, not that way," Beth interrupted. "If you're going to stand, put your legs together - you're standing like a man."

143

"Let her stand like a man," Mark heckled from the rear, "she makes a wonderful Joan. You're wasting her on *Candida*."

"Go mind your speech class," Beth retorted, "Anne needs to learn poise."

Anne's forehead throbbed. She could not stand on the stage anymore, not with Mark and Beth there. "Please excuse me," she said, "I feel sick."

Anne ran from the stage and back to the small toilet, slammed the door behind her. She sat down and sobbed violently. She had to stop thinking of Beth. She had to stop thinking of Beth. She had to stop behaving this way. She had to stop --

"Anne. Anne," Beth's voice came from behind the door, and then the door was flung open and Beth grabbed hold of her. "What are you doing here, you crazy kid!" She folded Anne into her arms and let her cry as she walked her to the small office and sat her down. "Mark's not worth all that! "

It's not Mark, not Mark, it's you! Anne ached to blurt out, but her throat choked with sobs and she had no more breath.

Beth stroked her head and put her soft cheek to Anne's temple and it was soothing. Anne's sobs grew quiet and her eyes and head let themselves rest on Beth's shoulder. Beth was talking strangely, as if she did not believe what she said but said it loudly so that others could hear. "You mustn't take Mark seriously. He flirts with everyone."

She knows it's not Mark. She's covering for me.

But that was too much to hope for. Beth wasn't really aware --

Mark stood in the doorway now, broad-shouldered and careless, and looked down at them. "Mustn't take who seriously? I've been trying to date Anne for weeks."

"Oh, go away," Beth said. But he stood there persistently, looking down at them with impish laughing eyes.

The regular acting class was beginning to arrive and Beth sighed, patted Anne and gently made her let go. "There goes our lesson," she said, giving Mark an angry look. "Come back tomorrow, Anne."

Anne's grip tightened on Beth's shoulder. Afraid to leave her so soon, she choked a new sob.

Beth held her firmly one more moment, giving her strength, and Anne felt again, vaguely, that Beth was aware of her in a way controlled and full of friendship. It made the world stop turning.

"Tomorrow, Anne," Beth repeated.

Her eyes met Anne's and were strong and definite. Anne saw them and realized that Beth knew what she really felt, and recognized in them a strong determination to help her fight against those feelings.

"Thank you," Anne said.

She quickly rose and ran back to the dressing room.

"Hey," Mark called after her, "how about that lunch?" The door slammed on his question.

The dressing room was small and shared by both sexes with a curtain in the middle that was constantly violated. When Anne entered, Marcel was fastening Jennie's bra while she was busy painting her eyebrows. "That was some scene you threw out there," he whistled. "But why Mark! What's he got?"

"Absolutely nothing," Anne said. She turned around and took off her tights and replaced them with a dress in the same motion. Then she bent over Jennie to glance in the mirror and dabbed her face with a damp towel.

Her hair needed combing but she would let that go. She had to leave quickly. She couldn't bear another moment.

But when she opened the door Mark still blocked her way, smiling and confident and offering her his arm. "So accept a free lunch," he said, "or wasn't I the one who upset you?"

A cold fear splashed through Anne. He knew about Beth and was forcing her to go out with him. He knew she wouldn't embarrass Beth. She set her jaw and limply took his arm.

He led her quietly across the street to Frank's Pizza and then to a corner table and sat her close to him. "I've been trying to talk to you for days," he said. His perennial smile exposed itself to her with all its charm.

Anne remained silent.

"Say, Anne -- " he tried again, putting his hand on hers.

She drew it away.

He shrugged and stopped smiling, became serious. "Anne, you don't have to act this way. I'm just trying to help. I know what's wrong with you."

He broke a crumb on the table with his nail.

Anne's expression remained lifeless - she did not want to talk to him.

"You're in love with Beth," he said.

It was a simple statement, not an accusation. Anne knew he had been going to say it but it startled her all the same. She could not answer.

"You crazy kid." He put his hand firmly on hers and would not let her pull away. "You need to talk to someone about it. There's nothing really wrong with you."

Anne looked at him. Without his cocky smile Mark was a different person. Truly handsome. Even likeable. His stage career was just starting but everyone knew he was well on his way to stardom. She was a fool not to like him. Sooner or later they would have to play a love scene together - and Anne had never even been kissed before! How could she become an actress without even knowing how to physically relate to a man! And here was Mark, worldly and much sought-after Mark, more than willing to teach her.

But it was Beth who had first made Anne a woman.

It was Beth who had put her through a complete fashion remake - high heels, feminine clothes, hairdos, stage-walking and talking. What years of high school peer pressure had never been able to accomplish Beth had achieved in only a few short classes.

But soon there would be a time when bland ingénue roles and costume classics would give way to modern parts requiring physical intimacy with the opposite sex, with a man like Mark. (Anne dreaded that time but knew it had to come if she were truly to pursue a career in theater.) And it was Beth who had first cast Anne opposite Mark -- Mark, her special protégé, already well on his way to the top.

Like Anne, Mark also came from the suburbs, but from a broken family, with an alcoholic father in and out of a mental institution and a mother who refused to leave him.

The Army had been Mark's way out and he had been lucky enough to enlist between two wars. His two-year tour of duty had transformed from a scrawny brooding underachiever into a veritable man's man, supple and muscular and seemingly self-assured. But he lacked a college education and his low grades would doom him to follow his father in some blue collar trade - unless he could find a better path. Meeting Beth, touring in the USO, and playing opposite her, had pointed him in a new direction. He had great looks and acting talent, and all of his Army buddies had urged him to give it his best shot.

Now he was out of the Army but still seeing Beth. She was still mentoring the progress of his career -- if not ultimately in theater, at least as a male model. Either way, Mark was on his way to the top and Anne was a fool to keep rejecting him.

Might she not at least try to work with him?

"Look," Mark went on, "it's safe to talk to me, Anne. I'm A-1 understanding, honest."

His manly smile came back and then went again. She looked steadily at him and then forced herself to nod.

He straightened, feeling he had won a step forward. He broke another crumb on the table, more happily.

"How about Monday night?" he said. "I get free passes to all the off-Broadway shows."

She smiled and then began to laugh. He was so persistent and yet so practical. Perhaps she might be able to endure him on an off-night if they were both watching a play.

Now Frank brought them veal and peppers and they both lay down their arms for a truce.

But Anne could not rid herself of Beth's presence - her touch, her fragrance. She dreaded going back tomorrow, to face Beth again. Beth would behave as if nothing had happened today and Anne would again watch her from the corner of her eye, conscious always of a need to hold her and a horrid burning frustration.

Perhaps Mark was right.

She would someday get over it.

She had to get over it.

She looked up desperately at Mark.

He sensed her glance and met her eyes.

"All right, we can date -- but on one condition --"

"Shoot," he said.

"What happened today, can we pretend that it was really over you?"

He laughed. "That's a twist! I don't know if my ego can take it."

"I'm sure your ego will survive," Anne answered bitterly.

"All right," he shrugged, laughing. "But before I'm through, you really will feel that way about me!"

She laughed. Somehow that was very funny.

Later, he walked her to the subway and they stopped at the entrance.

"Look," he said, "seriously, let's be pals -- just acting partners. You need the polish and I can help you. I'm harmless - and passive." He put up his hands to show her. "I can wait until you decide to really fall in love with me."

She smiled. He was doing his best to be sweet and it was gaining ground for him. She needed a friend, and an acting partner, and Mark was a prize choice - even if her pulse never quickened when he touched her like Beth touched her. She did need a male friend - she had never dared to have close friends, certainly not boyfriends, and not close girlfriends either. Not since she was twelve. Not since --

"All right," she said, "but just acting partners."

She extended her hand to him and they shook, then she turned to go down the subway stairs following the sign that said TO QUEENS.

Anne lived with her family in a modest part of the suburbs where forty-year-old houses, none exactly alike, were crowded side by side. Tall trees stood in front of them on poorly kept sidewalks hard to walk on with high heels. The smell of fresh rain on wet leaves was ever-present even on clear days and the sun could scarcely shine through branches that had been allowed to grow until they touched the branches of other trees across the narrow one-way street. At the end of the block, a new apartment project had begun to encroach upon the treasured empty lot of her childhood.

Anne loved the old neighborhood, but she loathed going home. There was nothing for her at home -- nowhere was really home except near Beth. Now that she had just turned eighteen she planned to leave home, live on her own, find her own way.

She reached her house and turned the key in the front lock. She hoped she would not be heard. She wanted to run directly upstairs and shower and change, without being noticed or talked to. She wanted to be entirely alone to think of Beth.

She entered quietly.

Mom could be heard in the kitchen.

The french doors of the living room opened to the hall, revealing the television set standing dark and silent. Dad had not yet come home. Her kid sister, Dori, was out on a dinner date. There was no one blocking her way to the stairs. Relieved, Anne went upstairs, her thoughts full of Beth.

The shower cooled her, took off the sweat of dancing and rehearsal. Anne wiped her skin sensuously with the wash cloth full of perfumed soap, then rinsed and repeated the ritual another time, finally wiping herself dry and spraying herself with cologne. She was, after all, about to become an actress - perhaps even a movie star. Shouldn't she begin to look the part?

She folded the long white towel around her like a toga and looked at herself in the foggy full-length mirror. She let the towel fall and admired herself. There was nothing wrong with her body. Her skin, white and sensitive, was unblemished, her muscles were taut and shapely. She was now a woman. There could be no denying about that.

Once she had been sad about it.

As a child she had strapped her breasts tightly, hoping they would not grow full. She had insisted on wearing jeans to school despite bad marks in grooming. She had snipped her straight brown hair in fits of rage despite Mom's attempts to make it grow. And most of all, she had refused to play with the girls - preferring to remain a tomboy, always trying, and failing, to make the team.

Anne was different - not like anyone else in her family, and though she loved them, try as she might, she could never feel close to any of them. She could never confide in them. They would never understand.

Anne stepped up to the mirror again and looked at her face: first one profile, then the other. Then she held her long hair up -- she had finally grown it, but only to please Beth -- the hair that now had become her pride. Her face was beautiful and feminine - not the face of a lesbian. How could she be a lesbian?

Yes, she knew that word -- had always known it. She could not remember when she had first heard it, but always knew that it pointed to her. Now, it was no longer an unusual word - it was even a common word, used indiscriminately. Everyone in acting class threw it around recklessly, would point to someone on the street and say, "Will you just look at that dyke fight up the street!" or "Just look at those two queers coming out of that bar!" joking with each other, imitating effeminate men or burly women almost with secret envy. There were plenty of them in the neighborhood, which at night drew many perverts and prostitutes.

Anne thought she knew the faces of lesbians. They were fat and ugly and cruel. How could she be like them? Panic returned to her: *If I let myself go on thinking of Beth this way, I soon will be like them!*

She snatched up the towel and ran from the mirror, from her own image, out into the hall to her room.

She had barely dressed for dinner when Mom called up to her from the bottom of the stairs. "Eva, are you home?"

Anne sighed. She would have to answer. She came out of her room and to the head of the stairs. "Yes, Mom?"

"Telephone for you," her Mom announced. (Her hands were full of meatloaf and she was anxious to get back to the kitchen.)

Anne hurried downstairs to the living room. She seldom got calls and wondered who it might be.

The living room was dark except for the dull light of the television set. Dad was sitting in his chair, in his undershirt, unwinding before dinner.

Anne went to the telephone and answered shyly.

"Anne?" It was Beth.

Anne paled. Beth seldom called and each time Anne had been paralyzed with fear. She hoped her excitement would not show on her face, hoped Dad would not look up from the flickering black-and-white screen.

"Anne, I'm worried sick about you," Beth said. She paused, "Can you talk?"

"No," Anne managed to say. A wonderful whirlpool was again flowing around her. Beth cared. Then the thoughts in front of the bathroom mirror gripped her and filled her with terror. *I don't want Beth! I will not be a lesbian!*

"I'm all right, Beth," she whispered shakily. "Mark and I had a talk. Everything's fine."

"So it really *was* Mark," There was a sound of disbelief in Beth's voice. "I'm glad," she said skeptically.

"Yes, it was Mark," Anne lied shakily. "But we're just friends now. I'm sorry it happened. I didn't mean to come between the two of you."

Again Beth paused for a long time and then said clearly, "There's nothing serious between us, Anne. I want you to know that. He's all yours if

150

you want him."

There was another long silence and Anne did not know what to say.

Beth's voice came through the phone again, full of concern and warmth. "Anne, be careful. Don't go off like that again. Call me if you're in trouble. Remember, you can always talk to me."

"Thank you," Anne whispered. "I'll be all right, I promise." She hung up quickly. She could not bear to talk to Beth another minute.

"Hey, who was that?" Dad's voice spoke innocently above the newscaster on the screen.

Anne whirled, frightened. "Just Beth," she stammered, then rushed toward the stairs.

"Who's Beth?" he called after her.

"Just a friend," she shouted back.

Mark didn't sing in his shower, he recited Sophocles -- so seriously it made Anne laugh as she listened in his living room, marking movements on her script.

"You'll never make Oedipus," she shouted.   "Ah, well, maybe you will," he joked.

He put on his shorts and entered the living room, wiping his face and hair, letting her inspect him.

"How do you like the new after-shave?" he said.

Anne hated the smell of it. "Perfect," she lied. "Beth will love it."

"She most surely will," he said cockily. "Will you be all right here by yourself?"

"A perfect place to be alone with my lines," Anne said.

He went to the bedroom and took another five minutes to put on black-tie, and then he was ready for the Opera.

"Kiss Beth for me, will you?" Anne joked -- she had learned to joke about her feelings.

Mark laughed then blew her a kiss and said "Done."

Anne knew he wouldn't. Mark would kiss Beth for himself, and would sleep with her. Casual sex, so what! Beth would think nothing of sleeping with Mark even if she had no real feelings for him. For Beth, sex was just a proper nightcap after a night on the town.

The door closed after him and Anne knew Mark would not return until late, if at all.

Now Anne was left to the four walls -- expensively decorated walls but lifeless all the same -- and she could not concentrate on her script. It had been three months since that day when she had acted so foolishly. Talking about Beth to Mark had helped, but there was something terribly lacking from the world, and even Mark's constant attention would not fill that gap.

She tried to remember how good it should feel to just be alive, to enjoy the fresh air and golden sunshine. But Mark's dating Beth made the entire world that much worse -- she could not help feeling jealous and it was painful to sit memorizing lines, all the while longing to be sitting next to Beth in Mark's seat at the Opera.

She tried to analyze her state of mind. It was natural for her to react this way to Beth. Mark had told her so. Beth was the real Mom she never had. After Dori was born, sickly, needing all of her attention, Mom, exhausted, had pulled away from Anne, had even been loathe to breast feed her. (Yes, Anne vividly remembered that earliest rejection!). Since the age of three Anne had been left to fend for herself while Mom focused on Dori. It had forced her to become entirely independent and resourceful. But she had grown up without any real sense of belonging to her family -- it was only natural for her now to respond to someone older whom she admired, someone beautiful and womanly, someone who cared enough about her to scream, *For God's sake, Anne, listen and learn!*

But there was something else nagging at her -- a fierce unhappiness that she had known all her life. She felt entirely out of place. And she could never remember when she had not longed for some woman -- first Mom and then her teachers. Never, not once, had she longed for or sought the company of men. Not even Mark made her feel alive, and Mark was the closest because now he could talk to her and she to him, freely.

Anne decided to leave the script and dream of Beth. She fell asleep on the day couch, where Mark found her when he returned the next morning.

"My God, they'll think I slept with you!" she said.

"You did," Mark joked, crunching on another piece of toast.

"I mean, you know -- " she was embarrassed, "I didn't, did I?"

"Hell no," he laughed. "If you had you'd remember it." And then he paused, still laughing. "Perhaps I should be worried. How old are you?"

"Nineteen," she lied.

He sighed with false relief. "Safe!"

"Mark," she said slowly, "if we had slept together, would anything be different?"

"Sure," he said absently, concentrating on his eggs.

"How?" she persisted.

He shrugged. "You'd be grown up."

"Mark," she pleaded, "no one's ever sat down and actually told me about what it's like to have sex."

Mark stopped eating breakfast and looked at her. "What are you driving at?"

Anne paused and looked down. "I can't go home this morning. I won't be able to explain it to Dad."

"Tell him you stayed at Beth's," he said unconcerned, "She'll cover for us."

"It's not that." She shook her head. "I've just decided not to go home again. I can't bear it there anymore. I'm so confused, Mark. I don't know which way to turn."

He put his napkin down, stood up and went to her side of the table. He took hold of her shoulders and rubbed away the tightness there. "Has your turn come, Anne?" he said softly.

"I don't know," Anne said. She rose and walked away from him. "Did you have a good time with Beth?"

"Uhuh," he nodded, watching her.

She turned and gazed at him. "I'm terribly jealous of your times with Beth," she said. "I can't bear the thought of your being with her. I do love her, Mark. There's nothing I've been able to do about it!"

He gave her a look of impatience and sat down again to his breakfast.

She turned and traced the lines of a vase with her fingers. "Mark, just exactly what do you want of me?"

"I couldn't begin to explain it to you," he answered distantly with an air of boredom.

"How does one go about having sex?" she persisted.

"Why do you want to know?" he retorted.

"Does Beth like you? Is she pleased?" Anne insisted.

"Yes." He was growing impatient.

"Mark," she said. There was great strain in her voice and she turned from the vase to look at him.

He turned, summoned by the tone of her voice, and paid attention to her.

"What exactly do you want of me?" she repeated.

"I want to make love to you," he said seriously.

"In graphic terms," she insisted.

"Why do you want to know?" he repeated.

"I want to know so I'll be able to please Beth," Anne said.

Now he laughed, a jeering laugh aimed at her.

"You can't do that," he said. "It's impossible."

"Nothing is impossible," Anne replied.

She returned quietly to the breakfast table and slowly buttered her toast. She felt him watching her through the whirlpool that again was splashing her. She couldn't bear to live this way anymore. The time had come to push herself out of her depression. Yet losing her virginity to a man would be like dying. What would it be like, to die? She felt the cold steel of the knife in her hand. It was a dull knife. In the bathroom there was Mark's razor.

Anne closed her eyes and put down the toast, gripping the knife desperately. Somewhere beyond the whirlpool Beth's words resounded in her ears: *You can always talk to me.* But Anne knew she could never bring herself to talk to Beth. Her life had become a meaningless droning obsession. She had to break away from it now, had to do something decisive -- had to either die, or change.

"Mark," she managed to choke through the whirlpool, "Mark, make love to me."

Mark did nothing. He sat watching her, his eyes carefully studying her face.

Anne saw the knife in her hand and dropped it.   It lay on the table, reflecting the light from the window, a simple, dull thing that symbolized Mark's razor, safe in the bathroom.

She forced herself to look at him again and rose, facing him, almost like playing out a scene. "Well, what are you waiting for? It's what you've wanted, isn't it?"

He hesitated, went over the thought in his mind then decided. He rose too and faced her, took her firmly.

As if a part of her was standing off and watching, Anne felt his arms come around and pull her to him. She felt the roughness of his beard, his clothes, and finally the warmth of his body pressed against her own. She felt his mouth take the nape of her neck, moving downwards, felt his fingers opening her blouse, exposing her bra, undoing it. And when the wetness of his mouth moved over the mounds of her breast the fear growing inside her mounted to the edge of panic. This was not an acting scene and she really did not want him. She raised her hands to stop him.

"Mark, no," she gasped.

He would not listen, pushed her hands aside, put his wet mouth on her breast.

"Mark, no," she gasped again, but she knew it was too late to stop him now.

She closed her eyes and let him take her, take all of her - felt his body invade hers, on and on, endlessly until he was satiated, all the while thinking how meaningless it all was to her, how foreign, how wrong. His after-shave was offensive, his sweat, his passion -- his entire presence, oppressive. And the colder, less responsive she grew, the more frenzied he became, the more determined to fill her, to make her feel him.

Finally he pulled out and ejaculated outside her.

Anne lay there sickened, wondering when he would let her go home.

The Players spent lunch and afternoon breaks around the corner from the theater at a café called The Florentin, where one cup of coffee, priced twenty-five cents, was sufficient to hold a table reserved all day through a series of shifts. The management did not discourage this because its reputation depended upon the "Bohemian" atmosphere which drew many tourists, and the actors, poets, musicians, were certainly all part of that atmosphere.

Anne surveyed her fellow students. Each was involved with himself and this strange process of transition to adult life. Each had a lingering childhood problem. Each was experiencing some form of adolescent love - or nameless lust - or need that could not be fulfilled except by children's magic.

Jacques belonged to the group, too short and boyish for his age, effeminate yet perhaps still unaware, followed incessantly by the fat and simpering and servile Carol, his childhood sweetheart from his Bronx neighborhood, now still pursuing him at the urging of his parents, always like a dog at his feet.

Then there was Marcel, who played the lute and sang medieval folk songs while trying to grow a beard. And his steady girl, Jennie, whose voice was high-pitched and whose mind efficiently catalogued clichés, snatching bits of culture from others' conversations, repeating them at the best times.

And also Ronnie, the big tall fat boy with a Shakespearean voice and a magnificent talent for acting - who had brought tears in all their eyes as King Lear; he too was affected like Jacques, but was ashamed of it and went to great lengths to prove he was manly.

Yesterday, Anne had been one of them. Today, Mark, the grownup, the graduate, had severed her from the group.

Today Anne was neither here nor there, having become one entirely alone. Today the world was truly colorless and all her virgin dreams were gone. Today she felt wiped out, so completely, in all her limbs, and her eyes saw only black-and-white shadows. She sat quietly in her corner by the large window and watched them all, not listening to their talk, not drinking her coffee.

"Anne, you look ghastly," Jennie said, stopping her incessant flow of words to seriously look at her. "Are you sick?"

"Just a cold," Anne lied. She wanted so much to tell them the truth, but it would have been awkward and silly -- telling them that she had just lost her virginity -- telling them that she was no longer a child. She was glad that later she might go home to rest. (She wondered how Mom and Dad would react to her having been out all night -- to her not even having called them. There would be hell to pay. No matter -- she would not be living at home for long. She would find a job and move out by next month.)

Then Beth arrived with Mark, snatching a ten-minute coffee-break, and Beth sat next to her.

Immediately Anne was aware of new strength and her pulse quickened.

Beth seared her with her eyes and Anne wondered if Mark had told her.

No, Mark had not told her. Beth didn't appear to know anything had happened. She was only concerned about the rings under Anne's eyes. "You ought to get more beauty sleep," she said.

Anne nodded and smiled, embarrassed. She could not look into Beth's eyes -- Mark had thrown a barrier there.

Mark was watching her too, with a firm, knowing gaze. "How are you, Trooper?" he said.

"Okay," she said feebly.

In a few minutes Anne tried to slip away, but at the end of the street Mark caught up with her and took her arm. "Where do you think you're going," he asked protectively.

"Home," she sighed.

She stopped and regarded him more strongly. "I'm sorry if I seem cold. But I can't be warm. Mark, I don't really want you again."

He walked with her, his hands in his pockets, looking at the ground. "You make me feel responsible. Was this really only the first and last time?"

"I'm sorry," she said.

"Look," he spun her around, "you're not giving it a fair chance. It takes practice to get used to the idea. It doesn't always work out the first time."

"You've already got Beth," she retorted, "You don't need me. Mark, you've had me, and now it's over."

He looked down again and did not answer.

They walked quietly to her subway.

"Look," he said with his steady glance, "I want to see you again. Beth is not the only woman in my life. I'm free as a bird and I really want to see you."

Again Anne shook her head. "I'm grateful to you, Mark, for showing me what it's all about. But there are some things I just can't feel. Please let's just be friends."

He held her shoulder and would not let her turn from him, stood regarding her firmly. "Look, Anne, there's nothing wrong with you. You're every bit normal. Please help me prove it to you. Please give me time."

"Poor Mark," she smiled. "Don't feel so guilty. I asked for it. I got it. Now give me a week or so to think, to take it all in."

He pinched her cheek and straightened. "That's more like it!"

She watched him walk away with a whistle and a bounce and Anne wondered why she felt so blank about him. Deeply she knew that watching Beth walking away would have been different.

The day was lingering an extra hour on the tree tops and Anne thought as she walked home: *How right it is that it is Spring.* Spring is the time for moving and shaking dust out of old corners. Tomorrow she would look for a job and an apartment; but by early morning, she planned to leave home, suddenly. It would have to be a sudden move, so sudden that her parents would be too overcome with shock to try to stop her. Once she had escaped there would be time and opportunity to ease their feelings.

With the coolness of thought that springs from unpleasant necessity, she laid out her plans. She would stay up all night to pack her belongings in light suitcases and paper bags, and her treasures in a small trunk -- her sketches, attempts at poetry, uncompleted books and plays, all her childhood efforts at trying to find herself through self-expression. For three years they had collected in secret places, hidden from Dad's criticism and Mom's concern.

Ever since the day Dad had put his foot down. He was difficult to speak to, set in his ways, half-stuck in an old-world culture that had no respect for American educational advantages - especially for girls:

"You cannot go to Bennington," he had said.

"But the scholarship-- "

"Scholarship? Another word for charity. No! Your mother needs you here. You have enough to learn right here about choosing the right husband and becoming a good wife."

But that wasn't the real reason he had said No. He was afraid to see Anne better herself, grow out of the multi-ethnic neighborhood they had all grown up in, climb up the social ladder.

She had heard him arguing with Mom who was trying to take her side: "What, so she can come home all ivy-league uppity like Novak's kid and give us the bird? No way! Not in my family!"

Dad was blue-collar but extremely successful at his trade. He owned a small moving company serving the Park Avenue antiques and fine arts crowd, did none of the heavy work himself, and pocketed the profits mostly in cash, off the books. He had stashed away a small fortune - but neither Anne nor Dori would ever get hold of it - that was going straight to their husbands, when they married men he could approve of. Only husbands could be trusted to manage money.

Now Anne reached her house, ran up the steps and unlocked the front door. Portia, her cat, greeted her with a meow.

Anne bent down to pet her. The soft fur felt good in he hands and she felt the tension in them ease.

No one was home. It didn't look as though they even had missed her. Perhaps they thought she had gotten home to late last night and left again too early this morning. Maybe she wouldn't have to explain her being out all night. Or she could tell them she had stayed at Beth's. But at least the house was empty for the moment. They had probably all gone to a movie and wouldn't be home till late.

She hurried upstairs to pack.

For three years she had worked as a part-time cashier at the local supermarket, then also as a receptionist in a dentist's office, and through both jobs had been able to save enough money, ostensibly to pay for night classes at the Circle Players, although Beth had soon awarded her an acting scholarship. Thanks to that, her bank account had accumulated close to a thousand dollars and now she felt financially secure enough to leave home.

Receptionist jobs would come easily to her - her natural looks, and her new training in fashion, would now give her an immense advantage. Perhaps she could start on a modeling career, make the rounds. No matter what, she had never had a problem being hired on the spot and apartments should also be easily found, even if only sublets.

There remained only for Anne to pack up her belongings. Now she could not wait another day. Even planning to wait until the next morning seemed too long. It had to be done now!

Anne packed hurriedly. There were many things that would not fit in bags -- her books and childhood keepsakes. But they would be safe until she could come back for them. She would take only the most essential things. The rest if need be she could replenish from scratch. But she had to leave now, secretly, or she might be stopped. Particularly if they should find out that she had been out all night and didn't call them. She could never explain why to Mom and Dad, not in a way they would understand.

When everything was packed she brought the heavy canvass suitcase and duffle bag down and called for a cab that would drive her into the city.

She began to write a note: *Dear Folks, I guess I've run away from home.* She stopped. It sounded childish. How could she explain about Beth or Mark, about not wanting to get married and have children? She could not even reason out her revulsion at the parade of ethnic marriage prospects to whom she had been subjected at Saturday night Church gatherings. All these things, to her parents, would seem such strange motives for leaving home, for wanting to be left alone in a world full of strangers.

Anne tore up the note. It would be better to call them and assure them by telephone that she was safe and well and then perhaps to arrange a meeting with them at some public place where she could try to explain to them that she had turned eighteen and was now grown up and had a right to go her own way.

Her cab arrived and with the help of the driver she loaded it with her things. Only Portia remained to meow goodbye.

Anne paused, cursing mildly under her breath and took the cat in her arms. "Come along, I can't leave you," she said.

With the help of the cabbie she found a slightly-roachy medium-priced hotel that would take both of them in.

2.

THREE weeks passed and the decorating was nearly done. Anne and Portia found themselves alone, sitting by the telephone with its unlisted number, waiting for it to ring. She had found a perfect place -- a year's sublet with adequate furniture, and convenient to The Florentin and the Circle Players. Needing to be alone until she felt fully settled and secure, she had skipped classes and temporarily dropped entirely out of view. Now she was ready for guests, but no one knew where she lived or how to contact her.

Whom should she call first?

Beth first came to mind but Anne painfully rejected the idea. There was Mark - but seeing him might be too great a strain right now. What a pity they couldn't just be friends. She didn't want to be touched by him, but not because of fear or deep revulsion -- it was just that he had left her with a nothing feeling that broke all illusions and put it blankly to her that she was indeed different, not interested in men, not even Mark.

She decided not to sit and brood about this and picked up the phone. She would call Jacques; he was safe, possibly even already Gay. She wondered whether he knew of women who were, and if they were not all scary-looking perverts.

"Hi, Princess," she heard him say, "where have you been? Your folks have been pounding at my door."

"I'm sorry," Anne said.

(She had called them just after she left, tried to explain to them. But they were still angry, anxious. She volunteered only the most minimum information and still hadn't told them where she lived. She was afraid to meet them in person, even in a public place. She wanted to see them, wanted to invite them to her house, but only when she could be certain they were resigned to her having left home.)

"Want to come see my new place?" she asked Jacques.

"Sure," he said. "I'm free tonight. How about now?"

"All right, tonight," Anne laughed.

"The address, please, and the telephone number."

Anne hesitated. "You won't give it out -- "

"Hell no," he said.

Anne paused for another moment, then laughed at herself. She couldn't go on being a recluse, not when she wanted her telephone to ring so badly. She gave Jacques the number and the address and told him to give her an hour to make tidy.

The apartment suddenly grew real. Even the loathsome ashtrays Anne personally had no use for. Anne felt that the dream her childhood ordeal had passed and that she was finally alive again, in a different world full of new things to do and think, free from parents and adolescent fears.

She gained new courage and now dialed Beth then waited, barely able to speak from the excitement that welled in her.

Then Beth's voice, clear on the telephone, forced her to speak.

"Beth? Hi."

"Well, hi," Beth said. "We've missed you. Your Dad's been frantic."

"I left home," Anne said. "Want to come up and see my new apartment?"

"Sure!"

Beth turned away from the receiver and said, "Hey, Mark -- it's Anne." Anne's heart sank.

So now Mark would also know where she lived. She had hoped to catch Beth alone.

"When do you want us over?" Beth said.

"Tomorrow night?" Anne stammered. At least Beth would be with him. Mark would be easier to handle. And it was better if Anne did not see Beth alone -- she knew somehow that it would be better.

"Okay, around seven," Beth said, "but only for an hour - we have tickets to a show."

Anne gave her the address and then too soon the conversation was over and the telephone receiver was down again, silent.

Anne remembered Jacques would be over and began putting away paint cans and underwear for his arrival, patting Portia as she hurried back and forth.

She called the corner deli and ordered canapés and beer to be delivered, then sat down and waited.

Jacques was temporarily staying at the Y some twenty blocks away. He arrived soon after the delivery boy and rang the doorbell eight times in rhythm to identify himself. She buzzed him up and he leaped two steps at a time up the five flights to where she stood in the hallway, waiting.

"Anne," he embraced her playfully, "so what are you doing living in the Village?"

She gave a sphinx smile and led him in, displaying her flair at interior decorating. She had rearranged and spread new cloth over the furniture so that it had lost its dumpy look. Her sketches, hung on the walls, reflected the sublet's new occupant.

"What you can do with next-to-nothing," Jacques whistled.

"Beer or what?" she asked, efficiently going to the refrigerator. "The or what," he said.

She poured scotch in a kitchen glass for him and then came back to sit on the day couch.

"Hey, what a location," he said, "straight across from the Oval."

"The Oval?" Anne was puzzled. "What's so special about that place?"

Jacques flipped. "Don't you notice?"

It was amusing to watch him - he took pride in being effeminate. The entire Cast had gotten used to it.   "No, seriously," Anne said, "Is that a queer place too?"

"For butches," he nodded. "Strictly rough trade."
He sat back and looked at her. "You've changed. What's happened to you? Why the sudden move?"

Anne paused for a moment, fingering her beer can, then looked directly at him. "Can I tell you a secret?"

He nodded, returning her glance and leaned forward.

"I had to move," she continued, "because I think -- somehow I know -- that I'm queer."

She looked at him and waited.

He paused for a moment then guffawed. "Alice, welcome to the club!"

Now they both laughed, Anne blushing, but relieved.

She sat nearer to him and said, "Tell me more about the Oval. Do girls really go there?"

"Mostly drag," he nodded.

"Drag?" Anne had often wanted to ask what was meant by that. The rest of the Cast seemed to know.   "With men's clothes on. You know -- tough. There's also a lot of pimping too. Bull-Derricks hustling their fems. Strictly low class. A real dive."

Anne smiled bitterly. "Thanks for the vocabulary lesson."

But now they knew they could really be friends and Jacques spoke more freely of himself. He was in love with a boy named Gene who would have nothing to do with him. Jacques chased him from one leather bar to the next and scored new tricks along the way even while constantly giving Carol the slip.

Then he spoke of other things, news of the Players and how Anne had been missed at rehearsals and how her replacement was a dog. And then there was a long silence again and Anne spoke slowly.

"Do you know of better places than the Oval?"

Jacques shook his head. "I'm the wrong one to ask -- brave the joint some afternoon before the crowd comes in and ask one of the waitresses. But stay away from the customers -- they're mostly weirdoes. Seedy. Maybe even dangerous. They'll steer you way off track and God knows where you'll end up. The women too. Be careful."

His words filled Anne with dread. But the information was invaluable. At some point she knew she would have to dip her toes in Hell in order to get directions to a better place. For some reason venturing into a snake pit seemed easier, less dreadful than simply confronting Beth with her feelings.

"Thanks," she said. "I guess I'll work up the nerve to poke my face in there one of these days."

When he was gone she looked out of her window for a while, toward the Oval, trying to make out in the dark whether the figures entering were men or women.

"Hi, there!" Beth came first up the stairs and took both Anne's hands and inspected her. She fondly pressed cheek against cheek. "You look wonderful!" Mark, coming up behind her, nodded knowingly and said, "What's your tonic!"

"Freedom," Anne said. "Come on in."

Indeed, she felt free. Her talk with Jacques the day before had given her new assurance and she had prepared for their visit with great calm. A new sensation for her - she was usually frozen with expectation.

"It's a swell place, Anne," Beth said.

She seemed more excited than usual. Anne wondered if Mark had told her his version of what had happened between them. Beth was making a great effort to be friends.

"Just a sublet," Anne said, then took their coats.

"Just a block from the theater," Mark noticed. "Convenient. When are you coming back?"

"I'm not," Anne said. "I'm giving up acting for a while."

"That's a shame, Anne," Beth went to her, took her hands again and squeezed them tightly. "You shouldn't quit - you have real talent."

A lump welled in Anne's throat. How could she stop seeing Beth? But there was Mark -- and there was that impossible barrier still standing there!

"I'm sorry. I have to," she blurted. She avoided looking at Beth.

"Can I pour you drinks?"

They nodded and went to sit on the day couch, but on opposite sides.

Anne felt Beth knew about what had happened with Mark. She behaved as though she knew and had decided to let Mark handle it. Had decided to give Mark to Anne -- as if Anne were in greater need of him. *How awful,* Anne thought. *I don't want him. How can I convince her of this? How can I convince Mark?*

She brought their cocktails and they made small talk and Beth laughed more than usual. Her composure was tarnished at the edges, Anne noticed, and she also drank four martinis within the allotted hour of their stay. When she got up to straighten her dress and say "Well, let's go," she was wobbling slightly.

"Come back soon."

Impulsively Anne took her hands and looked deeply into her eyes.

Beth looked away and said, "Thanks."

Mark brought their coats and there was nothing more for Anne to say except the usual goodbyes.

Mark gave her a meaningful glance as they left.

Anne returned it icily.

Now the door was shut and Anne was alone. It brought back that dreadful tearing in her stomach and she knew the reaction had finally come down. Beth still beguiled her, despite Mark, despite the talk with Jacques, and even despite Beth!

There could be no relief.

She would lie in bed all night with her eyes fixed on the ceiling, picturing Beth in all the secret ways she had dreamed of in adolescence, of their arms and thighs locking in long embraces, of a phantom penis making love to Beth. Marks? No, Anne's.

There could be no relief.

The phone's ring jolted her from her reverie. It was Mark.

"It's too late to call, Mark," she said.

"When am I going to see you," he insisted.

"I don't want to hurt Beth," she evaded.

"Beth and I are through," he said emphatically.

"I don't want you, Mark," she said more strongly.

It had no effect.

"I want to see you," he demanded. "Be right over."

Before she could answer him he had hung up, and in a matter of minutes he was ringing and banging on the downstairs door. She finally let him in, afraid to annoy the neighbors. And when he entered, again he took her, and took her, and took her.

"It takes time to get used to it," he insisting. "Just because you can't feel anything yet doesn't mean you're a lesbian. Give it a chance, Anne!"

Those were the magic words. *Give it a chance.* Perhaps he was right, she might grow used to it.

In the weeks that followed, she was finally getting used to it, giving it a fair chance. Now it had become merely tedious but no longer unbearable.

Feeling sorry for him, Anne convinced herself that if she gave him what he wanted then perhaps eventually he would tire of her. Perhaps if she faked it, his own obsession with her would fade.

But it didn't. Try as she might, she couldn't reason with him, couldn't get through to him.

"Look, just because you satisfy me doesn't mean you satisfy me. When a man craves lobster and you fill him up with steak until he can't eat another bite, he might still crave lobster!"

He laughed. "I'll be glad to serve you steak with lobster anytime." Then he grew more serious and held her tightly so that her arms felt bruised. "Anne, I can do anything and everything a lesbian can - and better!"

"You don't understand," she pushed him away, "It has nothing to do with *doing*, it's *being*! Your athletic prowess doesn't impress me at all."

(A memory would quickly flash of lying on his bare, hard chest and finding it alien, of pawing at his chest and trying to make the nipples full and soft and hearing him laugh, *What the hell are you doing!* And when he held her she was always made sick by the odor of his flesh and the taste of his mouth. *Perhaps if he weren't a smoker and stopped using that after-shave,* Anne thought. But no, it was all of Mark she couldn't stand.)

As usual, he left soon, determined not to let go of her, and as more weeks and then months went by, he continued to make himself convenient under the plausible excuse that it would further both of their careers to be seen together.

Beth's talent agent had already signed him to a contract and his career both as actor and as rugged male model was about to spring forward. He took Anne to press parties almost every night and made certain they were photographed together. Columnists started taking notice, calling them a pair. And rather than being jealous, Beth selflessly urged them both on, encouraged Anne to continue with her acting and dancing lessons, pointed with pride to both her protégés.

But unlike Mark's, Anne's career, even with Beth's help, was far from certain. Female talent was in too great abundance and the road up was also encumbered by constant sleaze. Steadily being seen with Mark did make a small difference, protecting both of them from showbiz predators. Now small-time agents began to approach Anne and she got a few calls for minor photo shoots. If she had been inclined to dump Mark and go out with one or more of them, she might have landed a major modeling contract -- but she was holding back. *This is not what I want to become,* she kept saying inside her.

And all the while Mark's body was becoming a habit with her so that she would even ask for him, wanted the quick release she had learned to get from him that momentarily stopped the other craving.

But she still felt only half there whenever she was with him and nothing could keep her mind from wandering to a searing fantasy of making love to Beth.

But Beth herself was gone.

Mark no longer spoke of her and Anne did not mention her. She had gone on the road with a musical and had sent only one post card.

"What date should we set the wedding," Mark ventured one night.

"Not ever, Mark," she said dully.

"A June wedding, I think. Tell your parents."

"I don't want to marry you, Mark," she repeated. "Nor do I want you to ever meet my parents."

"You'll marry me even if I have to make you pregnant," he said.

At a press gathering he spontaneously announced their engagement and to keep her parents at bay Anne played the game with him, all the while insisting it was only a game.

Her Mom and Dad were not especially happy to learn of Anne's engagement from a newspaper column.

"Who is this man! Why are you not bringing him home to us," her father kept demanding on the telephone.

"It's not real, Dad, just publicity. Don't believe a word of it!"

And in the weeks and months that followed, Anne continued to make one excuse after another to keep Mark away from them, even while using his address instead of her own to discourage them from invading her privacy. Even if being engaged to a stranger would not quiet their anxieties, at least it presented a barrier to their demands she return home.

And so a year went by and her parents resigned themselves to her refusal to involve them in her life. And Anne and Mark continued to be seen together, now a steady twosome at all the right places. Then one evening, when the party was especially wild and they both drank too much -- Anne to escape Mark, and Mark to stone himself -- after six martinis Mark proposed again and Anne thought, *What the hell*, and said yes.

He pulled her right up then and made her say good night and took her to the car and they zigzagged through the night to Maryland and woke up a Justice of the Peace.

When Anne awoke the next morning she remembered and thought, *What have I done!* Mark lay next to her in a sweat, wrapped and knotted in the sheets, groaning as he did with a hangover.

She looked around. It was a motel room. She knew then that what she had remembered was true.

Her head hurt. She got up and went to the bathroom and wet two face cloths and brought one to him and then waited for him to wake up.

"Mark," she said, "I want an annulment."

He looked at her groggily. "Now wait a minute. So we were high. That doesn't change things."

"If you don't give me an annulment I'll get a divorce," she stated with finality.

They drove back to New York and Mark let her off at her door.

"Start packing. You're moving in with me," he said. But when he drove off she called Jacques who gave her the name of a hip attorney and he immediately began separation proceedings.

Mark received the summons a day later and was at her door. "My God, Anne, why can't we talk this over?" "I tried, Mark, but you wouldn't listen."

She was quiet but near tears. She could not bear another night with him but still felt she had to let him in, had to try again to explain.

"Anne, I'm going to fight this," he said. "There's something wrong with you. You're sick. I'm not going to let you go."

"Do what you like," she said. "Nothing I say seems to matter to you." She buried her face in her hands, weary.

He went to pour them both some scotch then came back and put the glass in her hand. She wept quietly and absently took a sip then put the glass down in distaste.

Everything was still.

The television upstairs had been shut off and the hi-fi next door was silent.

Then the telephone rang. Mark seemed to expect it and took up the receiver.

"Hi, Beth," he said. "Come on over."

Anne raised her head. Beth was calling -- calling her, not Mark. Her show must have folded. Was she back in town?

A new strength surged through her. She was impatient with the four walls and with Mark. She wanted to snatch the telephone from him. How dare he go on speaking to Beth! Beth was phoning *Anne*!

"Beth, you're the first to be told," Mark was saying, "Anne and I got married."

"Give me that phone," Anne said, enraged. "How dare you!"

She tried to take the receiver from him but he held it high.

"Come over for a toast," he continued, taunting Anne. Then he hung up and looked at her. "She called me this morning and I told her to call us tonight." His face was hard and his mouth had a mean curve. "Anne, I'm going to finally spoil your dream."

Anne gripped the day couch, feeling helplessly weak. This was not the Mark she had once known -- or was it?

Without wanting to she had wounded his pride and now he was hitting back -- through Beth. There was nothing for her to do but sit and wait now for Beth in quiet rage.

For nearly a half hour they lingered in silence until the doorbell rang.

"Answer it," Mark said.

"It's your show," she defied.

He downed his drink and rang the buzzer, then waited for Beth at the door.

Beth was carrying yellow roses and champagne.

"Hi, kiddies," she chimed, smiling brightly. "Happy honeymoon and what's the idea of not telling me sooner?"

"A surprise," Mark said, taking her coat.

He pretended to have cast off his sullenness and was being light and social.

Anne sat blankly, seeing through him.

"Anne," Beth turned toward her, concerned. "You're pale. Are you sick?"

"I'm fine," Anne said. Seeing Beth's eyes gave her new strength.

Beth handed her a small package. "It's all I could find for a house warmer," she said.

Anne accepted it gracefully and held it in her hand. Somehow to Beth it must have signified a peace offering - to show Anne she had no hard feelings.

"I'm so happy for the two of you, really I am," Beth continued.

She squeezed Anne's hand warmly and Anne cherished the warmth in her palm. It gave her strength to blurt out quickly, "Thanks -- but we're getting a divorce."

Beth's smile transformed, grew serious. "What happened?"

Mark returned with martinis and spoke before Anne could. "She's got a fool notion about wanting to be free."

"We got drunk one night, Beth," Anne blurted out, trying to tell her everything. "It was an accident."

"I don't get it," Beth shook her head, fumbling for a cigarette. "I thought you two were in love."

"We are," Mark interrupted, "but Anne thinks she's a -- "

"Mark, shut up!" Anne rose, shouting. "Don't you dare!" She gripped her glass, poised to throw it at him. No one else had the right to tell Beth how she felt about her.

"A what?" Beth asked, concerned, perhaps even comprehending.

Mark shrugged. "Forget it."

Anne looked down at her dress. In her rage she had spilled her drink. She went to slip into another and decided instead to put on jeans and one of Mark's shirts. Rebelliously she decided to tie her hair tightly into a pony tail and tucked it further out of sight, into a bun, reclaiming her tomboy style. Defiantly she returned and sat down.

Mark had changed the subject and was asking Beth about the show.

"It hasn't folded," Beth was saying. "As a matter of fact, I called you this morning to tell you there might be more than just a bit part in it for you. We dropped a few in the cast and we're back in New York, for more rehearsals and rewrites before we go on the road again. It may even get to Broadway. Auditions are tomorrow and I've already put you on the short list."

"Thanks," Mark said, fingering his glass.

(Anne knew that at any other time he would have been whooping with joy.)

"But no thanks," he said. "I'm staying in town." His look was openly sullen. Then he changed and refilled Beth's glass. "Tell us more about you, and the show."

Beth was filled with information and spoke nervously in a long monologue as they listened, pretending to laugh at her imitation of the stars at rehearsals and the gossip about the director's new mistress, and the two transvestites who had sneaked onto the chorus line.

Mark was getting high, on purpose, and taking Beth along with him, refilling her glass, mixing her drinks. Beth was used to drinking a lot and it was easy. With distaste, Anne saw the end of the night's game and wanted to leave -- but it was her own apartment, where else could she go?

Then Mark sat beside Beth and began to kiss her. Beth responded instinctively, too drunk to notice, then remembered and brought up her hand to push him away. "Mark, what the -- ?"

"It's all right, Beth," Anne said from across the room, then took her coat and left.

Outside, it was almost Two A.M. - if the clock tower could be believed.   Anne walked through the chill air to the Square and then decided it was not safe to sit on the benches at that hour. She counted her money. She had enough for a hotel room. There was an acceptable hotel in a brownstone across the street. She entered the narrow lobby and booked a room, but she wasn't ready to end the evening. The Oval was still only a few doors down. She would go there first, or perhaps not.

Third Street was still trafficked with tourists - it would be safe if she just stood there for a while, gathering her nerve, trying to see through its dark windows. Then a woman in men's clothes staggered out the door and paused, stepped on her cigarette and looked at Anne blankly.

Panic again gripped Anne, and revulsion. She hurried back into the hotel lobby, anxious to escape her eyes.

Anne woke late in the morning just before checkout time and was grateful that it was Saturday and that she did not have to go to work. Daylight filled the room, making it seem less dingy. The wild sounds of the night were gone and only the maid's vacuum cleaner was heard next door. She rose and put on her clothes and went downstairs to call her own apartment from the public phone.

There was no answer. Beth and Mark were not there. With a feeling of freedom she ran across the street and up the stairs to her own door.

It was such a relief not to have spent the night with Mark. It almost made up for the loss she felt over Beth. But in the apartment the gloom overtook her again. There were the empty glasses of last night and the full ashtrays.

And the rumpled bed.

Suddenly she realized that all night she had burned with an intense jealousy and now she hated Mark completely.

Mark had thought to prove something to her last night, in a cruel way, intentionally to hurt her. But she was beyond being hurt by him.

She knew Beth would react normally to him. But Mark had been merely using her to get at Anne. Mark didn't want a woman who wanted him. That would have been too simple. Mark was determined to hold on to Anne precisely because she didn't want him.

And Beth was the victim.

Anne would never have misused Beth that way.

"Damn you, Mark, I hate you!" She sat on the chair, not wanting to sit on the bed where they had lain. "Beth, Beth, no one loves you like I do!"

Much later, the telephone rang.

"Anne?" It was Beth's voice, searching and timid, not the strong voice that had always greeted her.

Anne's heart swelled. There was so much she wanted to say to her.

"I'm sorry about last night," Beth continued. "I was dead drunk --"

"Beth don't -- " Anne found it hard not to cry. "It's all right, really it is."

"What a horrid mess!" Beth did not listen to her. "How can you ever forgive me?"

"Please don't, Beth -- " Anne said. "Look, come over now and we'll talk. I have so much to say to you, in my own words, not Mark's."

"All right." Beth's voice was still timid, lost. "I'll grab a cab."

Now Anne put down the receiver and changed to a fresh pair of jeans. She marveled at the calm with which she gathered the glasses and emptied the ashtrays. She had begun to grow up, she decided. She was expecting Beth, only Beth, if only just to comfort her.

This was a new experience. She was no longer the lost young kid who cried on Beth's shoulder. Now she felt strong and able to protect and provide for a woman weaker than herself.

When Beth arrived, the apartment had been cleaned and breakfast was almost ready.

"Hi," Anne let herself be pecked on the cheek, cheerful as she took Beth's jacket, straining to make her feel at ease.

Beth's face was tired and she wore no makeup, showing her age. Her hair was tied away from her face in a kerchief and she was wearing her dance tights.

Anne handed her a Bloody Mary with only a whiff of vodka and said, "Hair of the dog."

Beth said "Thanks," and took it, went to a chair and fumbled for cigarettes.

She looked at the day couch with discomfort.   Then   Anne brought her eggs and toast and coffee on a tray and set the tray down on the coffee table, sitting on the couch, reclaiming it.

"Mark means nothing to me," Anne said nervously, searching Beth's face for a reaction. "Please believe me, Beth."

"I believe you." Beth looked at her.

Anne realized now that it was not guilt that Beth felt, but distaste. Mark had behaved badly and Beth felt soiled.

"Exactly why did you break up," Beth asked her.

"Mark didn't tell you last night, did he?"

Beth shook her head.

How like Mark, Anne thought, *too possessive to let Beth know.*

She rose and paused, choosing her words carefully. "Beth, you once said I could talk to you," she began. "How I wish I really could have talked to you." She stopped. It was so difficult to get it said. It had been so simple to tell Jacques, but now it was so difficult.

"Beth," Anne began again, "you remember that day in the theater -- when I behaved so foolishly and cried?"

"Yes," Beth nodded. "Over me."

The statement was so simple. Beth had known the truth all along. "I thought you had gotten over that," Beth added softly.

Anne shook her head. She could barely speak. Beth knew and understood everything and it brought the whirlpool back and the weakness in her knees.

Anne was no longer in control of herself.

Beth rose from the chair and went to sit next to her. "Anne," she began, "I'm glad you took the long way round."

Anne looked at her, puzzled. "I don't understand."

Beth smiled, brushing a lock of her hair back with a finger. The morning sunlight made the platinum shine and Anne thought her even more beautiful.

"If you had talked to me months ago," Beth started, "I would have done my best to help you get over it, to go out with Mark. But you found Mark all by yourself and you decided all by yourself that you don't want him. I'm glad I had nothing to do with it."

"Beth," Anne forced the words because she had to know, "are you a lesbian?"

Beth smiled and rose. She took her time to answer, walked to the window and looked out to the street below.

174

"No," she finally said. "I can't honestly say I am."

Anne's heart sank. Beth understood, but Beth did not desire her.

"Anne, I wish I could explain what I am to you," Beth said. "I don't exactly fall in any category. Right now, I don't even feel capable of love - I've been hurt too often and it's turned me into a good-time-charlie. Even my affair with Mark was strictly for laughs. Last night, if you had stayed, if the three of us had been involved -- it wouldn't have been a new thing for me. What disgusts and upsets me is that Mark used me to hurt you."

She turned now and looked at Anne and Anne knew that Beth was waiting for her to say something, and Anne said feebly said, "More coffee?"

Beth nodded and looked through the blinds again. The sunlight bathed her face. Anne paused to look at her from the kitchen, holding back the trembling that still threatened to overpower her. Then she controlled herself and brought back a fresh cup.

Beth took it, continuing to stare at the street below. "Anne," she said finally, "are you terribly unhappy?"

Anne nodded and forced a "Yes."

Beth turned her back on the window, casting her eyes now fully on Anne. "Come here," she said.

The same cold nervousness gripped Anne and she could barely move, but she came to stand beside Beth at the window.

"Take my hand," Beth said quietly.

Trembling, Anne reached out and took Beth's slender hand. The long fingers wound around hers tightly and for a moment Anne could not breathe as she felt Beth's touch surging through her.

"Back in college," Beth explained, "my best friend fell in love with me. We had an affair but I outgrew it. She has a new friend now and they're very happy." She paused, searching for the right words. "Some women are happy with other women because it's natural for them to be that way. You may or may not be one of those," she said. Now Beth brought her hands to Anne's face, spoke directly to her eyes. "No one in the world can make turn you into a lesbian, Anne," she said. "The same way that Mark couldn't make you love him. The same way that I couldn't possibly live as a lesbian for very long."

"Are you in any way attracted to me?" Anne managed to ask.

"Of course!" Beth answered. "How could I possibly be otherwise?"

She stopped again and now gripped Anne's hands more tightly than before.

175

"Can you bear my going away afterward? Anne, afterwards I won't want to see you again, not for months."

"I can't bear not having known what it's like to be with you," Anne said.

"Once and only once then, Anne," Beth said.

Anne nodded, unable to let go of her hand, unable to move.

Beth drew her closer, took her in her arms slowly and tenderly. It sent a shaft of pleasure through Anne -- Anne now knew it to be pleasure and not pain, was conscious only of a superb softness and an unbearable attraction that would not let her body stop pressing to Beth's.

Beth's flesh was familiar.

Beth's mouth was sweet.

Anne's lips clung to Beth's, not wanting to ever stop kissing her -- until Beth forced her to stop and brought her mouth to Anne's breast, her sensuous hands gently removing the folds of clothing that separated their bodies until they both lay naked, somehow having found the day bed through the whirlpool, and Anne could not bear to wait any longer and cried, begged for Beth to take all of her.

Anne awoke to the telephone jarring her from a blissful sleep. She kissed Beth softly before she turned to answer.

It was Mark. He called to let her know, he said, that he had told her parents that she was abnormal. "For your own good. Because you're sick. You need help, Anne. You're my wife and you need help!"

"Talk to my lawyer!" She slammed the phone down in a fury and turned back toward Beth, her eyes now open.

"It was Mark," Anne said. "He's told my parents I'm a lesbian. Now there's going to be hell to pay!"

Anne returned to the bed to hug Beth. She now knew Mark was the sick one, that there was absolutely nothing wrong with her. She felt right for the very first time, and all she could think to say was, "poor Mom and Dad, what a shock!"

"The bastard," Beth said. "I could wring his neck!"

She lay next to Anne, fitting so well in her arms, and Anne knew this couldn't be wrong!

"There's one thing I can do," Beth said. "I can testify. But whatever you do, for both our sakes, don't *ever* tell anyone about us."

Now they kissed again, passionately, letting the tension ease, and finally both laughed over Mark's threat.

Beth was confident the divorce would never come to trial. A separation was in process and once Mark was hit with the bill for Anne's support he would rethink their relationship. He had a burning ambition, valued his career more than anything. And Anne's rejection had been final and backed up by legal process. Even so, for a while Mark might still be a problem.

Beth sat up and kissed Anne one more time - a goodbye kiss before pushing her away gently. "I'm going to have to leave now, before both of us change our minds," she said.

Anne accepted it and said nothing and lay on the bed hugging her pillow.

It had grown dark outside and Beth turned on a small lamp to dress by. She was upset and moved slowly.

Finally she said, "You think I'm being cruel to leave now."

Anne shook her head. She was choking back tears; she couldn't speak.

"Oh Anne," Beth went to her, put her hands on her shoulders, "cheer up, my resolutions are never very strong. If you came to me one night I wouldn't turn away from you -- I couldn't!"

Anne looked at her. How beautiful she was in the half-light! She resisted the impulse to kiss her once more.

"Look," Beth went on, "it would be hell if this went on. You'd grow too fond of me and one day -- one day there'd be a bloody mess!"

"It's all right, Beth," Anne managed to say. "I understand. You feel about me as I felt about Mark. You're right. It's best we stop now."

Beth pressed her head against Anne's. "You'll be okay, won't you?"

"I'll be fine," Anne said.

Beth turned, put on her blouse hurriedly and took her coat. She paused at the door one last time: "Show's going on the road in two weeks. I'll look you up again in six months or so."

"That will be fine," Anne said feebly.

"I'll send you clippings and post cards -- " Beth added.

"Thanks." Anne could no longer hold her tears now and she cried into the pillow. "Thanks, Beth."

Beth paused, hesitated another moment, and then left, closing the door softly behind her.

3.

WITH strong determination Anne prepared herself for the Oval -- and beyond. It was the next Friday night and Jacques was sitting on her day couch, drink in hand, approving her outfit.

"Alice, whatever you do, don't speak to strange men," he camped, "Do speak to strange women!"

Anne laughed and spun around to let him see how she looked. She wore a pair of colorful slacks and a Mexican shirt made of virgin linen.

Jacques whistled, "They'll sure know you're femme in that."

"But I'm not," Anne laughed. "I can't stand to look at those butches. I'm out after the girls."

He roared, "Well, Mary, don't pick up a drag queen by mistake!"

"I know the difference," Anne returned with a smile.

She felt so free. Once in a while she thought of Beth and cried for her, but still she felt free. She was out to look for a new Beth, one that would stay with her and love her and accept her love -- somewhere beyond that strange and ominous world across the street.

"Don't get stuck in the Oval," Jacques was now warning her. "Find out where the better bars are and get the hell out to them. I don't think that place is safe."

"All right, Mother," Anne said.

"Are you sure you don't want me along?" he asked again.

"I'll be fine," she smiled. "Besides, I like to walk into lions' dens alone."

He laughed. "It's more like a cat house than a lion's den."

"Very funny," she said. "Now let's cut the conversation and get on over there."

He got up and took his coat and went out with her. "I'll be in the Florentin if you need me," he said. He left her in front of the bar and waited as she climbed the three steps to the door.

It was early and the rough crowd had not gathered yet. It seemed fairly safe. Anne was afraid but walked in through the swinging door and stood, surveying the interior. The Oval was round like its name, dark and painted dirty red with overt murals of half-men, half-women dancing together and drinking.

The bar was peopled like the murals and Anne's unskilled eyes had difficulty determining the separate sexes. She walked to a table in the corner and sat down.

There seemed to be no waitress and she sat there, waiting. Her eyes were becoming more accustomed to the darkness and she was able to distinguish the sex of several of those at the bar. They were mostly girls in men's clothes.

One in particular, a tall young tomboy at the end of the bar, dressed in jeans and lumber jacket, had seemed to notice her. She was looking at Anne through the corner of her beer glass and then turned again to look at her through the mirror behind the bar. Her hair was black and slicked back, but her face was ghost pale even in the red light as though she lived only for the night and never allowed the sun to touch her.

Anne did not find her attractive, yet there was something likeable about her.

(Anne marveled at her own lack of fear -- the fear that had seized her when a girl had come out of the Oval a week ago. *Beth has healed me,* she thought.)

Then a man sat at Anne's table and broke in on her thoughts. She turned to him angrily. "I'm sorry, this table is taken."

"That's all right, baby," he said. "I don't mind." He might have been drunk.

He tried to pat her hand.

Anne withdrew it quickly and looked for the bartender. She was at the other end of the bar.

179

Was there a bouncer?

Anne felt trapped. She had sat in the corner and there was no way to get up from the table without going past him.

"What'll you have," he insisted.

"Nothing," she answered, trying to get up and past him. He pushed her down again and her anger flared.

"Get your hands off me," she said, and pushed back.

"So you want to play rough," he said, grabbing her hand.

"That's enough, mister," a dark voice said.

It was the girl at the end of the bar. She had come over, holding her beer bottle. "Let go of her." Her eyes were hard and her expression strong.

"What's the idea," he said, not getting up.

"Moe!" the girl called out, not turning.

Now Moe appeared, a heavy-set man over six feet tall. Anne had noticed him sitting at the door. Why hadn't he bothered coming sooner?

"He's annoying a customer," the girl said.

"Back to the bar," Moe motioned to him.

"What's the idea?" the man repeated. But Moe motioned again and he got up reluctantly, mumbling obscenities.

"Yeah? And the same to you!" the girl shouted after him.

"The management is sorry," Moe now said to Anne in his best manner.

"Thanks," Anne said.

He shuffled back to his post.

So this was a bouncer! Anne thought, amused. *How much like a scene from a honky-tonk Western!*

"Can I get you a drink," now the girl said, "I work here."

"Scotch and coke," Anne said.

The girl turned and shouted to the bar, "Hey, Toots -- a Cola 69!"

The bartender saluted and poured out a shot of scotch and let it and a Coke slide down the bar. The girl put them both on a tray and came back to Anne's table. "Straight or mixed?" she asked.

"Mixed," Anne said. The waitress poured half the Coke into the scotch and put both on the table. Then she stopped and waited. "Will that be all?"

"Guess so," Anne nodded, then, "Won't you join me?" she ventured.

The girl smiled and said thanks and pulled up a chair across from her.

"I'm Skippy. What's your name?"

"Anne," she said.

"Fem?"

"Maybe, maybe not," Anne returned, letting both the model and the tomboy show. She remembered Jacques' slang and laughed to herself. She too could play the same game.

But now that Skippy had spoken to her she did not seem so strange. She was even attractive.

Again Anne marveled at herself. An unattractive man did not grow more attractive when she spoke to him, only more repulsive, and yet Skippy, in her boyish way, was making her feel at ease.

"Hey, don't you belong in Paradise?" Skippy said.

"Is that a compliment or a place?" Anne asked.

"Both," Skippy laughed. "It's across the Square. Girls only."

"Is it in the telephone book?"

"Yep, Downstairs Paradise. You won't have trouble finding it."

Now Skippy sat up and looked at her warmly. "This your first time in a bar?"

Anne blushed; she had hoped to seem more worldly.

"Tell you what," Skippy said, "if you want to hang around until I get off, I'll take you there."

"How long will that be," Anne asked.

"Couple of hours."

Anne hesitated, and then decided.

She could handle this. After Mark, and Beth, she could handle anything that came along.

"Maybe." she finally said.

"Fine," Skippy saluted then rose and went back to the bar with her tray.

She continued to keep a protective eye on Anne from the mirror behind the bar.

Anne sat back, relaxed, and waited, like a tourist taking it all in. The juke box was playing *Earth Angel* and she listened, watching the people at the bar getting up to dance.

But she kept her guard, still felt apprehensive there, as if someone might approach her again at any moment. She sensed danger in the Oval as Jacques had said, either from a drunk or a man with a knife. The place seemed to cater to men who hated women. She was glad both Moe and Skippy were watching her.

Then Skippy returned and set her tray down on Anne's table and said, "Do you rock?"

Anne listened to the music. It was compelling. "Sometimes," she said, "but I like to lead."

Skippy laughed. "That's a turn! Okay."

She extended her hand and helped Anne slide around the booth.

They walked to the inner room to the middle of the floor where the tables had been arranged so that there was dance space. It was still early -- now they were the only couple on the floor.

"Okay, let's," Skippy said, falling into the rhythm.

Anne was nearly a professional dancer. It had been part of her drama training and she often led Jacques in a rock-and-roll. Now she let herself loose and soon lost Skippy who swung to the side and watched her, shouting. "Wahoo!"

This made her self-conscious and she slowed down, dancing with Skippy again.

"Now let me lead," Skippy said. "I can't follow that."

Anne laughed. "All right."

Skippy pulled her close so that their bodies touched full-length and this slowed up the rhythm.

Anne realized she had been wasting time.

This was much better. Skippy's arms were long and sure, but they were soft. Anne suddenly knew it was not only Beth who could make her thrill, that she could feel the same yearning for another woman. It suddenly dawned upon her that this was the purpose of dancing closely in a bar. She had never been able to understand why Mark wanted to dance closely -- what could possibly be so exciting about it? She had preferred to exhibit and let loose -- and yet now she knew that she preferred to dance closely, that awareness of her partner, a woman, was the purpose of dancing.

"Do you mind going so slow?" Skippy now whispered in her ear.

"No, I'm enjoying it," Anne said.

(Deep inside her she was slightly shocked at her own ability to let go. Skippy was a stranger, someone who could never be her type emotionally or culturally; yet Skippy was a woman and this made her exciting -- for one evening only, perhaps, but still exciting.)

Then convention overtook her and she broke away. "I'm sorry." she said, "I don't mean to lead you on. I'm already involved."

Skippy smiled. "Forget it. My technique's too fast anyway."

They walked back to Anne's table and sat down.

Anne was silent.

She did not want to be Skippy's date for the evening. It would have been simple to let that happen, but there would be no point in it. Skippy was not the Beth she sought. Anne would sit for a while and then would go and find Paradise alone.

She wondered how she might explain, but Skippy spoke for her.

"Look, I know I'm not your type," she said. "But taking you to Paradise was just a friendly offer. Honest."

Anne looked at her. She was smiling with great understanding and Anne knew that despite her apparent coarseness she was sensitive and aware of others' thoughts and feelings in a way that was rare.

"What makes you think you're not my type?" Anne said. She did not want to demean her.

"Experience," Skippy replied.

Anne smiled and their eyes met in friendship.

Now Jacques came through the swinging door and broke their glance. "Doll, there you are! I've got someone I want you to meet. She's waiting for us at the Florentin."

He tugged her arm, but when he saw Skippy he apologized.

"It's all right," Skippy said. "You run along. Maybe we'll see each other later, at Paradise."

"It's a date," Anne said and let Jacques lead her out of the bar.

"Mary, you picked the weirdest trade," Jacques said to her when they were on the sidewalk. "I thought you could handle yourself."

"It's not the women I have to be careful of," Anne laughed. "She's really a damned nice kid."

"Well, come and meet Esther."

He was impatient to get far away from the Oval.

Anne was amused. Jacques really couldn't stand masculine women any more than masculine women could stand feminine men.

"Just a minute," she stopped him before they entered the Florentin, "exactly who is Esther? Male or female?"

183

"Doll, I'm not exactly sure," Jacques joked then sighed impatiently. "She lives with Carl, who is one of my johns, in a townhouse. She's Kosher French and spent her childhood in convents hiding from the Nazis. I think she was also in the Resistance. Anyway, she's hard as nails but simply dashing."

He would say no more but pulled Anne by the wrist into the coffee shop and through the maze of tables in a direct line toward the back.

But Anne could not just walk into the Florentin without the usual ritual and they were hindered by Marcel who ran up and embraced her and said "Princess, where have you been?" and then Jennie who extended her hand and said "Welcome back, femme fatale," and then sniveling Carol who tried to corner Jacques. But Jacques would not let himself be stopped and pulled Anne onward until finally they reached the rear and stopped at a small table.

Then Anne saw her. A girl -- no, a woman -- or perhaps a young man -- ageless-looking, thin and pale, with slender fingers and short, black hair, deep-set pitch-black eyes.

"Esther," Jacques called and Esther turned, the full depth of her eyes striking Anne.

"Hello," she said.

Her voice was low and matched her eyes, contrasted dramatically with her pale skin.

Anne let their glances touch and smiled.

"Meet Anne," Jacques said. He pulled chairs for the two of them and then made Anne sit down.

"Hello, Anne," Esther said again. She had a half-smile and her mind seemed fogged with other thoughts and yet her black eyes seemed to burn clear through to Anne's spine, making Anne dizzy and weak.

"Hello, Esther," Anne forced herself to speak.

This was silly. She was behaving like a child again. She ought to have better control. Anne forced the dizziness to fade and brought the Florentin right-side up again.

"Jacques tells me you're looking for lesbian bars," Esther said.

"Yes," Anne admitted, embarrassed.

"I'm on my way there now," Esther said. "We can walk together if you like."

"Swell!" Anne said.

She hoped she did not seem too anxious.

Esther still regarded her with that amused half-smile, knowing exactly what her eyes were doing to Anne.

Anne held her expression motionless, though she could barely keep her lips from trembling. Finally she said, "I heard you were in the Resistance."

Esther laughed. "Who told you that?"

"Jacques said he thought you were."

She dismissed it. "I was eleven years old."

Anne looked away, awkwardly fingering her coffee cup, searching for Jacques. He had left them to avoid Carol and had joined the Cast at the other table.

"Shall we go?" Esther invited.

Anne rose and followed her out of the Florentin.

The night air was clear and they walked slowly, not speaking, through Washington Square Park now filled with people, Gay, Straight and indeterminate -- artists, troubadours, tourists, sitting on the benches, at the chess tables, or on the rim of the dried-up fountain.

Esther's long legs unconsciously took longer strides that would take her way ahead of Anne before stopping, waiting for her to catch up -- and yet they were walking slowly!

When she was ahead of her, Anne could see and admire her - her expensive, tasteful clothes and slender ankles. She was wearing toreador pedal-pushers, obviously imported from Spain or Capri, and though the late Spring air was cool, she wore sandals. Her stately legs and feet were beautiful, like her hands and face. There was a warmth around her despite her outward aloofness. Anne wondered if Jacques had seen it. But she decided it was only for women's eyes.

"How old are you?" Esther asked.

"Twenty," Anne fibbed.

"That's too bad," she said and smiled.

"Why?" Anne asked.

"Not twenty-one."

"What happens at twenty-one that doesn't already happen at eighteen?" Anne said, thinking of Mark.

Esther laughed and stopped to sit on a bench, her slender legs apart, and looked at the ground.

"How old are you?" Anne returned.

"Twenty-four."

"Too bad," Anne chuckled, "Not twenty."

"Are you really Gay," Esther asked.

"No, I'm terribly sad," Anne replied. "I can't find a lesbian anywhere!"

Esther did not laugh. "Seriously -- how do you know?"

Anne grew serious too. "I'm certain, I think. When I'm with men I don't feel alive -- but with women -- "

"Have you slept with men?" Esther interrupted, perhaps skeptically.

"Just Mark -- my husband," Anne began to explain.

"And with women?"

"Yes, once."

Anne stopped. She did not want to discuss Beth. She could talk about Mark but Beth was sacred.

"And you don't like this Mark," Esther said after a while.

"No." Anne said.

"You weren't compatible?"

"Oh no, that wasn't it." Anne felt she had to explain but it was so difficult. "I just didn't feel alive or happy with him. I could have gotten the same result from an electric vibrator."

Esther laughed loudly. "But you were happy with this woman?"

"Yes."

Esther did not speak but sat looking off in the distance for a while. Then suddenly she got up and said, "Come."

They resumed their walk and reached the other side of the Park and went down a side street to a place with a half-lit sign. The lit part said PARADISE. It was downstairs, in a cellar, under a dark set of steps and through an obscure blue door.

The bouncer, a small baldpated man, challenged them at the coatroom and demanded they prove their age. Anne resisted asking if his name was Pete.

His eyes were quickly sizing both of them up and he seemed to approve of how they looked and the way they were dressed. Meanwhile, Esther took out her driver's license and Anne showed him her learner's permit. This was enough to satisfy him and he let them pass.

Paradise was clean, not like the Oval, and with all the walls painted blue. It might have passed for a campus hangout. The customers looked like they might have been ivy-league sorority types and the waitresses were women dressed like male waiters on Park Avenue.

Esther headed for the bar and Anne followed her. Her eyes were searching the dark corners for someone. Absentmindedly she told the bartender to bring two beers.

"Are you meeting someone?" Anne asked.

She nodded. "I have three dates tonight. It depends on which of them shows up first." Then she looked up at Anne and smiled. "Tell me about Mark. Are you still married?"

"Our annulment is in progress," Anne answered.

There was another long silence while the music played and then Esther said, "Do you enjoy art?"

Anne nodded. "I've even gone back to painting lately."

Esther was not impressed, but said, "Come with me to the Museum sometime."

"When?" Anne asked. She had decided to be bold.

"Perhaps next Saturday?"

Esther took out a card with her name impressively gold-etched on it and wrote down her telephone number. "Carl had these made up to amuse me," she said. "Call on us, will you? And bring Jacques."

Anne took the card and put it carefully in her wallet. "I'd like to very much," she said.

Now Esther became silent and Anne knew they were done talking to each other and so she sat silently too and surveyed the bar.

More women were coming in and Anne watched them. Each one was different and some were attractive; most were masculine but there were no distinctively masculine or feminine types; each might have passed for either with proper clothing. Then a tall woman came in, alone. She wore paint-stained levi's and a man's old shirt which somehow made her look very feminine - full-breasted and statuesquely beautiful. Her hair was close-cropped but styled and not butch, and her face was classic. Anne thought first of a Michelangelo and then of a Greek bust depicting Orpheus.

Esther turned then, saw her, and waved.

How dazzling it was, Anne thought, to be looking at both of them -- both of them so agonizingly, breathtakingly beautiful!

187

The tall woman who came toward them wiped perspiration from her forehead.

"Hi," she said to Esther. "Sorry I'm late. I got involved. I've got to go back to it soon, though -- but you can sit there and watch me work, if you don't mind."

"I don't mind," Esther said. Then she turned to Anne and said, "Do use that card."

Anne nodded.

The two turned from her and walked toward the back, toward a table behind a pillar, and Anne watched them, envied each of them. She felt like a mere mortal spying on two goddesses in an embrace. But she had little time to pine for them. A familiar voice said behind her, "Can I buy you a drink?"

Anne turned and saw Skippy. She was smiling happily because they had met again.

Paradise made Skippy look less sinister. She was simply a plain girl now, perhaps from the Lower East Side, with barely a high school education.

"Let me buy you one," Anne countered.

Skippy laughed. "There you go again. Okay." She ordered beer and Anne switched to scotch.

"Did you meet up with your friend?" Skippy asked.

"Uh-hu," Anne grunted with a sigh.

"Oh," Skippy paused. "I guess that means you're alone for the eve."

Anne hesitated, then decided.

"Yes."

She looked down at her glass.

Skippy laughed and slapped her back. "Cheer up -- there are lots of others."

Anne half-laughed. "Are you looking for someone too?"

"Me?" Skippy shrugged. "Naw, not yet. I just got off a ten-day binge over my last one."

"Why?"

"A long story," Skippy said. "I used to work at Cora's -- up to two weeks ago."

"What's Cora's?" Anne became interested, Skippy was becoming "people" and she wanted to know what made her tick.

"A dive way over East," Skippy said. "It's better than the Oval, but not as fancy as here."

"Why did you break up?"

"Mary likes men," Skippy said; now she seemed annoyed and irritated and drank her beer more determinedly.

Anne put her hand on Skippy's wrist and stopped her from lifting the glass again. "Want to dance?"

Skippy looked at her and laughed. "Oh no," she said, "you're dynamite."

Anne smiled. "I'd never danced that way before -- with a girl."

"I should've known," Skippy said. "Where are you from, anyway?"

"Queens. My parents were born in Slovenia."   "Yeah? You don't sound like a foreigner."

Anne laughed. "I'm not. And you?"

"East Side," she said. "Three generations Italian-American. *Napolitana.*"

They both laughed and Skippy drank some more.

Anne looked toward the back to see if Esther and her date were still there. The two had gotten up and were paying their check. A sudden loneliness gripped her. She watched them leave and wanted to follow. There was no more reason to remain in Paradise.

"Want to come to Cora's?" Skippy seemed to have read her mind. "It's noisy there and wild, but it's safe -- if you're with me."

"Sure," Anne said.

She waited for Skippy to down her beer then went out into the air again, Skippy following.

A little rain had fallen and it made the cars swish as they passed and the trees smell sweet.

Anne took Skippy's arm and they walked more quickly.

"We'll need to look out for dyke-bashers," Skippy said. "The neighborhood's not as safe. If I give you the sign, be sure to run like hell."

Anne nodded, now more determined than ever to explore the entire landscape. She was getting quite an education -- one that might prove invaluable in the near future.

"This girl you were meeting," Skippy said while walking, "know her long?"

Anne shook her head. "I just met her tonight. It'll probably come to nothing."

"Aw, don't say that," Skippy returned. "There's no reason why you can't make out. You've got what it takes!"

Anne smiled. "Thanks."

A late full moon pointed their way back across the edge of the Park and past Third Street toward way over East. The streets were spotted with a new kind of crowd - rough young men and servicemen out to pick up girls. Anne and Skippy walked quickly, enduring the wisecracks and dodging the hands and bodies that tried to block their way.

"They ought to put a cop on this street," Skippy said as they hurried. "We could use some real police protection instead of all the plainclothesmen they've got out trapping queens."

"Do they really trap homos?" Anne asked. "Every once in a while. Especially around elections," Skippy said.

They walked further, past the crowds, and Anne asked Skippy why she had left Cora's to work in the Oval.

"Cora kicked me out until I got sober," Skippy said.

"Then you're going back tonight?"

"Yeah," she said. There was a lack of enthusiasm in her voice as if going back to Cora's would bring back the past. And yet she seemed to be drawn back there, as if it were home.

"Do you like working in bars?" Anne asked.

"There's nothing like it," Skippy said. "You're free to dress and be what you damn please. The pay's lousy, though. Girls are bad tippers."

They were on a lonely side street now and in the night it seemed a cold and concrete world -- as if someone had poured cement over the whole earth. Skippy quickened her steps and Anne followed her, conscious of the danger of an empty street. Then at the far corner they spotted a crowd of loud young men.

"Come in here," Skippy said, and pulled her into a doorway. They went half-way up the inner stairs and waited. "What's the matter?" Anne asked.

"I don't like their looks," Skippy said.

Soon the crowd had passed the doorway and they waited a while longer. Then Skippy took her down again and they resumed their pace. After a while she explained. "They like to rough up Gays in this neighborhood."

190

"I don't understand," Anne said. "Then why does Cora have a bar here?"

"No cops either," Skippy said.

This seemed logical in a queer way and Anne followed Skippy's long steps around a corner and to the middle of the block where a dimly-lit neon sign said CORA's.

They quickly entered and were greeted by another bouncer who resembled Moe but not the man at Paradise.

"Hi, Sol," Skippy said. "Cora here?"

"Skippy, baby!" he held her hands. "Sure, come right in -- she's been asking for you."

Anne followed them through the inner door and was immediately overwhelmed by smoke and loud music.

Cora's was a cellar painted dirty yellow and crowded like Coney Island on a Saturday and Sunday combined.

Wild rockers impeded their way in.

"Some joint, hey?" Skippy said to Anne proudly. "Come on, let's find Cora."

She took Anne's hand and pulled her through the dancers and then through narrow spaces between the tables to the back where an older woman, eating spaghetti-marinara, sat in a booth with a crowd of long-haired girls wearing scoop blouses and mascara.

"Hi, Cora," Skippy waved sheepishly.

Cora put her fork down a minute and looked up. "You sober?" She wiped marinara from her mouth with the corner of a white napkin tucked like a bib all the way up under her chin.

"Yep, like a judge," Skippy said, her hair slicked back and looking neat and ready.

"Good, get back behind the bar. They're going nuts without you." She forked more spaghetti in her mouth, eating with gusto.

Mafia Mom, Anne decided, *right out of a Lupino movie.* She expected to see Mercedes Cambridge and Joan Crawford walk in at any moment.

Cora's skin was a yellow tan and there were streaks of white in her red hair. But she was not ugly -- in fact, Anne found her inexplicably attractive in a way that both frightened and intrigued her. Her eyes were large and green, her mouth full. She might have been forty, but a trim forty, with a woman's breasts and slender waist. Her hands were small and strong and had the same golden tan. She was dressed in a brown and obviously expensive suit - probably Italian - but her voice was low and tough, strictly Lower East Side.

"First meet my new pal, Anne," Skippy said, pulling Anne forward. "Anne, meet Cora."

"Move, kids," Cora said to the girls in the booth. They slid off, smiling and waving at Skippy, and went to dance with each other.

"Siddown," Cora motioned to Anne.

Skippy helped Anne slide into the booth and then sat beside her. Her eyes were bright and full of admiration for Cora and she seemed very young now.

"I just canned Mary," Cora said, marinara around her mouth again. "You were right, fella."

"You bet," Skippy agreed. "I've had it too! No more bi's!"

Cora wiped her mouth and laughed.

Her table manners may have been coarse, Anne thought, yet she was not repulsive. Decidedly *mia casa,* she enjoyed what she ate unselfishly, offering them antipasto and wine as she talked.

"Where did you get this bimbo?" she asked Skippy.

"I found her in Heaven," Skippy answered. "Wait till you talk to her. She doesn't know from nothing."

"That's not quite true," Anne interjected, but Skippy and Cora paid no mind.

"How do you like my place?" Cora said proudly, gazing seductively into Anne's eyes. "Terrific, eh? I been all over Europe and there's none like it."

Anne smiled and nodded shyly. The place was beginning to wear on her nerves -- the noise and the smoke, the wet tables and dirty floors. She felt a sudden urge to leave.

Cora sensed this immediately and stopped eating. "What's the matter, kid. Too much atmosphere?"

Anne looked down, embarrassed.

"Hey, Skip, did you take her upstairs yet?" Cora said, punching Skippy's shoulder.

Skippy shook her head. "We only just got here."

"Hey, what's the matter with you. What kind of hostess are you anyway?" Cora said. "Take her up, stupid."

Skippy smiled, relieved Cora had given the sign.

"Forget about the bar. You come back to work tomorrow," Cora said. Skippy's face beamed. "Okay!"

"What's upstairs?" Anne asked apprehensively.

Memories of pulp novels darted quickly in her mind, of opium dens and white slave markets, of extortionists and pimps. Cora might be all of these. Upstairs might be a trap.

"That's where the real party is," Skippy reassured her. "There's a better crowd."

"Don't be scared, kid," Cora said. "It's all legit."

Anne laughed at herself. Cora was no villain -- she was too open and her gaze was too honest. She let Skippy pull her past the dancers again and through a door that said NO ADMITTANCE, amused as she noticed another sign over the bar that said NO DANCING. Apparently all the signs that said NO meant YES.

She followed Skippy up a flight of stairs to another door which opened to a darkened room. It was red-walled like the Oval, but the murals were discreet. The floor was clean and instead of booths there were plush sofas and low coffee tables. Not many people were here -- the juke box was mellow and the dance floor was almost empty.

Anne looked at the couples and could not distinguish in the darkness whether there were any men there, or only women dressed as men. She supposed the crowd was mixed.

"Swank layout, hey?" Skippy said.

Anne politely agreed. "Ritzy."

They found an empty sofa and sat in it, waiting for the waitress. When she came Skippy ordered scotch and beer. They sat back and relaxed. "Cora'll be up later," she said. "She gives every new customer a grand welcome."

"That's nice," Anne said. "I like Cora."

"Ain't she tops?" Skippy sat up eagerly.

(Anne wondered if Skippy had a girlish crush on her -- like her own crush on Beth.)

The juke box began to play *Earth Angel* again, now *their* song, and Skippy stopped to listen to it, twisting with the melody. "Dance?" she finally said.

Anne hesitated. She wanted very much to dance closely to a woman again, and yet she did not. It would be the same as at the Oval and she was afraid. Skippy sensed her reluctance and pulled her up gently.

"A yard away," she promised.

Anne followed and they danced apart until they both laughed at themselves and Anne pressed closely to her. It was a good feeling. A warmth grew in the pit of Anne's stomach. Skippy's ample bosom was pressed to hers and their thighs touched intimately.

She closed her eyes and pressed her cheek to Skippy's and thought of Beth. Then the music stopped and Skippy slowly let her go.

"Wow!" she said. "We'd better go easy!"

Anne nodded and turned back toward the sofa.

Cora was there.

"Swell place, isn't it?" she said proudly.

"Classy," Anne returned, again politely.

"Skippy, go bring me a drink," Cora said.

"Sure thing, Cora," Skippy saluted. "Be right back."

Anne was left alone with Cora and in the quiet atmosphere she did not seem so sinister. She even seemed a little old and tired and quite normal.

"Where else have you been?" Cora demanded. "The Oval? Paradise?"

Anne nodded. As yet she had scarcely been able to say one syllable to Cora.

"What the hell are you doing in here?" she now scolded roughly.

"Trying to meet women," Anne said, somewhat defiant.

"Skippy's not your type," Cora countered. "Don't mess her up."

"Why not?"

Cora now sounded very much like Dad. Anne resisted being told what to do.

"She's a good kid," Cora said. Her tone was quiet and more friendly now. "She goes overboard too easy."

"What's she to you?" Anne countered.

"She's just a good bartender." Cora tried to seem cold but that was a poor try. "I don't want her on another binge, hear?"

Cora stopped, became more personal.

"You don't belong here. You're out for kicks. Pick on somebody your size."

"What do you mean?" Anne was wary now. Was Cora trying to move

194

in on Skippy?

"I mean you're not really queer," Cora said bluntly. "You're just a crazy mixed-up kid still looking for Mom."

"You think I'll grow out of it?" Anne's tone was sarcastic now. Cora must think her quite young -- a virgin afraid to sleep with men and choosing masculine women instead -- like the fems at the Oval.

"You know," Cora went on, "a girl could get in a lot of trouble talking to strangers and going to rough places. She could be inviting the undertaker. She can expect to be robbed, roughed up, raped -- your parents know where you go?"

Anne laughed. "I left home some time ago."

"Why?"

Anne paused. She couldn't easily say why. "For one thing, I didn't like being bossed," she decided. Cora ignored this and sighed. "I'd like you to meet my son sometime," she said. "He's just about your age."

Anne did not answer. It would not have been polite to say no.

So Cora really was a Mom! It might have been what made her look beautiful despite her coarseness and her occupation. She wondered how Cora had become a mother and decided it had to have been an early mistake -- like marrying Mark had been for her.

"I guess I'd better go home," Anne said.

"Do that," Cora said, "and don't come back for a while -- not till I find a new girl for Skippy."

She rose now and punched Anne's shoulder lightly. "Thanks for listening."

Anne smiled and gave her a salute. "Don't mention it, Mom."

Cora laughed and walked away.

Skippy had come up with Cora's high-ball and stood there. "I guess she bought one of us a drink," she said, and sat down next to Anne.

"Not us, me. You're on the wagon!"

Anne took the glass and downed it quickly.

(It tasted innocuous, well-watered.)

"Hey, take it easy," Skippy said. "I'll have to carry you home."

"No, Skip," Anne said. "I'm sorry, but I think I should leave now."

"Why?" Skippy was puzzled. "Did I do something wrong?"

"No," Anne smiled. "But as you said before, I'm not really your type -

195

- so I'd better go now."

Skippy shrugged. "There goes a good try!"

Anne rose, and Skippy said, "I'll get Sol to get a cab for you."

They went downstairs and stopped in the dark hallway before the door. Skippy took Anne in her arms. Anne did not want to resist and let herself be kissed. Skippy's mouth was sweet and tender and she thought for a moment, *I really do want to take her home.* And then Skippy let her go and opened the door, pausing to talk to Sol who already had a cab waiting outside.

The open air cleared their heads of the smoke and the liquor. Skippy opened the cab door for her. "Come again," she saluted.

"I will," Anne promised.

It was only a short ride home. Anne got out in front of her door and paused to let the night air clear her lungs and cool her face. She was sad and there was a fierce longing in her heart and thighs, but she felt free and full of life, and aware, so much aware of the world.

4.

THE telephone woke Anne the next morning. It was 11 A.M. and the sun had tried to nudge her for hours. She covered her eyes against the light and reached for the receiver. It was Jacques.

"I was worried sick last night," he said. "I went over to Paradise after you and heard you'd left with a bull-derrick for Cora's."

"A bull-derrick?" Anne was trying to clear her throat and her eyes.

"A drag butch," he clarified. "Honestly, Mary, I can't leave you alone for a minute!"

Anne wished Jacques would not swish so early in the day. It was hard enough to bear in the evening. But she reasoned that she had to be broadminded about his affectation. It was, after all, merely a defense against a world that was calling him queer. He would play the part for them, with a flair.

"I had a lovely time at Cora's," Anne said, knowing it would make him groan. "As a matter of fact, those 'derricks' aren't as bad as I thought. -- It takes all kinds, you know," she added teasingly.

Jacques groaned again, much to her amusement. "I never thought you'd go for that kind of trade."

"They're all right," Anne said, "for a night."

(She knew she was imitating Beth now -- Beth's sophistication, her humor.)

"Anyway," Jacques continued, "get dressed. I'm coming to pick you up. We're having lunch at Carl's."

"Carl?" The name was familiar, but Anne couldn't remember from where.

"You know," Jacques reminded her, "Esther's john."

"Oh?" Anne sat up with interest. "Will Esther be there too?"

"Unlikely," he said, "But you'll like meeting Carl - he's a great find."

Anne yawned. "I don't see how meeting Carl is going to get me anywhere with Esther, but all right. Just give me time to brush my teeth with yesterday's coffee."

He said okay and goodbye and she hung up.

Anne rose lazily, stretched the sleep out of her and scratched her head. A hangover on a Saturday morning could sometimes be pleasant and there was something wonderful about this being the beginning of a weekend. Most of all, she was secretly happy about going to lunch at a stranger's house to learn more about Esther. She needed more friends now, after Mark, after Beth -- new interesting friends.

She wondered what sort of man Carl might be and why he was keeping Esther. Whatever his reason, it was of small importance. Nothing might come of seeing Esther again -- but she was a symbol. Esther was a means of meeting up with the right crowd, and being introduced to Carl might be the way to see Esther again. Esther was DOWNSTAIRS PARADISE, and Anne by no means preferred CORA's.

She lit the gas under the coffee and then proceeded to dress. She wondered what she should wear. She wanted to wear jeans, but that might not be appropriate Uptown. *Let me see,* she thought, *Jacques always flips over my skirts.* She decided to slip on a black skin-tight one-piece, and a touch of costume jewelry.

She had barely finished with her makeup when Jacques rang the doorbell.

"Alice, you're not going to wear that!" he exclaimed.

Anne hesitated, embarrassed. She had made the wrong choice. "Will Carl mind terribly if I wear a dress?"

He shrugged. "Not really, I guess. But don't you dare turn him on -- he's *my* date."

Anne turned and picked up her purse. She wasn't going to change into jeans after all that preparation. She ushered him out the door and down the stairs.

"Wait till you see my new car," Jacques told her. He was happy this morning, anxious to meet up with Carl for himself.

Anne smiled inwardly, knowing herself to be only Jacques's excuse to connect with Carl.

"What sort of man is he?" Anne asked.

"He's sort of semi-invalid. Sits home mostly. Drinks a lot."

They reached Jacques's jalopy -- a 1941 Cadi Convertible, and Jacques proudly opened the door.

"Do enter my Royal Model Q," he camped. It was covered with authentic plastic leopard skins from authentic plastic leopards; proudly, at the center of the windshield, he had hung a huge white Madonna.

Anne slid into the front seat. "Mary, this is too much!" she laughed.

"High Camp," Jacques agreed.

Anne sat back and waited for him to start the motor, wondering whether he might have to roll it downhill to jump-start it.

"You were telling me about Carl," she said once the car was moving.

"Oh, yes," Jacques said absent-mindedly, trying to avoid an Austin that was angling into his parking spot. "Well, he's really Gay, you know."

"That's a relief," Anne said. "But what's he doing keeping Esther?"

"He likes to surround himself with beautiful things -- and people. Father complex maybe."

Jacques had successfully avoided the smaller car and now drove down the street damp and slippery from the water from a recent sanitation truck.

They cut through Washington Square driving through the Arch and proceeded Uptown on Fifth Avenue, dodging the light two-way traffic.

"But then you're sure there's nothing between them," Anne said. She wanted to see the situation clearly.

Jacques laughed. "Carl couldn't do anything if he wanted to. But wait till you see him. He's so Old-Money refined!"

Anne laughed. "You look at him. I'll think of Esther."

Anne sat back in the car seat and closed her eyes. She wanted never to forget Esther's image -- her deep-set eyes and pale, silken skin. It was an image that did not exactly belong in this world. She seemed ageless and sexless and all Mind -- the classic pale, wan intellectual. Anne had always found that type irresistible.

Perhaps it was her long hands that were so beautiful, the way they gestured or held things, each finger sensitive and independent. But no, it was Esther's whole self. Beth's body, in contrast, was very womanly, her breasts full and her thighs round and soft-muscled. Esther's lines were jagged -- the nose of a Semite and the bearing of a medieval youth, yet the ever-present grace and nakedness of a small-breasted maiden.

(Even with clothes on, Esther was naked. She wore clothes as if they did not matter, as if they were not fastened but merely draped around her in perfect balance, easily slipped off and yet clinging.)

Again Anne laughed at herself. She was romanticizing. But it was fun to describe someone in her head, and to fall in love with that description. Particularly now, when she would have to forget Beth -- at all costs she would have to forget Beth!

A small shiver went through her and she determinedly pushed away fear. Beth was becoming a legend in her life. Beth's scrapbook had always been in her keeping and she pasted new clippings that Beth sent her just last week -- Beth's picture in a local newspaper, Beth's name mentioned in a column. And Beth's fragrant note accompanying them: *How are you? I worry. Do write, love, Beth.*

Anne had not yet written her. She was afraid to because of what she wanted to put in the letter, what must go in the letter. She did not want to burden Beth with words of love. She wanted to cry. Again she forced herself to think of Esther.

They had reached the Sixties and Jacques turned East and immediately parked just before Madison. Carl's Georgian double-wide townhouse was white and had three floors. A wrought-iron gate and narrow setback blocked the steps to the front door. There was a small ivy-covered fountain there, trapping their eyes.

"What a waste," Jacques sighed. "Carl lives in all of it and won't even rent me the attic!"

"Why should he?" Anne laughed. "It's marvelous that he can live in a whole house in the middle of the city."

Jacques rang the door chimes, loudly, and they waited, feeling awkward in such impressive surroundings.

The sculptured iron door finally opened and a small Spanish maid recognized Jacques and let them in. The interior was very dark and smelled of lemon-oil-polished oak. At the end of the long hallway they saw an open door and a light. "He's in the study," the maid said to Jacques, led the way to that door and immediately disappeared when she had done so.

From the study they heard Carl shout, "Do come in. Don't just stand there." He had a Bostonian accent. Decidedly ivy-league Anne decided.

They entered timidly and saw books from floor to ceiling and a Degas on a white wall. Carl was on a library-ladder, replacing a book. The hi-fi set's turntable was revolving silently at the end of an album. "Do come in," Carl repeated. "I just want to put this away before I forget."

He wore a dressing gown of pure silk -- Egyptian or Arabian in its geometric dentate design and most likely antique and authentic. "Darlings, I'm so glad you decided to come," he said, descending carefully down the ladder. "I thought I was doomed to an afternoon of drink." He walked slowly and unsteadily to two green leather easy chairs and motioned for them to sit. "Now at least I'll have company. What'll you have?"

It was a bit early for drinking, but to be polite they both said scotch and he poured three on ice and brought them on a tray to where they were sitting.

He is handsome, Anne decided, *lean and sickly, perhaps even jaundiced, but nevertheless handsome. If only he wasn't rotting his liver! And why must they both smoke so heavily!* (Anne did not smoke. She loathed heavy smokers, loathed it in Mark, and Jacques, and even in Beth.)

"How nice of you to come," Carl said to Anne, smiling warmly although it distorted his face -- perhaps from a minor stroke. "I hope Jacques warned you that Esther isn't home."

Anne nodded. "We came to visit you."

"That's nice, that's very nice," he said. He put their glasses on the coffee table then sat down on the carpet in front of them, looking quite oriental in his patterned robe. (Anne noticed that his feet were bare -- he had left his slippers by the french windows.)   "Jacques, will you put another album on?" he requested.

Jacques immediately rose and went to the phonograph.

He's being so obedient, Anne thought, amused, *just like Skippy*.

Jacques found a symphony by Sibelius and refilled the hi-fi.

They sat listening to the music while Carl drank and Anne and Jacques scarcely touched their glasses.

Carl finally broke the long silence.

"What sort of girl are you, Anne?"

"She's Gay," Jacques quickly volunteered, thinking to clear the air. But it did nothing to further the conversation.

Carl smiled and winked at Anne. "I meant, what do you do?"

"I paint," Anne said.

"She acts, dances and models too," Jacques interjected. "It's too bad she's given all of it up."   "It wasn't my calling in life," Anne smiled, turning to Carl. "What do you do?"

"I drink," Carl said flatly. He put his glass to his lips wickedly and then sat looking at his toes.

Anne decided that he was not as old as he seemed, perhaps not more than thirty-five. But he seemed older. She wondered what was making him drink.

"Carl was a captain in the Navy," Jacques said meaningfully after a pause.

"Please let's not talk about my past," Carl dismissed him with some annoyance. "Let's talk about you, Anne." He leaned forward. "Jacques didn't tell me you were so -- pretty."

He hesitated. For Carl, *pretty* was a wrong word, a polite understatement.

201

"I'm not," Anne countered. Inwardly she rebelled at his remark -- as she always rebelled when men complimented her looks.

"She's a mad bull-dyke inside," Jacques laughed nervously. "You haven't seen her in drag!"

"My mistake," Carl smiled. "I saw the dress and thought she was femme."

They were both now just teasing her and it irritated Anne. She rose and went to look out through the windows of the french doors.

The garden outside seemed larger than it was and filled with sweet-smelling roses, ferns and moss like those of a cloister. There was enough space between the townhouses across the yard for her to glimpse the skyscrapers beyond, reflecting the sun.

She continued to look at the garden impatient for Esther to burst in on them unexpectedly. She did not belong in this room with the two of them -- possibly she was even intruding and became anxious to leave.

Carl and Jacques were in a conversation while the symphony was in crescendo, then Carl broke through her thoughts. "Are we boring you?"

"I was hoping to run into Esther," Anne said.   "A pity she's not here," Carl said, "but at least let me try to entertain you. Would you like to see the rest of the house?"

Anne nodded, half-curious, but mostly just polite.

Carl reached for the bell and rang for the maid who appeared a few seconds later. "Please escort them to the elevator," Carl said, "then start putting out lunch."

The small maid nodded, curtseying, and waited for Jacques and Anne to follow her.

"Jacques, you show Anne around," Carl said, "I'll wait for the two of you in the dining room."

Jacques took Anne's arm and they followed the maid through the dark hallway to a small cage-elevator. There was just enough room for the two of them in it and it took them slowly and precariously to the top floor.

"How do you like him?" Jacques said excitedly.

"He's more your type than mine," Anne teased. Then she added, "He's really quite decadent."

"Isn't he?" Jacques returned. "I wish to hell he wasn't drinking himself to death."

"Is that why he left the Navy?" Anne asked.

"No. They stripped him of his rank for being Gay, publicly drummed him out, the whole bit. That's what started it all." There was a short pause and then Jacques added, "He's been drinking himself to death ever since."

"What a waste," Anne said. "He should be mad as hell at everyone else, not taking it all out on himself!"

"I agree, Alice," Jacques said, " but I'm beginning to think he's a lost cause."

They both sighed then went first to the second floor and began systematically viewing all the rooms. The doublewide townhouse was like a museum. There was an orange room -- a Chinese-orange room with hideous ornaments -- and then a medieval room, a colonial room, an ultra-modern room, a Victorian, a Louis XIVth -- and not a single room for real people to live in.

(Carl's bedroom was on the ground floor, by the garden, Jacques mentioned.)

The third floor was an attic with servant's quarters. Jacques paused meaningfully.

"That's Esther's bedroom," he said.

"Is Esther a servant?" Anne asked.

"No, she's sort of an exchange student," Jacques answered. "Carl is her Sponsor."

Anne looked at Esther's squatted attic door. She was bursting with curiosity to see what kind of bedroom she had but she decided it would not be right to enter; she would wait until Esther invited her.

They decided to walk down from floor to floor rather than brave the elevator again. On the ground level they passed by the kitchen where another woman was preparing the meal, and following their noses, found the dining room.

Now Anne was more impatient than ever. Esther's bedroom, her door -- such a plain door not in keeping with the other décor -- had made her restless. She wanted to leave, to walk a long distance by herself, to do anything but sit with Carl and Jacques when she wanted so much to be with Esther. But Carl was fussing with the buffet table, supervising the savory meal that would be served to them and Anne could not now politely leave.

"Seen everything?" he greeted their return.

"Just about," Jacques said.

"Good. Soup's on," Carl said and sat with great appetite at the head of the long oak table.

Anne let herself be helped into her chair by the small maid and Jacques sat opposite, both on either side of Carl.

The dining room was even more elaborate than the rest of the house, with antique polished silver gleaming on the magnificently carved, many-drawered side-board that stood majestically between red velvet curtains. But the room was too somber and the bright light from the chandelier above the dining table was largely absorbed by the ancient tapestries on the walls around them.

A smell of sherry filled the room. "I hope turtle soup is not too exotic for you," Carl said, himself ladling from the serving bowl.

"Not at all," Anne said. He had revived her curiosity. She wondered if gourmet turtle soup would taste better than the one from Campbell's in a can. She tasted it. It wasn't much different. (Might the cook have used Campbell's?) Still Anne said, "It's very good."

"Fine!" Carl responded. "You must come to lunch often." Then he added, "As a matter of fact, why not tomorrow? Esther will be here then and we can all listen to Bach. I've just acquired an extremely rare young Ricci album of his *Unaccompanieds*. It's superb!"

Anne was pleasantly surprised and said thank you. (Jacques, meantime, winked at her reassuringly.) "Where is Esther now?" she asked them.

"With her aunt," Carl said briefly.

Anne put her spoon down. So! Esther did have some sort of family. Carl's house was a place for her to escape to, like Mark's apartment had been a retreat for Anne.

At once Anne felt a kinship with Esther and wondered again in what way Carl fit into her life. There had to be more to their relationship than Jacques was willing to see. Carl had to be more complex than that.

"Tell me about Esther," Anne said to Carl. Hearing his opinion of her might give some clue.

"What would you like to know?" Carl asked.

"Is she Gay?" Anne asked boldly, "I mean, really so?" She knew this was a loaded question to ask -- Carl's answer would betray his own feelings for her.

Carl looked up at her, disturbed by that, and then looked down and quietly finished his soup. Finally he said, "She thinks so. Let's put it that way."

He almost mumbled this and then put his spoon down and the maid took this as a signal to remove all their bowls.

"Then you think with her it's mostly psychological, perhaps even curable," Anne said to Carl, pursuing his answer.

Carl paused for another long moment and then looked up at her. "Yes," he said, challenging her. "At least - that's what my therapist says."

Now both servants brought in the main course and Anne dropped the subject.

Carl fumbled with the carving knife, his unsteady hands attacking the eye-boned sirloin -- heavily marinated in shallots, garlic, mushrooms and bourbon. Jacques got up to help him while the cook prepared each plate with buttered cauliflower and browned parsley potatoes.

They ate in silence.

The menu was truly mouthwatering but Anne ate with little appetite. Carl's attitude toward Esther had soured the meal. Minus his self-hatred, he was, fundamentally, the same as Mark. He refused to admit to others or to himself that Esther's preference for women was anything more than a temporary state of mind -- as if women, eventually, would always choose men over women.

Anne wondered why even Carl should feel this way. Surely he was not the same as Mark -- didn't seem to be interested in women the way Mark was. Then why was he interested in Esther? Was it because Esther, in being unobtainable, fulfilled a double purpose -- an opportunity to assert his normalcy, and yet no obligation to follow through?

Anne decided she would have to watch Carl carefully. He was not about to let Esther slip from his grasp; he was not about to let Anne or anyone else make a lasting impression on her.

They had finished the main course and part of the brandied cherries that followed before Carl decided to break the silence.

"I hope you two planned to stay all day," he said. "I have new first editions I'm dying to show someone and albums waiting to be unwrapped." Then he added, almost pleadingly, "It gets so lonely here -- won't you stay awhile?"

Anne looked at Jacques, who was anxious to remain, and sighed. Carl was pitifully alone with his bottle, sitting in a dull house with priceless books and records. She prepared herself for a tedious afternoon. Her one consolation was that Jacques at least would find it interesting.

And so they rose from the table and went back to the library and sat, and allowed themselves to be shown things that were in their own right magnificent, but in the present setting, in Anne's present mood -- her impatient mood of hoping that Esther might eventually arrive after all if they waited long enough -- were oppressively boring.

Carl meanwhile was leaving a wide berth between himself and Anne, addressing everything indirectly to Jacques, his willing convert. He seemed afraid of Anne, and yet determined to be friends, determined to amuse himself with a harmless -- or nearly harmless -- game with Anne, where Esther was the dangled prize. It was a strange, strained afternoon -- and then, Esther finally arrived!

It was by now Five o'clock and the conversation had entirely died. Anne was holding an eleventh-century manuscript wrapped in plastic which asserted the existence of *Papissa Joanna*, and was nearly impossible to read. The hi-fi had just finished blasting a chorus of *castrati* and the phonograph's arm was again stuck defiantly, despite its pretense at being automatic.

The sound of the heavy wrought-iron door to the outside world broke through the monotony, as the sculpted portal creaked open then shut again with the determination of a vault.

Anne looked up and saw Esther standing at the library door. There was a tense pause, then Esther's dark velvet voice said *"Bonjour."*

The dull light from the chandelier made her seem ghostly; her skin was stark white and her hair raven black. She was wearing a dress - a many-colored Indian print. There was a wide suggestive belt around her waist.

"We've been waiting for you," Carl said as if he had half-expected to see her.

(Anne wondered if he had actually kept them there all this time for that reason.)

"I couldn't get away," Esther said coldly.

Now she stepped out of the light, kicked off her high heels, and sat bare-stockinged on the sofa opposite Anne.

"Good to see you again, Anne," she said casually.

Anne did not reply. She was studying Esther. Esther in a dress looked like an entirely different person -- self-assured, almost cruel, yet in many ways very much like Beth in one of her leading-lady roles. Esther in a dress seemed to belong to Carl.

"What are you staring at?" Esther laughed nervously, uneasy at Anne's gaze.

Anne looked down, embarrassed. "Just studying you," she apologized. "I paint, you see." She felt she had to add that in order to give an excuse.

Esther smiled victoriously. "I'm glad you came. I'm sorry I got here so late."

"Carl has kept us well entertained," Jacques interjected.

"I told Anne she might visit with us tomorrow if she wanted," Carl said.

"*Bon!*" Esther said curtly. Her eyes were trained far into a dark corner of the room. "You must come back tomorrow, Anne." She rose and walked to the far doorway. "Please excuse me. Unfortunately, I have a dinner date."

Now she was gone again and Anne found herself unable to make the adjustment between Esther's having been there and having left again so suddenly. She herself rose abruptly and said, "It's getting late."

Jacques took the cue and rose, reluctantly.

Carl came to them and shook their hands, this time not detaining them. "Until tomorrow then," he said to Anne.

Anne shook his hand with a firm grasp and realized how weak his handshake was. The sickness of his touch made her shiver. "Thank you," she said, but as if to a dying man.

They drove back silently in Jacques' Model Q. Anne was too full of thoughts of Esther to make conversation. Her nerves were also on edge and she wondered if Jacques could see the tremor in her hands. Seeing Esther in a new light after spending the afternoon with Carl had upset her. She could not hate Carl but she was beginning to loathe his connection to Esther, however lame that connection might be. Esther might tolerate Carl's constant presence, but Anne could not. Anne decided she could no longer allow the close presence of any man in her life. They smell bad, her mind repeated, with or without cologne, like animals of a different species -- men are alien, unnatural, to be tolerated only at a polite distance -- even Gay men.

They reached Washington Square. "Shall I drive you home?" Jacques asked. He too had been silent, probably thinking of Carl.

"Yes, thanks," Anne said.

"Did Carl upset you?" Jacques pried.

"I don't know what to make of Esther," she replied, skipping several spaces in thought. "She's so much like Beth, and yet nothing like her."

"Alice, you'll be seeing Beth all your life!" he exclaimed. "Don't you ever expect to find someone else?"

Anne gave only a sad laugh in reply.

"Are you going tomorrow?" Jacques asked, now worried that it might not be such a good idea.

"Why not?" she said cynically, "She's good for a night or two."

He winced at her new devil-may-care attitude, and Anne was amused. Jacques was more easily shocked than it seemed. Inside, he was still so young -- perhaps not even yet eighteen -- and not half as experienced as he would have her think.

She said her goodbyes in distraction, her mind full of plans for her meeting tomorrow. Again she was feeling the excitement of courtship, and again the fear, the deep-down apprehension that all would go wrong -- that Esther would come to mean as much to her as Beth, and then -- like Beth -- would leave, would ultimately prefer Carl.

5.

SHEER will enabled Anne to sleep that night. The light from across the street, flashing on and off through the blinds, seemed to keep in time with her pulse and the throb in her forehead. It was not so much the expectation of Esther but the knowledge that Beth was near, in town for a night before the show's New Haven opening. Anne ached to call her, had ached to call Beth every day since their time two weeks before. She had picked up the receiver compulsively and each time had stopped herself. Beth did not want to be called; for Anne's own good Beth did not want to hear from her so soon. Not even to be wished good luck? No. *Beth does not want to be called. Beth doesn't love me. Beth can never love me - I'm strictly for kicks, that's all.*

But by night the white princess telephone, so clearly defined in the dark of the room, was an alive and tormenting thing. It sat waiting, commanding to be used. *Dammit,* Anne cursed, *I won't fight with myself this way.* She looked at her watch -- it was past midnight, but Beth would still be awake. Anne picked up the phone roughly and dialed. Each second was full, then as she heard the quiet ring in the receiver stop and the phone answered, it was like a splash of cold water on her face. She awakened from being half asleep and realized that Beth had answered, and that she, Anne, was being very foolish. "I'm sorry, Beth," she said. "I shouldn't have called you. I'll hang up again." And before Beth could answer, the white receiver was down and the princess phone was perched on the table again, mockingly seductive.

Anne lay flat on the sheets, closed her eyes and tried to sleep -- until a buzzing current in her ears made her eyes open groggily and see the room. It was the doorbell. The full impact did not come to her. She rose automatically, wrapping a sheet around her, and went to the door. It was Beth, standing there in a raincoat, a kerchief around her hair. She looked very strong and concerned.

"Hello, sleepy," she smiled. It was the warm, loving smile that had thrilled Anne the first time she saw Beth. It woke her and she began to shiver. Beth covered her shoulders with her arm and closed the door behind them.

It was so good to be in Beth's arms once more, so good, so comfortable and soothing, so much like coming home. Beth kissed her cheek, then her neck, then each of her breasts on the nipples, gently, and they sat on the bed and Anne let Beth take away the shivers with her hands. "I've been such a fool," Beth said. "I should have known it would come to this."

Anne took her hand and kissed it fondly and rubbed her cheek against it to make herself aware that Beth was really there. "What am I going to do about you?" Beth sighed, taking away her hand and petting Anne's hair fondly.

"It's so good to see you again," Anne responded, holding her tightly. "I had given up hope."

Beth lifted Anne's head gently and kissed her full on the mouth -- a strong and passionate kiss that took Anne's breath away. Then she pressed her cheek against Anne's and kissed her ear and spoke softly into it. "I'm going to stay with you for a while."

Anne's breast surged with happiness -- too much happiness all at once. She held Beth tightly and cried. "I love you, Beth! I'll always love you!"

"No." Beth pulled her away gently and forced Anne to look at her. "You won't always love me. And I don't want you to always love me." Now she held her again, tightly. "What ever am I going to do about you!"

Anne ached to hold Beth as tightly, yet Beth herself was making her let go -- Beth did not want her. Anne's passion was imposing on Beth. Anne was being like Mark. She forced herself to say the words, "Please go now."

Beth looked at her, surprised, even reluctant. Her hands continued to hold Anne, firmly.

"Please go, Beth," Anne pleaded again, against her very soul. It did not sound like herself saying the words. "Please go now before it's too late!"

Beth still hesitated, giving Anne faint hope while Beth was deciding. Anne had not even dreamed that it might come to a decision for Beth. She had thought Beth was sure of her own feelings. There was hope -- but only for a moment. Then Beth's brows curved seriously into an agonized frown. She squeezed Anne's hands hard, then let go. Then as quickly as she had come, she took her coat and left.

The sound of the closing door seemed so final, so much like a nightmare. Anne would not see Beth again, would not touch her again -- not for years, perhaps. Not for many years.

The reaction did not come as a shock -- it crept up on her through the darkness of the room, leaving her too devastated to cry.

Anne awoke Sunday morning to the sound of a Bach chorale playing next door. The sunlight through the blinds told her it was late in the morning and a beautiful day. She forgot Beth for a moment and thought instead of the smell of fresh coffee from the hallway and of her own radio which should be turned on to the same music. And she remembered Carl and Esther, and her appointment that early afternoon. It was better not to think of last night and to put the image of Beth far away. It helped to think of Esther; it eased the frightened feeling inside.

She sat up and let the streaks of sunlight touch her legs. They seemed pale and thin in the light. She was nude and she felt pale and thin in the cool Spring on Sunday morning.

But somehow she felt strong. A masculine strength coursed through her, lifted her chest and limbs. She rose to let all her body meet the sun.

She did not put on her clothes and made breakfast still nude, feeling herself a child of nature with the sunlight -- not through venetian blinds but through imagined tree-branches on some countryside.

I must allow myself to feel free, and not allow myself to care so much about what happens to me.

Again she thought of Esther, how Esther might react to her nudity at breakfast. Would Esther like her body? She blushed for thinking so far ahead.

I mustn't anticipate this way!

It was One o'clock. Suddenly it dawned on her there was scarcely enough time to dress and get there. Anne gulped the remaining coffee, gobbled the second piece of toast and hurried to the shower. There was no time to prepare properly for Esther -- no time for an exotic bubble bath or facial or manicure. She let the warm water wake her and then half-dried herself and splashed on cologne. Today she would be informal -- she would tie her long hair in a pony tail and put on velvet Italian slacks. Tan Cuban shoes and a striped silk blouse from Marseilles finished the outfit.

Anne paused to consider wearing lipstick and mascara, then decided to appear *au naturelle*. Esther would see her today as she had seen Anne that first evening in the Florentin. She stopped to quickly feed and pet Portia, then rushed out and hailed a cab.

Carl's house was the only townhouse left out of the sun. It stood dark and cold despite its white exterior, with its ominous iron-grilled plate-glass door heavily curtained from the world. The hollow sound of the doorbell gave Anne a chill. But she would not allow herself to be frightened. She was here to meet Esther, not Carl.

The small maid appeared, white-aproned in the dark of the hallway, smiling a welcome.

Anne knew her own way through the hallway and walked past her to the library and stood, just as Esther had stood, in the doorway.

Carl was sitting in his chair, a breakfast tray still on his lap. "Come in," he hailed, "and have some coffee, etcetera."

"Thanks," Anne said, "just coffee."

She waited at the door, hoping to spot Esther.

"She's in the garden," Carl said, reading her thoughts.

Anne was embarrassed. Carl knew she distrusted him, knew she had only returned to see Esther. Then Esther entered from the french doors.

"Hello," she smiled. She was dressed almost like Anne, with a striped shirt and dark slacks, and wore no makeup. She was thin and tall and oh so beautiful! "Sit down and I'll bring your coffee," she said.

Anne sat on the edge of the sofa and waited for her to return from the buffet.

"Milk? Cream? Sugar?" Esther asked.

"Just black, thank you," Anne said. She waited silently again, not speaking to Carl. She sensed an air of hostility in him today -- worse than that of yesterday. But perhaps it was all in her own mind. She couldn't be sure.

"Don't fret," Carl said bluntly. "She likes you."

He was being sarcastic and now Anne knew why. They had discussed her before she came, and Carl had lost -- at least for today. Esther wanted to be alone with Anne. Carl would be left to his mausoleum, and his bottle.

In a way Anne felt sorry. She did not mean for Esther to torment him. She smiled and winked at Carl and it brought a smile back to his face. And now Esther returned with two china cups and took a seat on the sofa beside her. She was pale.

"Nice to see you," she said.

Anne nodded and took a sip of black coffee. They sat in silence.

"Shall I put on Ricci?" Carl volunteered shakily.

Esther rose, addressing only Anne. "Let's go to the park."

Anne felt imprisoned by her eyes. She got up to follow her then suddenly remembered her good manners and broke free of them. She turned to Carl. "Excuse me, what did you say?"

Carl sighed. "Never mind. You can listen to it when you come back."

Meanwhile Esther had taken her hand impatiently and was pulling her toward the door. "Come on," she said.

Anne skipped quickly behind Esther on the sidewalk. It was only half a block to the park and an entrance was only another block away. They headed in that direction like two children out to play. Esther was acting young and carefree, but it was forced. Anne pretended not to notice.

They chose a path with new grass on either side and ran further, letting themselves be hidden by the flowering trees.

Finally Anne stopped, pulling Esther's hand, and said, "Here."

They were both out of breath. Esther stopped and paced slowly alongside her, still holding Anne's hand in a tight knot, her whole body taut.

"Let's sit," Anne said.

They found an unoccupied bench and sat, looking at the obelisk on the hill.

"Why are you upset," Anne asked.

It took Esther by surprise. "Is it that obvious?"

Anne nodded, lightly squeezing her hand. "Is it because of me?"

"In a way." Esther let go of her hand and hunched over the back of the bench, biting her knuckles, thinking.

Anne watched her quietly. Esther was in some kind of quandary and Anne did not know what to do to help her.

Finally Esther spoke. "Why are you here with me? I'm really an awful person."

"I didn't know," Anne laughed. "Why?"

"You're very beautiful," she answered.

Anne was silent. She wondered if Esther said that often.

Finally Esther said, "What is it you want of me?" It was a blunt question.

Anne shrugged. "Someone to love, I guess," she said.

Esther laughed. "And I just want someone to love me." She turned and looked intently at Anne. "That's the difference between us."

Anne paused to consider this. "Is it that you're not willing to love someone in return?" she asked.

Esther was silent. She stared outward for a while and then turned to Anne and brought her hand to her temple, pretending to brush back Anne's hair. "You really are very beautiful," she repeated.

Anne blushed. Esther saw this and brought her face very close. (Anne expected a kiss but there was none. They were already attracting too much attention. Had they been two men, the decency squad might already be upon them.) They both turned and glared back at the peering passersby.

Esther laughed nervously and said, "This isn't Paris. We'd better get out of this park."

Anne did not want to go back to Carl's but Esther's grasp was strong and she followed, back through the wrought-iron gate and into the dark hallway again.

The front door thumped shut behind them and it was pitch black except for the stream of dim light from the library.

Esther stopped and pushed Anne gently to the wall. Her body was suddenly very close. Their thighs touched and Esther's arms wound tightly around Anne, sending a shaft of excitement through her. Their breasts pressed and Esther's warm lips brushed Anne's, paralyzing her. "Don't be afraid," Esther said.

But Carl's voice intruded from the library. "Back so soon?"

They let go of each other quickly and whirled toward the light. Carl was standing up, in the library, but not watching them. Esther paused a moment then led the way into the room.

"It was too cold," she said.

"It must be," Carl said wryly. "Your cheeks are red."

He returned to his chair but before he could sit, he broke into a violent cough. Esther whitened and rushed to him, breaking his fall. Anne had never seen her so alarmed. "Bring me his medicine," Esther motioned to Anne.

Anne hurried to a small table and took the bottle of pills and a glass of water and brought them. Carl was quieter now, but he took a pill to be certain. When he could speak he forced a smile and said for Anne's benefit, "It's not contagious -- just chronic."

Esther covered him with his blanket and felt his forehead, then went to sit on the edge of the sofa. She was upset. Anne sat beside her and tried to take her hand, but Esther was still watching Carl.

Ricci's *Chaconne* was filling the room. The sound of Bach, though sublime, was now oppressive and Anne wanted to leave. Then the unexpected happened -- Esther excused herself and left the room.

Now Anne was stuck with Carl and his music, good manners not permitting otherwise.

Five minutes went by and the strain of listening was beginning to show in her eyes. She looked at Carl. His head was turned toward the garden. He would not see her leave. He might not miss her. She rose quietly and tiptoed out.

Anne reasoned that Esther had probably gone up to her room. She boldly got in the elevator and pressed the top floor button. Slowly, the small basket lifted her away from the music, away from the dim lighting, and up to the sky-lit top. She walked down the attic hallway toward the room that Jacques had pointed to. Her steps made the wide boards creak.

"Anne?" She heard Esther's voice at the end of the corridor.

"Yes," Anne answered.

"Over here," Esther said. She appeared hidden in the shadows in front of her bedroom. An attic window was streaking sunlight between them, making it hard to see her. Once crossed, Anne saw her plainly. She was almost nude, her long and bony body, well built and strong, half-covered in a bath towel. Now Anne could see that her hair was wet from a shower. She stopped, unable to go further without touching her. Esther laughed and entered her bedroom. Anne followed, closing the door behind them.

Esther's bedroom was different from the rest of the house -- barren and painted white -- spotted only by hanging bookshelves, a small desk and files, and a low, wide double-mattress on the floor, unmade and streaked with sunlight from the gabled window.

"I'm glad you decided to follow me," Esther said, sitting on the bed, dabbing her hair with the towel. "Come here and sit by me."

(Anne obeyed silently, the first paralysis of excitement now gone.)

"I don't know you very well," Esther continued. "Do you like books? Music? Put a record on if you like." She motioned to the phonograph.

"Not right now, thank you," Anne said.

She rose and looked around the room. The messy desk caught her attention, full of papers covering Esther's typewriter.

"Please don't look there," Esther said. "It's not finished."

"What's not finished?" Anne asked.

"My manuscript," Esther said.

Anne smiled and turned. She felt the same about her own unfinished work, her paintings. She took a book instead and went back to the bed, pretending to be interested in it.

Esther wrapped a dry towel around herself and sat next to her, curious at what she had picked out. It was Thurber, full of drawings -- Anne had chosen it because it would not require close attention. She was determined not to look too easy, not to make the first move, determined to wait for Esther to reveal her true self. Thurber was merely an excuse for sitting on the bed beside her.

It worked. Esther put her hand over the open pages and Anne turned to look into her eyes. They were playful and unsure. Suddenly it struck her -- it was Esther who was waiting for Anne to make the first move! Emboldened, Anne put the book aside and took Esther's hands. They were cold and knotted as before. All of Esther was knotted as before, and shivering.

Was it possible that she was the virgin?

Had Anne suddenly become Beth for Esther?

"Lie down," Anne said to her quietly, taking her shoulders gently with her hands, stroking away the shivers with a gentle but firm grasp.

Esther lay down, tangled in the blankets, and watched her.

Anne kicked off her shoes and knelt by the bed, undressing. Now naked beside her, slowly, patiently, her hands began parting the sheets hiding Esther.

She found Esther's ankles, cold and white, and began to trace the blue veins upward toward her thighs - thighs that invited her mouth as did the rest of Esther. An awesome, exquisite power now flowed through Anne from her hands, now touching all of Esther, up and down, inside and out, feeling Esther gasp at each touch. Then Anne brought her whole body up to her, thigh upon thigh, breast upon breast, mouth upon mouth --

But afterwards, there was something wrong. Esther lay silent, staring upwards at the late afternoon sunlight now streaking the ceiling.

"What's wrong," Anne asked.

"Nothing," she said.

"I can't help feeling that you resent what just happened," Anne said.

Esther laughed sadly. "I do. And it's my own fault."

Anne was speechless. "Why?"

Esther sat up and looked at Anne, her eyes deep and serious. "I feel violated," she said. "Because I let you enter me."

"I don't understand," Anne said. "Why should you resent my hand inside you? Isn't that what intimacy is all about?"

"I've never allowed anyone to go that far before," Esther said. She rose and put distance between them.

216

"I think we'd better just be friends," she said. She stood and looked out the window, one fist clenched and thumped against the other.

Anne rose and went to her, still puzzled. "Won't you please explain the rules to me? What have I done?" She stood beside her at the window, a head shorter than Esther, now almost afraid of her mood. "All this is very new to me," she pressed.

Esther avoided her eyes. "No woman has ever done that to me," she said. "I've never turned for any woman!"

"What do you mean by turned?" Anne asked, "Are you the butch in all of your relationships?"

"Yes," Esther admitted tautly.

Anne was incredulous. Was Esther inwardly a man? Had Anne's aggression wounded her ego? "Then show me," Anne persisted, invited boldly.

Esther took hold of her, her eyes wildly strong. Her grip on Anne's shoulders were as firm and decisive as Mark's. She pressed Anne's body to her and forced Anne's mouth to accept hers. It was like Mark's attack on her, and yet not like Mark. Esther was taking her in anger and Anne was afraid, exquisitely afraid!

It was dark outside. She felt for Esther's body beside her and found only a rumple of sheets. She remembered a lamp by the bed and turned it on. The room was empty and the door closed, so that the monastic white walls boxed her in threateningly. She did not know how long she had slept -- the lack of sleep of the night before had finally caught up with her when all of her tensions were released -- ever so passionately, tempestuously released! Esther had played her body like a musical instrument, searching, feeling, finding each pleasure point with her strong and sensuous hands, her mouth, her boy-like frame. Anne had felt thoroughly ravished, for hours, for an eternity it seemed. And now it was dark outside. It had to be past Eight.

Anne rose, covering her nakedness with the loose sheet and searched frantically for her clothes. She was in a strange house that was noisily quiet with the sound of her own mind. How dare Esther leave her alone! She put on her clothes and stepped determinedly into the hallway. She took the stairs instead of braving the rickety elevator and walked into the library expecting to see Carl. But there was only the small maid, cleaning.

"Oh it's you, Miss," she said a bit startled. Anne wondered if the house was always so frightening at night. "Is anyone home?" she asked.

"Mr. Carl is asleep," the maid said. "Miss Esther is out." Now she awaited orders.

"Thank you," Anne said. "I will also be leaving now."

Outside the chill air humbled her. Shivering, she hailed a taxi. *Esther is probably at Paradise*, Anne reasoned, but told the cabbie to take her home -- but when she left the cab she changed her mind and went instead across the street to the Florentin. She was angry to the point of tears. Esther had left her alone. Esther had left her as Beth had left her.

The Florentin's windows were condensed with fog, but it looked warm and light inside. Anne opened the glass door, entered, and stood still, crossing the room with her eyes, searching the many faces for a friend. "Hey, Alice," Jacques hailed her. "Over here!"

The world straightened again. Jacques and Company were all seated together at a table, many new faces, no time for introductions. Anne smiled and headed for them, grabbing an empty chair along the way.

Marcel was addressing the crowd and did not want to be interrupted. "I insist," he was saying, "sex and love are entirely different. I love a dozen girls and they're all still virgins."

"That's because they don't love you," Jennie subverted.

(Their coffee cups were stale, but no one could afford to order fresh.)

"Alice, what happened?" Jacques said to Anne in an aside. "Did you finally make out?"

"Never mind," Anne dismissed, annoyed.

Jacques's affectation was getting on her nerves -- he was still so adolescent for his age -- twenty-one? twenty-four? -- having been cheated out of that normal development and having constantly been set apart as 'queer' -- and now also quite drunk.

But he wouldn't drop it. "Something did happen, didn't it? Alice, you're fast!"

"What happened?" Marcel asked, hearing a fragment of their conversation.

"Nothing much," Anne said. Then an odd impulse overtook her and she felt she had to make a public announcement: "I've just become a lesbian."

Jennie tittered nervously. *"Chaucun a son gout!"* and Marcel and Jacques laughed.

Anne smiled with them. Marcel and Jennie thought she was joking. Only Jacques really knew. She wondered how they would have reacted if they had really believed her. She wondered how the rest of the world, the rest of her friends and acquaintances might react. *Accept it or else,* she would tell each of them. She would no longer hide her real self from her friends -- from her employers, maybe -- but not her friends. They would simply have to accept it.

But would they?

Suddenly the warmth of the Florentin was stifling and her company, dull. She could no longer bear Jacques, could no longer communicate with Marcel and Jennie. She rose. She no longer belonged here. "I'll talk to you tomorrow," she said to Jacques. "Right now, I'm due at Cora's."

All their jaws gaped at her exit line.

She left the Florentin, left Wolfgang Amadeus Mozart in full swing over the loudspeaker, left the discussion of Shakespeare, Strindberg, and sex -- left the smoky heat and smell of fresh coffee, and walked in the fresh air past the crowd of men standing on the street, past the whistling crowd of violent men, past the last lights of safety and down the cold dark street, down the street of violent silence, down the only street that led to Cora's. If Paradise was for the likes of Esther, then Anne preferred Cora's.

She was ready to immerse herself in noise from Cora's juke box, ready to exhaust herself in dancing. The noise in her own ears was ready to blend with Cora's. She ran down the steps and through the swinging door, and stopped.

It was Sunday Night and Cora's had changed. The juke box was subdued. The NO DANCING signs were larger and there was no one on the floor. The women were all gone and only male truck driver types were standing at the bar.

"Hi, kid," Cora stopped her at the door, perhaps not even recognizing her. "Can you prove your age?" Automatically Anne took out her wallet.

Cora glanced at her permit and said okay.

Anne was puzzled. "What's the matter," she asked. "Where is everyone?"

"Primaries," Cora said. "Why haven't you been in?"

(It had only been two nights since their last conversation!)

"I thought you didn't want me to come back so soon," Anne said.

"Did I?" Cora scratched her head. "I must have been drunk." Now a couple more women entered and Cora's attention shifted. "Go siddown," she dismissed Anne. "I'll catch you later."

Anne sidled through the empty tables toward the back. She saw Skippy wave at her from behind the bar and waved back. After Esther, Skippy did not seem so attractive. But Skippy's eyes were friendly and Anne was glad she had returned to Cora's -- here, she felt at home.

"What'll you have?" Skippy shouted across the room.

"A Coke 69," Anne said.

"Whoops," Skippy laughed. "I should've remembered."

She prepared a tray and put Cora's cocktail on it too and then Cora came and took it from the bar and brought it to Anne's table.

"It's great to see a pretty face around here," Cora said. "But we'll be back in swing in a coupla weeks."

"Does this happen twice a year?" Anne asked.

"Once, twice, whenever," Cora said. "Someone in the Department has it in for me."

Anne was tempted to ask Cora if she "paid off" but thought better of it.

"If I told you not to come back," Cora said, "then what are you doing in here?" She placed her hand fondly over Anne's.

Anne blushed, surprised. Cora was moving on her. "I wanted excitement," she answered.

Cora laughed and took her hand away. "You sure picked a great spot! Excuse me," she said, rising again to stop more people at the door.

Cora was right. Anne looked toward the staircase and saw the door to the Upstairs was marked Closed. Nothing, but nothing, was going on at Cora's.

She was glad the place was quiet after all. Why had she wanted noise? It might be soothing just to sit and chat with Cora and Skip, and then go home. She looked down at her drink and felt hungry. She hadn't eaten since breakfast -- perhaps she should order food. But the kitchen was also closed. That decided the issue -- she wouldn't stay too long.

But now Cora had come back to her table with some people, putting a hold on all her plans. "Meet some of my friends," she said. "Frenchy, Mel, Jane, this is Butch."

"The name's Anne," Anne corrected.

"It's Butch to me, I can't remember names," Cora said, and left again.

How frustrating! What was Cora thinking! Or had they tipped her for an intro? Now Anne felt like Pinocchio growing asses' ears. The threesome standing at her table were decidedly decadent. *The Wolf, the Fox, the Mouse*, she renamed them in her mind.

"Hello," Frenchy said gallantly, taking her hand European-style. He was a very old man, maybe sixty, dressed like perhaps a banker or investor, but very old and with glinting gold fillings.

"Hello," Anne replied politely. She did not offer chairs but they assumed she had.

"May we buy you a drink," Mel asked, helping Jane sit down. (Mel wasn't foreign, maybe a lawyer or a businessman or a politician or maybe a Mafia boss, but his buxom-blonde date was strictly Lower East Side.)

"No thanks," Anne said, "already got one."

"The next one," Mel insisted.

(Cora meanwhile had come back and then gone again.)

Anne submitted patiently to their intrusion, looking with nostalgia at Skip who was filling orders at the bar.

"What do you do?" Jane asked her.

"Office work," Anne said tersely, hoping to dampen the conversation. "And what about you," she asked all of them.

"We spend money," Frenchy said. "But only on girls," Mel added, winking.

"I do hope Cora will join us again," Jane said, shifting in the chair, primping her bosoms. (It was plain, from her low-cut blouse, that they had come by car.)

"We're expecting another couple," Mel said. "I hope you're coming with us to the party."

"I don't know," Anne answered.

She was feeling most uncomfortable now and wished Skip would come over and protect her.

Skippy read her mind. She came over with a tray. "Hi," she said to Anne. "Mind if I join you?"

"Please do," Anne said, moving over to make room for a chair.

But Cora immediately returned, bumping Skip. "You're needed at the bar," she said.

"How about some dancing, Cora?" Mel suggested. "It's past Eleven. Should be safe."

"Okay," Cora said reluctantly. But she did not sit and abruptly took hold of Anne's wrist. "Come on."

Anne let herself be led to the dance floor and followed Cora's smooth but sexy step to a slow mambo.

"What are you doing with those birds?" Cora whispered in Anne's ear.

"But you brought them over," Anne said.

"Never mind what I did," Cora said, "just don't walk out with them."

"I won't," Anne promised. She was annoyed. How could Cora assume she was so stupid as to pick up strangers in a bar like hers!

"I'm taking you home," Cora said. "You shouldn't be alone at this hour."

"What makes you so safe?" Anne reacted impatiently. She was not a child!

Her remark stopped Cora for a moment and then she laughed. "Honey, I don't need nobody. All the girls come to me." Then she softened and continued to dance. "Maybe you're not so dumb."

Cora's cheek was against Anne's now and Anne was both thrilled and amused. Cora was trying to act the Romeo and it was strangely sensuous to play her game. She pressed closer into Cora, now doing a foxtrot, and closed her eyes. If only Esther could be so uncomplicated!

When she opened her eyes again, they had danced near her table and Cora was ready to lead them back. A new couple had arrived and were standing there, waiting for introductions.

Anne froze. There was a tall handsome man -- probably an actor, and with him -- almost hidden behind him so that Anne had not seen her at first -- was Beth, glowing in a long black evening gown.

"What's the matter," Cora said, feeling Anne's grip tighten on her hand.

"Nothing," Anne said.

She composed herself and walked back to the table with Cora.

Mel made introductions. Anne did not notice the man's name, or anything else. Her eyes were fixed on Beth's and Beth's glance was soft, embarrassed, full of concern, as startled as Anne's.

"Hello, Anne," Beth said, pretending to be introduced.

Anne nodded and sat, unable to listen or to speak. Anger and resentment was forming inside her, against Beth's escort. How dare he be with Beth!

She felt the breaking, the awful tearing in her stomach of the night before. There seemed to be no one else in the room but Beth.

Anne could listen only when Beth spoke.

"Do you come here often, Anne?" Beth was asking, shakily.

"No." Anne blushed.

She was ashamed to have Beth think her a part of a place like Cora's.

"I've been trying to convince her to come along with us," Mel said.

His voice pierced Anne's ears as if through a cushion. She saw Beth whiten, more so than before, her eyes panicked.

"Are you really coming with us, Anne?" she asked apprehensively.

"Maybe," Anne answered.

She wanted to go with them now, to save Beth, to take her away from this crowd and take her home, to where she belonged, to Anne's house and Anne's arms.

Beth started to say something and then stopped. She got up, casually, addressing only Anne. "Which way to the powder room?"

Anne took the cue. She rose boldly and said, "I was about to go there myself."

They walked together with great composure toward the back, toward the dirty little room that said LADIES.

"Anne -- " Beth closed the door behind them and went to hold her, to press her against the wall -- but the wall was dirty and she stopped, and Anne stopped, and they looked at each other.

"You're in a bad crowd," Anne said. "Who are they? Angels? Producers? What kind of party are you off to?"

"Please don't come with us," Beth said. "I don't want you to see me this way." She looked away. "We can't stay here, we need to go back before they notice.

Anne would not listen.

She took Beth's hands and made her stay where she was. But Beth was not warm and giving tonight, she was frozen, unresponsive.

"We have to go back, Anne," she repeated. "I don't want them to know about us."

"Why? Why are you this way?" Anne pleaded.

"I told you why," Beth answered, her hands on Anne's cheeks, her lips brushing hers. "This is my life, the way I have chosen to live it. Now let's go back!"

Anne followed her back to the table, past puzzled Cora and Skippy, and stood, not sitting down again.

"Is it safe in there?" Jane said playfully.

"Like a Church," Beth answered, making all of them laugh.

"Are you coming with us," Mel asked Anne again, trying to take her hand.

Anne pulled her hand away quickly and took up her drink. "Afraid not," she said. "Cora's taking me home."

"Pity," Frenchy coaxed, "but why don't you both come along?"

"No thanks," Anne said firmly.

"We'll be showing movies," he insisted in what was thought to be a tempting tone.

Anne backed away, not wanting to hear more. "Excuse me," she said. "It's getting late and I work tomorrow."

She went to the bar to pick up Cora.

"Are you still taking me home?" she demanded.

Cora was surprised - and aroused.

She hesitated a moment then said, "Sure, baby. Okay." She stopped at the hat-check counter to pick up their jackets and then ushered Anne out. From the back of the bar the party waved at her -- and Beth's eyes, desperate and anxious, followed her.

"What went on between you two," Cora asked when they were out in the night.

"Just a friend of the family," Anne said as glibly as possible, still protecting Beth. "She won't tell on me."

They walked to the corner where Cora's car was parked -- a flashy red Cadi convertible. Anne was surprised. She thought they were going by cab. "Neat!" she complimented and Cora smiled.

"Where do you live," Cora asked as they got in.

"Across from the Oval," Anne said. She did not want to give Cora the precise address.

Cora stepped on the gas and, with expert disregard for speed limits and traffic lights in the scant Sunday-night traffic, got her there in just about three minutes. "We could have walked," Cora laughed.

"But this car is so impressive," Anne countered.

They sat with the top down in front of Anne's door and looked at the street that was now nearly deserted. The crowds had dispersed and only drunken forms were dragging on the sidewalk, stumbling home.

"This is no place for you to live," Cora said.

"I like it," Anne said.

Cora was silent for a minute and then said, "Do I see you again?"

"Perhaps," Anne said.

Now Cora pressed the button that brought the top up. The tan canvas roof slowly fanned up and over them.

"Are you going to kiss me?" Anne asked.

Cora sighed. "Don't ask questions." She reached over and found Anne's mouth with hers. It was a bit too slick.

What a professional, Anne thought, *so thoroughly rehearsed!* But after Beth, Esther, and Skippy, no big deal!

Cora let her go then straightened her collar and turned the key in the ignition. "Go upstairs and behave yourself," she said gruffly.

"Thanks," Anne said, then, impulsively, she planted a big wet one on Cora's cheek. "Thanks, Mom!"

"Yuck! Babes!" Cora shook herself, then guffawed. They both laughed and Anne got out, watched Cora race off again, leaving her alone on the street.

She quickened her steps to her door and it was not until she reached it that the running of footsteps behind her pierced the silence. "Anne -- "

Anne turned, feeling a chill in her spine. All at once the street was filled and she was surrounded, made helpless, awkward: Esther was running toward her.

6.

"I thought you'd never come!" Esther stepped in front of Anne, a little breathless. "I took time off for coffee. What's the matter? Surprised to see me?" She bent her head boyishly and smiled a guilty smile.

"But you left -- and I thought -- " Anne tried not to seem clumsy.

"I had an appointment," Esther said quickly. "Sorry."

"How about another cup of coffee," Anne said, turning toward her door.

"Hell no," Esther kicked a pebble. "Let's walk through the park."

"Now?" Anne held back. "I'm starved! I haven't eaten anything all day!" She looked around for someplace to go. Every shop on the street was closing. Only Nedick's would still be open, on the corner of Sixth and Eighth.

"Come this way," she pulled Esther. "Food first."

They found Nedick's and Anne gobbled two hot dogs with the works and downed a large orange drink while Esther watched her, amused.

"Come on, sleepy," she rushed her, "it's a lovely morning."

Anne was reluctant. The day had been a long one and she was tired. But Esther was wide awake.

"Are you high?" Anne asked her.

"Only on coffee," she said. They had reached the park surrounding the Square and sat on a bench near the street. It was safe to sit there, even at this hour. Esther put her feet up and yawned, stretching, then folded her arms under her chin, leaning over the back of the bench, looking at the newly-seeded grass. "*Sizzle, diddle, chimpanzidle,*" she chanted, "*Man is Mind and Mind's a riddle. Burn inside but play your fiddle.*"

"Is that one of your poems?" Anne asked.

"No, a good friend of mine wrote it," Esther said, a little sadly. Now she rose, pulling Anne up with her. "Take off your shoes. Let's walk barefoot on the new grass." She kicked off her sandals.

It was too much of a temptation. Anne did the same and now both were barefoot on the wet grass, moving too quickly to feel cold.

A new freedom had been won in going barefoot. Esther's poetic mood had wakened Anne and now there was that tingle in her spine and that refreshing awareness of Esther.

Esther turned, sensing Anne's eyes, and her own eyes rested fully on Anne -- a slow, sensuous smile forming on her lips. But her eyes were softer than usual and Anne glimpsed something that was not boyish about Esther -- something that was still girlish and kind, even gentle. "Let's lie down," she said carelessly, pulling Anne down with her in a dark protected spot behind bushes and trees.

Anne looked anxiously about, afraid they would be seen. But the park was deserted except for a lonely policeman patrolling the other side of the Fountain. He could not spy them.

Esther hummed to herself while Anne squinted at the sky, spotting stars. How perfect, how right it was to be lying here with a woman beside her, without a thought about being disturbed.

Then Esther's face came between her and the sky, obscured in shadow. Slowly her dark face came forward until it had blocked out all of the sky and her features were plain again -- her deep-set eyes and pale skin, her open, narrow mouth -- open and tender, tender and near -- until it was not a mouth but a kiss, a kiss with Esther's lips, her breasts, her thighs, a kiss that was more than a kiss and demanded more. But that would have gone too far, even for Esther. She pulled away and lay on the grass, breathing hard. *"Merdre!"*

"Come home with me," Anne said, forcing her tired back to lift her up. She looked around. No one had seen them.

Esther jumped up after her and they walked with pretended innocence out of the park, still flustered, still breathing much too quickly, their eyes searching for a dark corner, an alley, just any place, a doorway where they might kiss again.

But there was nowhere until they came to Anne's hallway and Esther wanted to stop there but Anne pulled her forward, up the five flights to her door. There they fumbled for the keys, Esther playfully searching Anne's pockets, making the fire in her thighs almost painful. And now the keys were in the door, and the door was opened and shut again behind them, and they were finally free to wildly partake as they pleased.

The faint alarm of the clock by the bed rang unnoticed under the street noise, now loud with the passing of trucks and shouting of school children. And then the telephone rang. "It's probably my office," Anne yawned. Esther reached over her for the receiver and brought it to Anne. "Hello?" Anne said hoarsely, not taking her eyes off Esther. "Yes, I'm sorry. I'm ill. I'll be in tomorrow." She hung up again and watched Esther smile.

"Will you still have a job?"

"Probably not," Anne said, "but who cares?" She had been planning to quit anyway. Scouts from the leading model agencies had repeatedly approached her. After last night at Cora's Anne felt she could deal with the sleaze, with the Fox and the Wolf, could set her own terms and her own boundaries, could resist becoming the Mouse.

Now she remembered Esther. Didn't she also have responsibilities this morning? "Shouldn't you call Carl?" Anne reminded.

"Why bother," Esther stretched, "he knows where I am." She was lying on her back, naked, her head turned toward streaks of morning sunshine on the ceiling.

Anne gazed at her for a moment and then laid her head on her shoulder, Esther's body now familiar although not as soft or familiar as Beth's.

She was not womanly, and although Anne had again just experienced the most intense feeling she had ever had, it had left her wanting. Esther was a man-child, not a woman. Up close, her face and body were hairy and muscular, like that of a female athlete or an adolescent male. Her hands and mouth had made up for what she lacked in physiology (and certainly no physical release from a man could even come close to what Esther's sheer passion and endurance could achieve in Anne or any woman!) but it was all lust, not tenderness, not womanliness.

And worst of all, Esther had not allowed Anne to touch her as a woman. Anne might as well have awakened with her head on Mark's shoulder. There was nothing womanly about Esther. Esther, though perhaps more appealing, was no better than Mark.

Well, no, Anne mentally corrected, *if I have to choose between Esther and Mark on a desert isle, then by all means Esther, hands down!*

Anne rose impatiently. "Shall I make breakfast or shall we go out?" she asked.

228

"Both," Esther said, rising eagerly.

Anne laughed, going into the bathroom. "I'll lend you my hairbrush, but my toothbrush is off limits."

"My finger will do," Esther said, joining her, putting toothpaste on it. She brushed her teeth then borrowed the razor.

"Where do you want to go?" Anne asked, now out of the bathroom and dressing.

"Don't know," Esther shrugged, "Church, maybe."

"Church!" that was a new one!

"It's a day for churches," Esther laughed. "Paris is full of churches. Wherever they want to put up something beautiful, they put a church."

"There's one on Fifth and Tenth -- " Anne started.

"*Merdre non!*" Esther came in and slipped on her pants. "Only the Cathedral at Reims, and then only in full armor, as *Jeanne D'Arc*," she said in her charming french accent.

"You're teasing me," Anne laughed, throwing her a shirt.

"Only half-teasing," Esther said. "I am always feeling like I am in the wrong time and wrong place."

"Come on," Anne said, "It's time for breakfast at the Florentin!"

They were silent as they crossed the street between parked cars. The Florentin had just opened and Marcel was already seated at the window, tuning his lute. The Village Outdoor Art Show would bring in many tourists and his breakfast had already been paid for by a group sitting in the back. He began with the usual automatic *Partridge in a Pear Tree* that would soon modulate softly into *Greensleeves*.

"Dahrling!" he shouted to Anne over his own music, "You must be unemployed!"

"Just for today," Anne laughed, giving him her cheek. "May we join you?" He bowed assent with a strum. They sat, ordering coffee and sardine sandwiches, *garni*. (The Florentin was above serving bacon and eggs.)

"This is Marcel," Anne introduced, "And this is Esther."

Marcel scrutinized Esther's face with his eyes.

Esther nodded, plainly finding him uninteresting and *faux*. Now Anne felt strained. Esther did not like Marcel and they were stuck here, already having ordered.

229

"I'm working nights at the Dickens Room," Marcel said to Anne in an effort to break the silence. He did not feel comfortable with Esther either.

"That's great," Anne said, trying to remain enthusiastic.

Esther meanwhile had appropriated a *Manchester Guardian* left on the next table.

(Anne wondered why they did not like each other. They were so alike! Minus the essential appendages, Esther was precisely like Marcel. Of course it was hard not to laugh at Marcel's affectations, but he was so young, beautiful in a Renaissance way, in his sandals and suede -- and though often mistaken for Gay, not at all in the same category.)

And why did Marcel not like Esther?

Was it because they were rivals?

Was he sensing her manhood?

And what about Anne? Was Esther's attitude catching? Was Anne also transforming? Anne realized that what she had expected had begun -- that everyone would soon realize she was different, that she had crossed over into a land too foreign for most of them to accept.

The Irish actress who waited on tables and had taken their order now brought them their food and Anne proceeded to put her salad in with the sardines in a large dagwood sandwich. Esther put down the *Manchester Guardian* and watched her, both horrified and amused, then she approached her own repast in the proper, continental way.

Marcel had begun to pluck his lute like a classical guitar. *"Oh can you see yon little turtle dove sitting under the mulberry tree... "* he began to counter-tenor in falsetto. (Pretty good for having been entirely self-taught, Anne decided.) *"See how that he doth mourn for his true love as I, my love, should mourn for thee... "*

The Florentin was now transformed into a medieval castle. Only an occasional Villager, stopping to peer through the window before hurrying on, reminded Anne of the outside world.

Through the window Anne had a good view of '69½', the rooming house where most of the Florentin regulars lived. It was sometimes nicknamed *Belle-View* because of its interesting residents. But on a Monday morning *Belle-View* didn't seem so colorful. Now only one head poked out of the ground-floor window -- a girl with a G.I. haircut that Anne now recognized as a barmaid at the Oval. Was this to be Anne's future?

230

Marcel was still at it, trying to get her attention. *"Ten thousand miles is very far away for me to find my way back, but before I am false to that maiden that I love the Noon-day shall turn black, my love ... "*

More coffee arrived and so did Jennie, skipping happily through the open door, her round model's case on her arm. Marcel finished quickly and jumped up with his lute, in a broad bow to her. "Now I live again," he announced dramatically.

"But I've been gone only ten minutes," she laughed. Nevertheless, he kissed her hand in pantomime for Anne and Esther's benefit and made room for her at the table.

(Esther had not bothered looking up.)

"Hi, Jennie," Anne greeted.

"Hi," Jennie winked, then proceeded to try on a new pair of long white suede opera gloves she had just bought. For a minute Anne watched her. She resembled Anne's sister, Dori, who seemed to have nothing better to do but try on new clothes.

Meanwhile Esther put down the newspaper and looked restlessly toward the back at all the faces. Anne put her hand over hers, squeezed it impatiently. "Let's walk."

Esther rose, threw some money on the table, and they left the Florentin.

The sun was higher, and the Outdoor Art Show was beginning to draw crowds. They walked through it, nodding here and there to familiar faces. Then Anne decided to break the silence. "Do you like me?" she asked Esther.

"Of course I do," Esther reacted evasively, "don't ask me such questions."

Now it was Anne who was silent as they walked, vaguely leading both of them back to Anne's apartment.

Finally Esther stopped, held back. "I won't leave Carl," she said.

"Why not?" Anne countered.

"He needs me," she answered. "And I need him."

"Will you marry him?" Anne asked.

"Perhaps," she answered pensively. Then she added, "But we're not lovers, if that's what you mean."

"I don't understand," Anne said. "Aren't you a lesbian?"

231

"No, I don't think so," Esther replied, looking away. "But I'm not Straight, either. I don't know what I am! I wish -- I wish I were a man!"

"Would you then be with Carl?" Anne asked, puzzled.

"No, of course not!" she replied, offended. "I would only want to be with a real woman, a passionate woman, a real woman such as you!"

The don juan in her revived, leaned forward.

"But if you were a man, I wouldn't want you." Anne pulled back, realizing the impasse they had reached. "Where does that leave us?"

"Just friends," Esther said, retreating with finality, then adding more softly, "Good friends?"

"Yes, of course. Always," Anne answered after a pause.

They continued their walk, looking mostly at the ground. Anne needed time to take this all in. Was Anne the only person willing to call herself a lesbian? Neither Beth nor Esther thought of themselves as lesbians. Beth was ready and able to play the game to win, in the Straight world, even while bending now and then; and Esther -- Esther was not really a lesbian but something else! Then there was Carl, who was Gay and attracted to Esther's boyhood, but Esther had no attraction for men. Esther wanted women, wanted Anne, but only as Mark wanted her, and Anne wanted Esther to be more like Beth. This was all very confusing!

Anne suddenly wanted to get home quickly, to leave Esther, to be left alone to think. She had allowed herself to begin to care and now she had to be alone to begin not to care. She would have to consider Esther nothing more than a sometime-companion, a friend to be with 'just for kicks!' *Oh, but what kicks!* she sighed.

They stopped when they reached Anne's stoop and sat for a while. "Coming up?" Anne asked finally.

Esther shook her head. "I have another appointment."

Anne said nothing. There was something very young and repentant about Esther now, as if she were a child who knew she had done something wrong.

"But I'll see you tomorrow, right?" Esther now took Anne's hand impulsively.

"Maybe," Anne said.

She stood up and brought her hand up to Esther's cheek. She brushed it lightly.

Esther smiled and looked down, put her hands in her pockets and headed toward Sixth Avenue. It was not the way to Carl's.

Anne walked heavily up the stairs to her door. She did not care at the moment where Esther had gone. She needed beauty sleep. A sick, dizzy feeling was in her head. She needed to lie down and catch up on the night before. She reached her door and unlocked it.

"Hello, Anne." Mark was standing by the bookcase, a drink already in his hand. She had changed the lock, but obviously he had charmed the Super into letting him in. She entered silently and slammed the door shut. She felt too tired to be angry.

"How did you get in here," she said, sitting on the bed.

He smiled wickedly and put his glass down. "Marriage license, remember?"

"I'll change the lock again tomorrow, and I won't give the Super the key," she said. "Now please leave."

"I just came to visit," he said, smiling.

"What about," she sighed. She was so tired.

His eyes defied Anne's and he came to stand over her. "I'd hoped that by now you'd have dropped your, shall we say, peculiarity?"

His smile was most annoying.

"I haven't," she said. She kicked off her sandals and lay down. "I'm too tired to argue with you, Mark. Please go or I'll scream."

Mark went to the cabinet, unimpressed, and poured more scotch into his glass. "There's no law that says I can't be with my wife."

"There's a protective order in force," she said. "I could have you arrested."

"No judge is going to sustain that -- " he laughed, "not when he hears my side of it!"

"Your side of it?" she now returned, furiously. "If you don't give me an annulment my lawyer will hit you for alimony."

"For what!" he defied.

"For adultery -- with Beth!" she said firmly.

(She wasn't certain now that Beth would really follow through, but she

233

had to sound certain.)

"I know what the two of you did that night, and when the judge hears it, he'll throw the book at you!"

That stopped him. He paled. "You can't be serious! Would you do that? To me? To Beth?"

"Try me," she said.

She was amazed at her own strength talking back to him. How much she had grown in just a few days!

But Mark was not to be so easily stopped. Angrily he went to her and sat on the bed, took her wrist first gently, then firmly. "Anne, you can't do this to me. I love you."

She softened slightly. "No, Mark, you don't really love me. You don't even know me. If you did you would know I don't want you, I never wanted you! It's just your pride that's hurt, that's all."

But this made him angry. He tightened his grip on her wrist. "Annie," he said, and his voice was hoarse, "tell me one thing. What do they use, huh? What do they use?"

His face was over hers. Anne could smell his breath, tobacco-foul and hundred-proof. But it was not only his breath that repelled her -- it was Mark, all of Mark after Esther.

"I'm going to remind you of what a real man feels like," he said.

That was it! She had had it with him. No more! "Let go of me," she commanded.

But Mark took her with both hands.

"That's not what you really want me to do."

"Yes it is, Mark, and you know it!"

She struggled against him but knowing he was too strong. She couldn't stand his breath -- she turned her back on him. "Mark," she warned, "this is rape, and I won't forget it!"

"What, between husband and wife?" he chuckled, pressing himself against her, pulling at her belt-buckle, trying to get her pants down.

She stopped struggling. It was useless to try and fight him off. Her coldness would be more effective. Whatever he did to her now would not matter, would be chalked up as just another unpleasant experience with Mark -- but she would have the last laugh.

"You rape me now and I'll make you pay for it for the rest of your life!" she said strongly.

He let go of her sharply and she rubbed the soreness in her wrists and waited.

"You really would do it, wouldn't you?" he said, suddenly sober.

She nodded. "It'll be nice to have you support me for the rest of my life -- especially since I don't ever plan to marry again."

The prospect sobered him, filled him with helpless rage.

He went again to the scotch, poured another glassful and gulped it down, then flung the glass across the room.

Anne faced him and saw his twisted expression, knew what to expect from him. She steeled herself.

Mark stood, his fist clenched, holding his breath. Anne did not take her eyes from him. "Go on, hit me and get out," she dared him.

He wanted to.

He was poised to smash both their lives with one blow from his powerful fist.

His father would have done so.

But he didn't.

He couldn't.

Sanity returned to his face.

He stood helplessly, panting, sweating, then suddenly whirled and left.

Anne covered her face with her arm, digging deep into the pillow, riding the waves of anger and fatigue and pain from the bruises Mark had left in her arms and wrists. She was crying, but crying in relief. She had won. Mark would probably never return. It was finally over. Exhausted, she closed her eyes and slept.

When Anne awakened, the room was dark.

It was twilight.

She had rested and now felt alive again. Her bruises were healing. She sat up, feeling hungry and ready for the evening. She would go out to dinner. She had wanted to try one of the restaurants up the street. Afterwards, she might go to Paradise and look for Esther -- or, perhaps, someone else.

She got up and went to the shower. The water would wake her and wash off Mark. Portia followed her and watched the process with the usual feline hesitation. "Come on in," Anne laughed, "the water's fine!"

Portia shrugged, shaking her long fur, and projected a loud purr, reminding Anne that it was long past feeding time.

The telephone rang and Anne wondered if she should ignore it. But it might be Esther. Or Beth. She turned off the water, grabbed a towel, and plodded wetly across the rug.

The telephone still rang persistently.

"Hello?" Anne said, trying to stop the water dripping down her nose.

"Hello." The man's voice was familiar and it made Anne feel sick. "Is this Eva?"

"Yes," Anne said. "Dad?"

"Hello," her father said again, clearing his throat. His voice was uncertain and contrite. "You sound strange -- are you with someone?" he asked.

"No, I was in the shower," Anne said. She was shivering now and dried herself where she could and sat on the bed, wrapping a blanket around her. "How did you get my number?" she questioned, trying to seem casual.

She knew what the phone call was really about. It had to be Mark's doing. He had often threatened to tell her parents about her lesbian crush on Beth. Now he had probably called them and told them that and more!

"It's a dreadful thing that your parents have to get your telephone number from an outsider," her father said, some of the anger breaking through his barrier of control.

"It's a dreadful thing that my parents won't let me live my own life and that I feel I have to hide from them," Anne countered. She always had to be hard with her father -- he walked right over her otherwise.

"I want you to come home," he said, controlling himself again. "We have been worried sick over you." Then he added, "This Mark fellow that you keep refusing to bring home -- did you really marry him? Without consulting us?"

Anne paused. How could she tell him the truth? "It was all a terrible mistake, Dad. I don't love him. I'm getting an annulment."

She heard him sigh with relief, but then again he took an authoritative tone. "You are to come home now and stop all this running away."

Again Anne paused. She did not wish to hurt her parents, but there was no way she could ever go home again. "I can't, Dad," she said softly.

"I'm almost twenty now, and I have to live my life my own way."

"You are still my daughter," now he shouted on the other end. "I don't care how old you are!"

"Eva -- Eva -- " Anne's mother had taken the telephone. She was crying. "We just don't want you to be a freak. My darling, come home, come home!"

"I'm not a freak, Mom!" Anne retained her composure. She did not want to hurt them this way. She cursed Mark for doing this. She could have broken the news to them more easily. "I can't come home. I'm not little anymore."

"Eva," her father had the receiver again, "if you don't do as we say, I will have to use force." His tone was strong and had the same dictatorial tone that Anne had heard all her life. It made answering him easier.

"You can't use force," she responded in the same determined tone. "I'm of legal age now and there's nothing you can do to me."

"I will stop you!" His voice was high-pitched now. "No daughter of mine is going to become a - a lesbian!" He said the word with intense hate.

"I'm afraid you have nothing to say about that," Anne said quietly. "I am what I am."

"You're a victim of this -- this awful woman," her father sputtered. "She has you hypnotized!"

"No, Dad," Anne continued quietly. "I have always been this way. I won't be changed by you or anyone else. This is the first time my life has really felt right and happy."

"You are breaking the laws of nature -- " her father said.

"The law I'm breaking is *against* nature," Anne returned strongly. "That law will have to be changed!"

She did not want to talk more. This could go on for hours.

"There's nothing more to say, Dad," she said. "If you want any connection with me, please try to accept me as I am."

"Eva, I'm coming up to get you," her father said strongly.

"Don't strain yourself! I won't be here!" Anne said and hung up.

The room spun around her.

She was cold despite the blanket and lay down, shivering. (Portia was close to her face, meowing for supper.) Anne wanted to cry but could not. She was too angry. She was angry at Mark for having done this, furious at the world for being so stupid and having done this. How dare the world deny her a place in it? She was not hurting others by her existence; she had not harmed anyone, while Mark -- Mark with the world on his side -- had harmed her.

Portia's meows were nagging at her now and Anne forced herself up from the bed. "Come on," she said to her, "soup's on."

She emptied a can of cat food in a clean bowl and watched Portia eat it carefully. The thought of food made Anne remember she too needed to eat.

She would still go out.

She brushed her hair quickly and then put on her slacks again and took her toothbrush with her -- she might not come home again tonight. Her father might be here, waiting outside her door when she got back. She would spend the night in a hotel -- that is, if she could not find someone at Paradise.

She left enough dry food and water to last Portia a day or two, and packed an overnight bag with a change of clothes.

She was unhappy about going out, felt driven out of her own home by Mark and her father. Now she would have to move again in order to be free of them. She put on her jacket with a sigh and left the apartment.

7.

THE narrow street was busy with evening shoppers. It was the most popular street in the Village and had its sidewalks crowded with clothing racks and imported merchandise -- Japanese baskets, modern furniture, paintings, pottery, fruit stands, all side by side. It was like a street from the Paris Esther had described. Anne had never walked like this before, looking at everything closely as she went. Easter Sunday was this coming weekend and the street was particularly crowded in anticipation.

Anne wished Esther were walking with her. She felt so much alone now, almost like calling Beth again, just to speak to someone close, just to hide her head and cry. *I'm going to have fun,* she said to herself, *I'm going to find someone who likes fun and we'll have fun together. I'm going to forget everything and everyone and break loose!*

She stopped in front of the small italian restaurant that was so expensive but advertised a *prezzo fisso.* She would eat here, by the window. She opened the door and entered shyly, wondering if the management would object to her slacks. But they did not. Odd apparel was normal in the Village.

It was warm inside and dark, the room lit only by table-top candles. Anne turned toward the table at the window and then stopped, disappointed. Someone had taken it already, a tall, beautiful woman also in slacks.

Anne went to sit at the empty table next to her, hoping remotely to catch her eye. She looked familiar. Anne could not place her at first -- and then she remembered the goddess in paint-stained jeans that had met Esther at Paradise. Of course -- this was the same one, that girl, the artist -- only now she looked older, better dressed and self-assured. What luck! Anne would have someone Gay to talk to for a while.

She broke through her wall of shyness and decided to speak to her. It was a new thing for her to do -- she never spoke first to anyone. But tonight was different. Tonight Anne was changing.

"Hello, there," she said, trying not to seem nervous. The woman looked up vaguely at her and smiled hesitantly. "Don't you remember?" Anne said. "We met the other night -- I'm a friend of Esther's."

"Oh yes," the woman recalled. She relaxed and her eyes became friendly, cordial. "Is Esther joining you?"

"No, I'm here alone," Anne said.

Anne was embarrassed. She was glad she had said hello, but now everything was awkward. There seemed to be nothing else for either of them to say.

The waiter came to take her order. She glanced down at the menu and picked out one of the cheaper meat items: *veal scallopini Marsala.* She was about to order wine with it but then decided no, she had better stick to water.

The waiter left to fill the order and Anne again had nothing to do. She glanced sidewise at the woman and then back at her own hands on the table.

"Do you come here often?" the woman now asked.

"I can't afford such luxury," Anne laughed, feeling relieved that she

239

had been spoken to. "And you?"

"I'm celebrating too," the woman said.

"Oh, I'm not celebrating," Anne volunteered spontaneously, "I'm consoling myself."

It was easier to speak to her and Anne relaxed a little. "What are you celebrating?"

"I just sold a mural," the woman said with pride.

"Then you're an artist, as I thought," Anne said.

"A commercial artist," the woman modestly corrected.

"Oh." Somehow this was disappointing to Anne. She had always looked down on commercial art. "I paint. A little," she returned meekly.

There was a long pause now and then the woman said, "Won't you join me? It seems a shame to be taking up two tables."

Anne looked at her. There was something wonderfully kind about her eyes -- they were living eyes, more alive that Beth's, more alive than Esther's -- eyes looking directly at her and not over her to some far away horizon.

"Thank you," Anne said impulsively. "I will!"

She quickly moved over and sat across from her at the window where she had wanted to sit before. "My name's Anne," she said.

"Mine's Johnson," the woman smiled.

There was a faint touch of business-like masculinity about her that lent her assurance. But it was Beth's kind of assurance, both soft and competent. Had Anne never seen her with Esther at Paradise, she would never have thought Johnson Gay. Even now, she couldn't quite be sure.

"Have you had dinner yet?" Anne asked, not seeing a plate before her.

"I just ordered dessert," Johnson said, "but I'll set awhile on coffee."

Now Anne's waiter brought water and a basket of hot italian bread. With abandon she began to butter all of it while it was still warm. "Please excuse me," Anne said. "I haven't eaten all day."

Johnson smiled in sympathy, playing with her spoon, then asked cautiously, "How is Esther?"

"What makes you think I've seen her since the other night," Anne said, not wishing to give Esther away.

Johnson smiled again, wisely. "I know her too well." She put her spoon down and looked at Anne. "Is your evening free?"

"More or less," Anne said. "I had planned to go to Paradise."

Now Johnson chuckled. "You must be new! I'm afraid Paradise is not too hopping on a Monday night." (Johnson was right. Now Anne remembered Jacques telling her that Monday nights were a waste of time everywhere. Only drunks patronized the bars then.)

"I'm going around the corner to a movie," Johnson suggested. "There's a Maria Montez film. Want to come?"

Anne looked at her again. Johnson had qualities that were much like Beth, and yet somehow more wholesome. For one thing, she appeared to be a nonsmoker, like herself, and that was refreshing -- for once spending an evening with someone and not having to constantly fight the air pollution across the table. "All right," Anne said. She had not been to a movie in months and it might be fun.

Anne's first course, *minestrone*, arrived and Johnson watched her wolf it down. She seemed in a happy silence and Anne wondered, between spoonfuls, what she was thinking. The small candle flickering on their table was making her sandy hair look silver. *She's so much like Beth in many ways,* Anne thought, *but not really.* Johnson was slightly taller than Beth and both stronger and younger, and her eyes were not nervous.

"Are you a New Yorker?" Johnson asked.

Anne nodded. "From Queens. But my parents were born in Europe."

"Oh?" Johnson looked up in interest. "Where?"

"Slovenia. But I don't know much about it," Anne said.

"Good," Johnson laughed. "I never got there so I couldn't talk about it anyway."

There was something winning about all of Johnson. *I do like her,* Anne thought, *I hope she likes me.*

Anne had barely finished her soup when the waiter brought the main course. The restaurant was crowded now, and there was a line waiting for tables. Anne refused to be hurried and attacked the *scallopini* slowly, not caring as much about the meal now as talking to Johnson.

There was silence for a moment as she took her first bite, then Johnson said, "What are you consoling yourself about?"

Anne looked up, puzzled.

"You said you were dining out to console yourself," Johnson clarified.

"Oh," Anne said, "I guess it's because I have to move again." (She didn't really want to think about that now.)

"Are you being evicted?" Johnson asked.

"No, that's not it," Anne answered. Then she lapsed into silence thinking of her parents and Mark.

Johnson saw her mood and did not press her. Instead, she asked, "Do you paint for a living or are you studying?"

"Studying," Anne said, "only I'm not sure it's what I really want to do." Sadness was returning to her now, despite the company.

Johnson's dessert arrived -- an overstuffed and flaky *cannoli*. She dug her fork in it.

Her hands were beautiful, Anne saw. They were large, strong hands but smooth and uncalloused, with long sensitive fingers. Anne wondered how she kept them so smooth despite her work.

"I'd like to see some of your paintings," Johnson said. "If they're good, I might be able to help you."

"But I thought you did commercial art," Anne said.

"I have to make a living," Johnson laughed. "I have a small shop around the corner. I mostly sell frames and decorative stuff -- but I hang myself and my friends on the wall," she added with a smile.

Anne laughed. "I hope they don't mind hanging."

Johnson winked amiably.

"I'd like to see your shop," Anne said.

"Sure," Johnson returned, then added, "I even have the traditional 'etchings'."

"I'd love to see your 'etchings'," Anne countered, her sadness now all gone. It was fun to banter innocently this way, half-flirting, half simply being friendly.

"That can be arranged," Johnson answered wisely.

Anne finished her food and hailed the waiter. She glanced at her watch before he came and saw it was almost time for the first show. Her dessert was not included with the meal. "The check, please," she said to him.

"What? No coffee or anything?" Johnson asked.

"I don't want to keep *Cobra Woman* waiting," Anne joked.

Johnson smiled and shrugged and then rose to help Anne out of her chair. As they stood next to each other, Anne thought -- *She's not too tall, just right.*

Anne paid the waiter hurriedly and Johnson did the same, both splitting the tip. Outside, it was brisk and they walked close together to the end of the block and then around the corner and across the street toward the movie theater.   They stopped and looked at the marquee. The main feature was *Sheena, Queen of the Jungle.*

"Should be stimulating," Johnson said. She went to the ticket booth and paid for two. "I invited you, so I'm treating," she said.

Anne protested slightly but allowed herself to be overruled.

They entered and since neither of them smoked they went to the front of the orchestra.

"I like to be right on top of the picture, don't you?" Johnson said.

Anne nodded approvingly -- Johnson had read her mind.

The newsreel was playing.

Johnson reached over and helped her remove her jacket. Then Anne did the same for her, not wanting to accept too feminine a role, and they sat back and looked at the screen.

Will she hold my hand? Anne wondered. *Should I hold hers?* She decided to wait and see what Johnson would do, heeding the voice with the halo inside her that reminded her not to be so fickle. After all, all hope was not entirely lost over Esther. Shouldn't she be concentrating on trying to make it work with her? But Beth's *Good-time-Charley* attitude had rubbed off on Anne and all the events of the past weekend had left her somewhat cynical. It didn't seem as if anything or anyone could be permanent, so why not go on and enjoy life fully?

The credits for the first feature were now on the screen. "I always get a great kick out of Montez," Johnson whispered. "Pity she died so young."

"But only when she's cast as the villain," Anne observed. "Do you think the script writers will finally let the bad twin get the man this time?"

But of course they both knew that wouldn't happen. The film was made to please men.

"Don't you just wish they would feed the good twin to the Cobra for once?" Anne whispered in Johnson's ear.

Johnson laughed quietly.

Anne had leaned over when she spoke and found her arm now resting on Johnson's. She looked at Johnson. It was dark, but Johnson seemed to be blushing. Anne took her hand away and rested it back in her lap.

Johnson's hand gripped the armrest tightly.

Anne watched it for a moment and impulsively brought her hand back up.

She filled the grooves between Johnson's fingers with her own and waited.

Johnson's hand came to life impulsively and held Anne's.

The touch sent a wave of pleasure through Anne and her own hand felt Johnson's palm sensuously. But then Johnson brought Anne's hand back to Anne's lap and deposited it there with a firm but gentle pat.

Anne was refreshingly amused. Was it that Johnson really wanted to see the movie, or was she self-conscious about their holding hands in public, the rules between women and women being different than the rules between men and women? Esther had boldly disregarded that difference, but Johnson seemed to prefer to be discreet.

Anne watched the screen, following Johnson's lead. The feature was dull, the ending predictable. And the next feature, starring an Irish blonde with oversized *decolte*, also promised to be directed strictly to a male audience. Now Anne was definitely more interested in getting to know Johnson better. She wanted to walk and talk, but didn't want to spoil Johnson's fun. Despite all the ham acting, Montez had been truly alluring. Anne wondered if Johnson was really still enjoying herself -- whether she could really stomach so much Hollywood trivia, or whether she too had had enough.

Johnson must have read her mind again, for she bent over and whispered to Anne. "This is pretty crappy, isn't it?"

Anne shook her head, relieved. "But I can stand it, if you can," she said to be polite.

"Let's get out of here," Johnson said.

They put on their jackets and walked back out into the air.

They walked toward the corner, their hands in their pockets, not bound for anywhere in particular.

"Have I spoiled your evening," Johnson asked.

"No, not at all," Anne responded. "I'm so glad we ran into each other again."

"Ditto!" Johnson looked at her warmly. They had stopped to wait for the light. "Where do we go from here?" she asked.

"I don't know." Anne paused for a moment. There were so few places to go. She wanted to suggest her apartment but then remembered her father. He might be waiting there for her. Then she remembered that she had to spend the night somewhere and the voice with the pitchfork kicked her.

"How about showing me your 'etchings'?" she ventured.

Johnson laughed, blushed, then looked at the pavement. "All right," she finally said.

They hurried back in the direction of the restaurant and went around another corner to a quieter street. It was a street full of loft buildings and studios. Johnson's shop was at the corner. It was in a small slightly sagging building painted blue.

"It used to be a stable," Johnson said, "and the house next to it was where the family lived. I still have half the yard."

The stable-turned-boutique had only two floors and it was much like a doll's house, not a place where someone tall would live. "The rent's controlled," Johnson added.

The store and Johnson's apartment above it were dark and Anne could only see a little behind the large window. There were paintings and frames and sculptures. "I make my living mostly on frames," she said.

Anne said very little, observing the street and the house, and now she followed Johnson quietly up the creaking wooden steps.

"It's not much inside," Johnson apologized, "but it's great workspace."

Anne thought Johnson too modest. She had dreamed of finding just such a place to live for herself. The apartment was bare and divided into adjoining small rooms without doors. All but one of them were filled with equipment and half-finished work. But one room was painted white and almost bare, with comfortable and brightly-colored canvas wing chairs, bookshelves, and a studio couch.

"You can tell I'm a bachelor," Johnson laughed. "I've spent very little on decorating."

Anne let Johnson help her with her jacket and then sat on the couch and watched her at the closet.

"Were you always a bachelor?" she asked.

"No." Johnson said quietly. Now she looked up and smiled and said, "How about that coffee you missed?"

"Fine," Anne said, and watched Johnson disappear into the small kitchen.

In her natural setting, Johnson did not appear so carefree and happy as she had been in the restaurant. There was a touch of sadness in her home, her life, and it reflected in her eyes.

"Would you like music?" Johnson asked, returning to sit on the floor beside the couch where Anne was sitting. Anne nodded and Johnson slid over to the phonograph and put on several 45's. The first was cool and modern, soothing. She slid back to her former place on the floor and looked up at Anne.

"It wasn't Esther, was it?" Anne asked.

Johnson looked puzzled, then smiled sadly. "No. Esther's just a friend." Then she added, "My roommate left me last year. She's married now."

Anne felt sorry -- Johnson seemed still to be in love with her. "How long had you been together?" she asked.

"Eight years," Johnson said, perhaps a little bitterly. "She couldn't give up her family -- they lured her back."

"I'm sorry," Anne said.

"Now tell me about you," Johnson said, changing the subject. "What made you sad in the restaurant?"

"My family's trying to lure me back too," Anne said. "I can't go home tonight because my Dad might be waiting there."

"Do you live with your family?" Johnson was confused.

"No, I have a sublet about four blocks from here," Anne clarified, "but my parents want to force me to move back home, to Queens."

"Are you over twenty-one?" Johnson asked, concerned.

"No, nearly twenty," Anne blurted spontaneously, "But I'm both married and separated, and my lawyer says that makes me a 'ward of the State' under his 'Guardianship' until I'm twenty-one. There's no way either my parents or my husband Mark can touch me."

Johnson took a long breath over that one.

"And what about your lawyer -- does he know you're Gay?"

"Yes. Well, not exactly -- he doesn't know I've come out yet. Only a couple of friends and Esther know, and now you," Anne answered.

It was Jacques who had recommended Anne go to that particular lawyer, Jacques who had said he could be trusted.

Anne stopped, waiting for Johnson's reaction.

Another long breath is what followed.

Now Johnson rose and went to sit far away from Anne, in one of the canvas wing chairs.

"There's nothing either my parents or Mark can legally do to me," Anne persisted from across the room. "But I don't want to face a bloody battle

246

tonight, so I've decided not to go home."

Johnson did not answer for a long time. Finally she asked, "Do your parents know you're Gay?"

Anne nodded.

Now Anne wanted to tell Johnson the whole story, about Mark, and about Beth, without naming Beth, of course. It was a long story but Johnson listened to it, full of concern. "And so I have to look for a new place to live," Anne finished.

Johnson sighed and thought for another long while. Finally she said, "I may kick myself later for offering, but if it helps keep you out of trouble until you can find another place to stay, my back room has an extra bed in it, if you want it."

"But you don't know me," Anne said.

Johnson laughed. "I take in stray cats -- why not stray women? Besides," she added pensively, "I too was once a runaway -- at sixteen."

Anne impulsively took Johnson's hand. "I really like you, Johnson."

Johnson blushed. "Would you like to see those etchings?"

Anne nodded and Johnson got up and went to the next room. She returned with a large portfolio and carefully untied the straps.

"Woodcuts, etchings, and scratchboard," she said, taking out sheets of paper. It was advertising art mostly, plus book illustrations. And on the bottom, a Certificate from Cooper Union. Anne was impressed: Johnson's work was both competent, and happy.

Johnson watched her and then said, "Here are my attempts at serious art."

She took out other sheets -- lithographs and etchings she had done with no thought to selling them. They were good, perfectly balanced and sensitive, and with none of the stark and depressing quality of neurotic art. They were original too, neither cubist nor surrealist but Johnson's own tightly graphic style.

"I like," Anne said, looking at several pieces now spread out on the floor.

"I like praise," Johnson countered, but Anne saw that her compliment had meant a great deal. She was admitting that she liked encouragement.

"You surprised me," Anne smiled. "I doubted that you had real etchings."

"Then why did you come?" Johnson asked, gathering the sheets and putting them back in the portfolio. She tied it neatly once more and put it against the wall then returned to sit on the floor near Anne.

"I thought it might be fun," Anne said.

But now the sound and smell of the percolator evaporating the coffee down to the bottom reminded both of them to take a break. Johnson hurried to the kitchen and took time to repair the damage and put on a fresh pot.

"Has it been fun?" she asked Anne from the kitchen.

"Yes," Anne nodded, standing and walking toward her. "Only I wish --" She hesitated. The thought had bothered her all evening.

"What do you wish," Johnson asked, distracted.

"I wish you had another name I could call you," Anne said. She laughed a little in embarrassment. It was not a polite thing to say in most circumstances.

Johnson laughed a little too and asked why.

"Because Johnson's too masculine," Anne said.

Johnson looked down for a moment, amused. "My first name is Prudence," she said finally.

"What a lovely name. May I call you Prudence?" Anne asked.

"Just Pru is fine," Johnson said.

They suddenly did not know what else to talk about. Anne felt they must talk or the evening would end. She wondered if Johnson would try to kiss her. She wanted it to happen, but if it didn't, she could wait. It was not desire -- too much of Esther and too much of Beth in the past day or so had taken all lust from her. But Johnson was good company, a right playmate.

"How are you and Esther making out?" now Johnson asked.

It was not to pry, Anne decided. Johnson simply needed to know. "Better than usual," she sighed. "But it's hard to compete with Carl." She wanted to tell Johnson all that had happened but felt it would not be fair to Esther.

"Are you in love with her?" now Johnson asked bluntly.

"I like her," Anne admitted. "But I'm afraid to love her." Now she turned. Johnson was asking her too many questions and Anne barely knew anything about her yet. "And just what, Pru, is your story?" she said.

Johnson laughed. "I told you -- I lost my girl a year ago!"

"How could you stay a whole year without someone?" Anne persisted.

"I haven't been without someone," Johnson said.

"I'm sorry," Anne said. "I thought for a moment -- " She stopped and decided to be bold. "Are you as attracted to me as I am to you?"

The last 45 had finished playing and the room was quiet for a moment except for the hum of the phonograph. Johnson first turned her attention to it, shutting it off. The complete silence made the room seem light and large.

"Yes," she now turned and said.

She smiled and brushed back a lock of her sandy hair. "I guess I'd better start making you a place to sleep," she said.

Anne looked at her. There was enough light here to study her face. It was a beautiful face, unwrinkled but serious, with light blue eyes.

"Pru," Anne said seductively, looking at her eyes.

"You're playing a game with me," Johnson returned, perhaps amused.

"Yes," Anne said, kittenish. "Do you mind?"

"No," Johnson said wisely. Now she neared Anne and bent down, touching her lips with hers.

Anne felt a want growing in her again, despite Esther and Beth. It was a good game -- it pleased her.

"Shall I go on?" Johnson asked competently.

Anne felt a wave of pleasure go through her. She could not speak. She nodded, serious now.

Johnson brought her head down again and kissed Anne's neck. It was another gentle womanly kiss, not like Esther's tempestuous half-bite or Beth's studied nibble. But it brought the wave of pleasure as intensely and Anne waited, waited for Pru's magnificent hands to sculpt the rest of her ...

"I love you," Pru murmured in the gray light.

Anne awoke, feeling herself turned in the wrong direction, and then saw the room in the haze and remembered she was in Johnson's house and not in her own apartment.

Johnson was murmuring "Helen" in her sleep.

Anne held her tightly. Her flesh was warm in the gray light and her cheek soft on Anne's shoulder.

They had not made love, not exactly. They had simply held and fondled each other all night, getting to know each other, going slow. Pru was beautiful to hold and lie next to. "Like a young Amazon," Anne whispered to herself out loud, "sleeping in my arms under the branches of a pine tree."

"Huh?" Johnson murmured, shifting slightly.

Anne kissed her forehead gently, filled with the smell of the warm body beside her, a woman's body, strong and young and naked, with no jagged corners like Esther's, limp, relaxed and sleeping with confidence. Anne could feel the touch of Pru's lips still on her, having claimed her so innocently and yet as no other lips had done before, having made her aware of herself, not quite exactly as a lesbian or even as a woman, but rather more simply, as a person.

How refreshing! After the roller-coaster ups and downs of the past two weeks -- how back to normal!

She yawned and closed her eyes and folded herself over Pru, not yet ready to face the morning. But there went the alarm, ringing harshly through her reverie and then Pru was kissing her chin, her cheek and her ear.

"Wake up, sleepy," she whispered.

"What time is it," Anne moaned hoarsely.

"Seven," Johnson rang out cheerily and pulled her up out of the warm sheet so that the air splashed Anne's skin. "It's a workday."

"To hell with work," Anne groaned, trying to get under the sheet again.

"Come on, sleepy," Johnson pulled her again, this time to a sitting position.

Anne shivered and let herself be led, half blind, to the bathroom where she stood in front of the mirror for a while, just getting her bearings.

But soon the aroma of percolating coffee and eggs on the griddle provided momentum to hurry up and get with it.

"Scrambled or fried?" Johnson called out to her.

"Fried," Anne said, "over gently."

She braved the tepid shower for three minutes then dried herself and remembered that she had packed her toothbrush -- *What foresight,* she laughed to herself.

The heat was coming up through the old noisy pipes now, taking the chill out of the flat. Anne came back to the living room shyly wrapped in a towel to look for her satchel.

Johnson heard her and called out from the kitchen, "There's a skirt on the bed that should fit you."

Anne found her clothes spread neatly over the bed. Pru had thought of everything. Anne's blouse and underthings would do for her office, and in a pinch even the loafers, but not her slacks. Johnson's skirt, a brightly striped, flair skirt -- although a bit klutzy -- fit her perfectly.

"Let me see," Johnson said, inspecting her, "I knew it would fit someone someday," she smiled. "My Mom sent it to me. She's always sending me the wrong size."

"It'll do," Anne said. "I'm planning to quit that job anyway." Now she asked, "Where is home?"

"Near Sacramento," Johnson said. Now she turned back toward the kitchen and hastily dished out the eggs. "Sit over there," she ordered Anne, "and start buttering!"

They sat at a small card table near the kitchen and got right to breakfast.

Johnson poured coffee. She looked happy this morning. Her eyes were bright and she seemed ready for a run around the block.

But Pru in the morning looked more like a big sister than a lover. Not exactly what Anne preferred.

"Are you always so awake in the morning?" Anne asked, trying to warm her hands and chest with coffee.

Johnson nodded and put her cup down.

"It's nice to have a partner for breakfast," she added.

Anne saw shyness in her eyes now. Pru was feeling awkward. "I'm having a lovely time," Anne said, putting her hand over hers.   She let her eyes meet Pru's and they looked warmly at each other for a moment. Impulsively Anne brought Johnson's hand to her lips. "Thank you for being so good to me."

Johnson squeezed Anne's hand with her own. "You're the first person I've really wanted to make welcome since Helen left," she said.

She quickly looked down at her eggs and ate silently -- then added, "I hope you're coming back here after work -- I'll have that room ready for you."

Anne did not answer, but her eyes said yes.

"Do I see you for supper?" Johnson asked, finishing breakfast.

Anne nodded. "I'll bring it, though."

Johnson smiled. "You can cook it, too, if you insist."

"Fine," Anne said.

"I guess we'd better walk you to the bus," Johnson said, putting down her napkin.

Anne rose too. "I'll have to stop home before I come over tonight." She paused. "I have a cat to feed," she tested carefully.

"What's his name?" Johnson asked, smiling.

"Portia," Anne said.

Johnson laughed approvingly. "Bring Portia with you." Then she rubbed Anne's head fondly and took her hand, and they went to the closet for their jackets.

Anne watched Johnson nervously remove them from their hangers. She was very aware of Anne's nearness. "Pru, turn around," Anne said, taking hold of her collar.

Johnson dropped the jackets on the floor and put her arms around Anne. "Still like me in the morning?" she smiled.

Anne smiled too and nodded and brought her lips up to meet Pru's gentle kiss.

"It's a pity you're sending me off to work," Anne said.

"You need your job now," Johnson said.

Anne nodded and sighed.

They were silent, with volumes of things to say as they walked to the bus stop. They waited quietly on the corner and smiled at each other in the light of the morning sun and the clear blue sky.

8.

ANNE watched Pru wave to her from the bus stop and then sat back in her seat by the window. The bus was always nearly empty at this stop, but when they reached 14th Street, people began to crowd on. Anne let herself be squeezed into the corner of her window seat and tried to avoid an open newspaper now dangerously close to her face.

At Fifty-Fifth Street she got off and walked the long block to Fifth Avenue, to her office.

She had never been fifteen minutes early for work -- she had always hurried to zip in two minutes before Nine. But this morning she was early, and it gave her time to notice the sun-filled sidewalk and time to look at the green of the small trees in front of the lingering brownstone holdouts between office buildings.

She thought she heard birds and looked up and saw pigeons, precariously too close on ledges above the sidewalk. *Does everyone love office mornings as I do?* she thought.

Then she thought of Esther -- Esther also loved mornings. *Whatever will I do about Esther?* Anne thought. She shrugged her shoulders and walked on in the same happy stride. "Oh sizzle-diddle! For once I'm not going to worry," she said half-aloud.

Anne was a secretary in a publishing house that had its own skyscraper. It was a white, new building with self-service elevators. Since everyone came late, Anne's elevator was empty. She pressed the button and rode quickly to the ninth floor.

Only the office manager was already at her desk, compulsively early as usual. Romantically named Juliette, she was enormously fat, middle-aged and still unmarried. She had worked for the firm eighteen years and still remembered its first crowded offices on Madison Avenue.

Anne waved to her on her way to her own desk at the other end of the room.

"Well good morning, stranger!" Juliette exclaimed, whether enviously or pleasantly surprised.

Anne hung up her jacket then went back toward Juliette's desk. "Did Phil miss me yesterday?"

"I'll say," Juliette laughed. "He was back and forth pouting like a spoiled brat all day. How's your cold?"

"Almost gone." Anne cleared her throat. She had forgotten that was the excuse she had given over the telephone yesterday.

"Hi, Anne, how's your 'cold'?" Now it was Alan, the office boy waving to her from the door. He was a small bespectacled youth with a slight Brooklyn accent -- almost a lisp. Anne always wondered if he was Gay.

"Much better," Anne said again, then excused herself and went back to her desk.

Alan and Juliette scarcely noticed -- they were so anxious to start in on the latest office gossip.

They're both so tense, Anne thought.

She pitied them. The firm had been losing money and many people had been let go. Alan and Juliette were the only ones left of the original staff on Anne's floor.

Alan had worked here for six years with no advancement. Anne wondered what kept him on here -- she could understand Juliette's predicament, it would be difficult for her to find another job, but Alan could certainly find another one at his salary or better.

Again Anne said to herself, *stop worrying about other people so much!*

She pulled the typewriter out of the desk and snapped it in place. She was a good typist but there was little opportunity for her to use any of her other skills here. Phil, her boss, was fresh out of ivy-league and the least burdened of all the executives. Son of a major stockholder, he had been hired as the axe-man for the Board and spent most of his time humoring the Chairman and dictating memos. He was in charge of the new staff-reduction policy and because Anne was his secretary both Alan and Juliette had at first resented and distrusted her. But she had won them over with her young innocence and honest eyes.

Anne had nothing to do until Phil came in, which would be around Ten, if at all. She pretended to be busy with routine tasks, but her thoughts were filled with Pru and she really didn't want to work.

She could hardly wait until the end of the day. She thought about giving up her apartment and decided to call Jacques, who had said he wanted it. She looked at her watch -- it was now Nine-thirty. He would be in his office. She took up the telephone and dialed.

Jacques was working in the Wall Street area this season. Anne heard the operator announce his shipping firm and asked for him. She was connected with Accounting. Again she asked for him and heard the young man who had answered call him to the phone. "Hello?" she heard Jacques say. (His voice still sounded Gay but more subdued and slightly hoarse.)

"Good morning," Anne said, imitating Johnson's cheery tone.

"For God's sake," he spoke louder, "we've been trying to get you all night!"

"Who's we?" Anne asked.

"Esther, Carl and I," Jacques said. "We all had dinner at Carl's."

At the mention of Esther, Anne hesitated. What was she going to tell Esther about Pru? "I've had to move suddenly," she said to Jacques. "I'll tell you where you can reach me later. Meanwhile, are you still interested in my apartment?"

"To live in? Sure!" Jacques said without hesitation. Long subleases with low rents were scarce, and in between visits to his parents and one-night stands from the bars, he was still staying at the Y.

"But what's up?" he asked.

"Mark's told my parents where I live," Anne said. "I'm staying with a friend."

"A new lover, I suppose," Jacques said naughtily. "Don't worry -- I'll take care of Esther."

"No, don't do that," Anne said sternly. "I'll tell her myself."

"Oh, Alice!" Jacques said.

(Anne hoped neither operator was listening in!)

"I need to get some of my stuff but I don't dare go home because my parents are probably waiting outside the building," Anne said. "Meet me at Nedick's at Five-thirty and I'll give you the key. We can talk about everything then and arrange for you to bring some of my stuff to me."

"And if your folks are already there, then what?" he asked.

"Just tell them I've moved out and you don't know where to find me. Hopefully, they'll give up and go away," Anne said.

"Parents don't usually give up that easily," Jacques said skeptically, "but all right, meet you later." He hung up.

Anne put the phone down and tried to focus. It would be impossible to concentrate on work today. Too many things were going on. For one thing, she would have to speak to Esther and clear the air, but when? And she had to meet Jacques and try to get some of her things, and of course, get Portia too. Then she also needed to go shopping for tonight's dinner. And there was a lot of thinking to be done about tonight, about dinner and afterwards, with Johnson -- with Pru.

Anne remembered Pru vividly. The memory had been with her all morning, making her arms and legs, her whole body weak with anticipated pleasure. And now she was afraid of Pru, afraid of falling in love too soon. She had not dared let herself go completely overboard over Beth, for she knew

Beth would leave her. And as for Esther, that would not be a problem although she had begun to care about Esther's feelings, about not hurting Esther. But Pru was a whole new equation. Pru seemed ready to love and be loved, but it was Anne now who wasn't sure she was ready.

Was Pru really as perfect as she seemed? Perhaps all lesbians were, in the end, unpredictable, neurotic, incapable of true love. Cora's crowd changed partners every six months and fell hard each time, but bounced back. And even Paradise seemed to be full of regulars only out for one-night stands. Only a few relationships seemed really permanent and even Johnson's Helen had left her, after eight years!

Remember the high incidence of divorce, she told herself. Men and women aren't making such a good average either -- and more of the breaks are on their side: family approval, the law, church -- even quiz programs and books on marriage and sex.

Anne shook off the fear. She would go slowly, would not turn Pru into Beth, not for a while.

"You still look sick." Juliette was passing by with a ream of mimeograph paper in her chubby arms.

"Do I?" Anne blushed. She decided lack of sleep was finally showing on her face.

"Better go right to bed after work," Juliette advised.

Anne wondered if Juliette suspected her of having stayed overnight somewhere -- perhaps with Mark. Mark had been a familiar sight around the office up to four weeks ago, but she hadn't told anyone they were married. Anne laughed silently. At least Juliette wouldn't suspect the real reason for Anne's "cold".

She wondered what would happen if Juliette knew.

Would it change her attitude? Would she be afraid of Anne, or full of hate? Anne wanted so badly to tell someone. She felt proud of being different. Like Jacques, she wanted people to know.

Still, now she was glad that she had suppressed an urge to cut her hair short and wear a tailored suit -- like Miss Barnes, the woman at the far corner of the floor in the production department. (*Miss Barnes is a handsome woman,* Anne often thought, *I wonder if she's Gay?*)

Now she was glad she hadn't cut her hair because shedding her femininity, her womanliness, would have made her less like Beth and Pru, and more like Esther, Skippy and Miss Barnes.

It was just after Ten now and Phil walked in deliberately with the *Times* under his arm. He was earlier than usual, perhaps anticipating Anne's continued absence.

(*Phil is affected but not Gay,* Anne continued in her inner dialogue, sizing him up against Miss Barnes, *he's just Old Money spoiled rotten, like Carl.*) It showed in the way he walked and talked, in his favorite expressions, in the perpetual twist of his eyebrows like a puppy wounded by its master, full of repressed hate.

"All better, Anne?" Phil said, unconcerned.

"Almost well," Anne coughed to emphasize, "just a cold."

"We've lots to catch up on this morning, so bring your pad in," he said, not really paying attention to her reply. He rolled up his *Times* into a swagger and strode into his cubicle, hitting his hand with the paper.

"Yes sir, lots to do."

Anne groaned silently. And this was just the morning -- his mood was always sweeter in the morning -- it was only after Two in the afternoons, after conferencing with the Chairman, when Phil really returned heated up to a sadistic frenzy. *Oh well,* Anne consoled herself, *perhaps the day will go faster if I'm kept busy.*

By Noon she was so backed up with work that she planned to order a sandwich at her desk.

But then Esther called. *"Bonjour, mon amie,* free for lunch?"

"A short one," Anne said, a bit afraid to see her. It would be hard to explain about Johnson.

"Meet you downstairs at the elevator in ten minutes," Esther said.

Carl's house was within walking distance and only now Anne realized how convenient her office location could be -- Esther could meet her for lunch often. But now there was Pru, and she really should break with Esther before things got serious. And if she broke up with Esther, who would rescue her from Carl?

Stop it! she said inside her head, *I'm still thinking like a child. Esther can take care of herself!*

She brought her attention back to the letter she was typing and finished it, then put it on Phil's desk for signing. He was already out on a two-hour lunch with the Chairman -- perhaps Anne could take a full hour for herself after all. She walked quickly to the closet and got her jacket then ran to catch the Down elevator.

Esther was five minutes late. She arrived dressed in a man's dress shirt and fly-front designer pants. She looked ravishingly feminine in the sensuous silks and satins of her Gay-male attire, more so than in a dress, but Anne winced, hoping no one from her floor would be coming out of the elevators now.

"Let's eat in the Zoo," Anne said, taking Esther's arm and quickly leading her out of the building.

"What's the rush?" Esther laughed, refusing to be hurried.

"Oh, nothing."

Anne gave up. Esther had no feeling for her environment.

They zig-zagged lack-a-daisycally past pedestrians up Fifth Avenue.

"What's this about your moving?" Esther asked.

"A long story," Anne sighed. "Mark told my parents I was Gay and where I lived." She didn't want to explain it all now, particularly to Esther. She had more important things to say to her.

"Where are you staying?"

"With a friend," Anne answered cryptically.

Now Esther was silent and they walked more deliberately until they reached the Plaza. They found an empty spot on the white steps of the fountain and sat. (A hot dog vendor nearby was probably where lunch would come from.)

Esther impulsively took Anne's hand. "Are you angry at me?"

Anne blushed. "Why do you ask?"

"You're acting strangely," Esther said.

"No, I'm not angry," Anne said. "I guess I feel guilty, that's all." Now she decided the best way to tell Esther was simply to tell her. "I met someone last night." (Anne didn't want to say it was Pru -- it might not be right to tell Esther that.)

Esther looked at her blankly for a moment and then became concerned and said a little sadly, "Oh. Another woman?"

Anne nodded. "I felt awful when you left yesterday. I wanted to hit back at you for leaving me, for choosing Carl. I went a little too far last night and now I'm very confused."

Esther paused for a moment and thought about this. Finally she concluded, "You like her."

"Yes," Anne admitted.

"But you also like me?" Esther said.

"Yes," Anne said again. Now she laughed, a little embarrassed. She had never thought such a situation would arise. But after so many years of not having anyone to be really close to, now that she had finally come out, she felt very much like a kid in a candy store -- so many ravishing women to choose from! Somewhere in the back of her mind she was afraid she was hurting Esther very much. She wanted to do something about it, but there was nothing to do.

But now Esther laughed boisterously and fondly rubbed Anne's head. "Don't take things so seriously! We've only just met -- and I haven't been reporting to you, have I?" She pretended not to have been hurt by Anne's revelation, but her face and complexion said otherwise.

Anne squeezed her hand. "I can't help taking things seriously," she said. "I want to find someone *I* can take seriously."

"I guess I haven't made you feel very secure," Esther apologized.

"I wasn't very secure to start with," Anne said. "It's really not your fault."

"And then there's Carl," Esther said.

"Yes, there's Carl," Anne agreed. Now she was silent and waited for Esther to speak.

"Let's walk," Esther said, getting up.

They started again toward the Zoo. There were many people out today, much traffic, and hundreds of flying and fluttering pigeons to avoid.

They crossed the Plaza and came to the park and walked down the path to the crowds around the elephant cages. On either side of them, old men and women, and even younger ones, some with baby carriages, occupied every inch of space on the benches.

Esther walked very close to Anne, holding her hand. Her nearness was pleasantly exciting, and Anne almost regretted Pru for a moment.

"I don't know if I can explain Carl," Esther said after a while. "I can only say I need him. We're engaged. Someday, I want to marry him."

"Why?" Anne asked, perplexed.

"Because that is what women do, in my country, in my family. Even lesbians. Only after marriage can they live as they please. In my country, and in my family, that is what is expected." Esther said, disturbed by her own words. "In my country, in my family, no woman is anything unless she is married."

The sudden gap looming between their worlds now dashed Anne's hopes completely. It was clear from the conviction in her voice that Esther really believed in what she was saying, that she embraced her culture rather than rebelled against it.

"But why Carl?" Anne asked.

(Someone younger and healthier would have been a better choice.)

"Because with Carl I can still be a virgin," Esther said. "Don't you understand? I don't want to do anything with a man."

"And you think you can marry Carl and still be free to go to Paradise every night -- and have his money and all that security, without giving anything in return," Anne said blankly. "You think that with Carl you can have something for nothing."

"You don't understand," Esther said, now very upset. "That's not it at all!"

"But I do understand," Anne said. The memory of her visits at Carl's was strong, the memory of the pained resentment in Carl's eyes. "You don't think that Carl wants anything from you but he does. He wants to have all of you. You'll never have a life of your own with him. If anyone else dares to get really close to you, dares to love you -- or if you love them -- Carl will smash them, quietly, subtly, threatening you with his sickness, filling up your schedule with a dozen other people."

"No, that's not true," Esther said.

They had stopped in the middle of the path now and their voices were quite loud.

"It is true," Anne said. "Wasn't it true with me? Wasn't I brought in to make you forget someone else you were interested in? Won't there be someone -- isn't there someone right now -- to replace me? Hasn't Carl invited someone new for this coming Sunday?" She stared fixedly at Esther and took her wrists, pleadingly. "Esther, think -- hasn't he kept you on a Gay merry-go-round? Are you really happy?"

Esther turned away from her. "Let's not stop here. Let's walk," she said.

They went further into the Zoo and then out again and found a bench that was vacant. They sat.

Anne persisted: "Is someone else invited this coming Sunday?"

260

Her tone was softer this time. She did not want to hurt Esther or put her through some third degree. But she felt it was necessary to get things clear between them. It was necessary before she decided about Pru.

"Yes," Esther said, sounding a little beaten, "someone else has been invited this Sunday."

"I'm glad Carl is keeping you suitably amused," Anne said bitterly. Instantly she regretted her tone. "I've been very hard on you. I'm sorry."

"Sometimes the truth hurts," Esther smiled sadly. "Everything you've said is true, and I've known it for a long time. But this is the way I have chosen to live, and I will marry him."

"I know," Anne said. "I really shouldn't have spoken up. I somehow knew you knew it. But I had to get things clear."

Esther paused for a long moment and tapped her foot on the pavement. "Will we still see each other?" she asked.

"I don't know." Anne said, thinking now not only of the gap between her and Esther, but also of the gap between her and Beth. "I just don't know!"

"Are you seeing that other girl tonight?" Esther asked guiltily.

"Yes," Anne said. "I'm going to be staying at her place for a while."

"When can I see you?" she pressed.

"Sunday morning," Anne said impulsively.

"But I can't -- " Esther was plainly torn.

"Are you always going to do what Carl says?" Anne challenged.

Esther was silent and then said, "Maybe Sunday, then."

"I'll be at the Florentin from Ten to Eleven," Anne said.

They got up from the bench. They had forgotten to eat lunch but it was time for Anne to go back to work. "Are you walking me back?" she asked.

Esther looked at her watch. "I can't."

"That's all right," Anne smiled. "See you Sunday." She extended her hand and Esther took it, limply, then held it tightly for a moment.

But her eyes were elsewhere.

Anne forced herself to turn away and walk down the path. She would leave the park and try to hail a cab. She was late.

9.

BY late afternoon the work was cleared away and Phil left at Four. Anne waited another half hour and then left. Juliette disapprovingly watched her leave but said nothing. Anne shrugged and mentally defended herself. She had often stayed after quitting time when work was piled up -- she was entitled to time off.

She took the bus down to Washington Square, then cut over to Nedick's for a hot dog -- just one, to make up for a lost lunch. Jacques was to meet her there and he arrived, by subway, just as she finished her orange drink.

"Alice, what an ordeal!" he said. "My car's parked on Charles Street today. Now how do we manage this?"

"Take my key and drive over to McDougal and make sure the coast is clear," Anne said efficiently. She had thought it all out. "Then wait for me. I have to stop at the A&P."

"Roger and out," he saluted, and turned toward Charles.

Now Anne walked down Sixth Avenue to the A&P on Bleecker. There was just enough time to get groceries for dinner and more cat food and kitty litter for Portia's stay at Johnson's. She would put them directly into Jacques' Model Q wherever he was parked on McDougal -- then Jacques could stand lookout from the Florentin and warn her by pay phone and run interference if her parents arrived.

So far, so good. The plan was working and once in, Anne hurried to the closet and took out enough to fill two suitcases. The rest would come later. Quickly, it was all done, and Portia was in her harness, tugging.

Anne gave the apartment one last look. It frightened her to be sitting here now. She was terrified that her father might show up, afraid of facing him because she realized she wasn't really sure she was right. So many things had happened too quickly, and no one in the world seemed quite capable of fully understanding her way of seeing things. Mark had called her sick, mixed up, incapable of knowing what was best for herself, and her father had echoed him.

Deep inside Anne she believed there would be no other way of life for her. But how could she explain that to her parents in a way they would understand and know her to be completely sane and in control of her own life? She felt guilty for hurting them, for not being able to be the kind of daughter they wanted. But this was the only way it had to be.

Ready to go, she dialed the pay phone at the Florentin where Jacques was stationed, and he told her the coast was clear. On the way out Anne stopped to get her mail out of the box -- there were mostly flyers, and a letter from Beth. Anne gripped it in her hand and left, hailing Jacques across the street. Together, they carried her suitcases to his car which was illegally parked half up the block.

They piled the baggage into it hurriedly then Anne went around and got into the front seat with Portia. Jacques started and throttled the engine and shifted into First. *Mission accomplished!*

"Your pain, my gain," Jacques said, referring to her apartment. "It's a shame you have to give it up."

"Wait till you see my new place," Anne laughed. She was sad to leave her own place but knew Johnson's house would turn Jacques green.

"When are you moving in?" she asked him.

"Tonight, Alice, tonight!" Jacques winked naughtily. "Only, can you wait for the rent until Friday?"

"Fine," Anne said.

There was still no sign of her father as they rolled toward the corner. Then Jacques said, "Duck!" and Anne with Portia sank to the floorboard and waited.

"Did you see my Dad?" she asked.

"No," he laughed. "I just wanted to see two pussies dive!"

"Ouch!" Anne winced. She wanted to kick him but his foot was on the gas pedal.

It was only four blocks to Johnson's, but all the street signs pointed to the wrong way and they had to circle around Seventh Avenue and back before they could get the car turned in the right direction. In the evening traffic that took ten minutes.

"We could have walked it," Jacques said, turning into the street. But when he stopped in front of Johnson's store he ground the gears and said, "Wow! Alice, what a trick. This setup's better than Esther's."

"Pru isn't a trick," Anne said. Jacques was especially obscene today -- life with his parents may have been worse than usual. "Come in and meet her," Anne said, "but mind your language."

It was getting dark now and Johnson's shop was lit. It looked warm and inviting. Anne, carrying Portia, opened the glass door and heard it ring, then held it open for Jacques and first the baggage, then the groceries.

They heard the buzz of an electric sander coming from the rear. "I'll be out in a minute," Johnson called out.

"I see she makes her own," Jacques said, trying out a chair on display. He had put the baggage in the only clear spot on the floor and now watched Anne wrestle with Portia's leash.

Anne looked at the shop. She had not had time to see it yesterday. It was crowded with wrought iron sculpture, long mosaic slabs and paintings, stacked or hung. In one corner were two drafting tables -- the kind commercial artists use -- with half-finished work on them. It was all so neat and self-sufficient. Anne wondered it there really could be a place for her here, if Johnson would have changed since this morning, perhaps had even forgotten about her.

"May I help you?" apron-clad Johnson said, coming to the front and removing her work gloves. Then she saw Anne and stopped. "Why didn't you holler?" she said, and smiled.

At once Anne felt welcome. Johnson's eyes were as kind as she remembered, and all of Pru came back in her mind, even to the tips of her fingers.

"Hi," Anne flushed. "I brought friends."

"So I see," Johnson said, coming near to pet Portia.

"And that's Jacques," Anne said, "He's taking over my apartment."

"Hi," Johnson turned and extended her hand.

"Hello," Jacques rose meekly, now slightly intimidated by Anne's admonition to behave himself, and also by Johnson's height and build.

She looks very masculine tonight, Anne thought. It made her feel a little strange. She wanted always to think of Pru as a woman.

264

"Well, I guess I'd better be going," Jacques said, feeling awkward.

"Wait," Anne said, reaching in her pocket.

(She felt Beth's crumpled letter there. She had not had time to read it. She patted it flat in her pocket to make sure it would not drop out.)

"Here." She threw the keys to Jacques, "Save my mail, will you?"

"Right, Alice," he winked and quickly exited.

"Hello, Portia," Pru was saying, now scratching the cat behind the ear.

Anne turned. "She likes you," she said. "We both do." She looked up at Pru now and enjoyed her nearness, felt calmed by her quiet eyes.

"What are we standing for," Johnson blushed. "Let's get everything upstairs."

"But the store -- " Anne began.

"Past Six," Johnson said, shutting the lights and locking the door, "Closing time."

She took the suitcases and Anne followed her upstairs through the dimly lit hall, with Portia still half-tugging on a leash and the groceries in her arms.

Upstairs seemed cheerier now than last night. Pru had added small touches to spiff it up. Anne followed her toward the back, to a room she had remembered as crowded with stuff that morning. It was cleared and clean now, and brightly furnished with items from the store below.

"Beautiful," Anne said, still holding Portia and the groceries.

"The bed's just for show," Johnson said. "Unless you want to sleep alone," she added, and smiled.

Anne blushed. She wanted very much to sleep next to Pru, but she found saying this difficult after having seen Esther that afternoon. She wondered what she should do. She looked at Johnson and saw she was blushing too. She didn't seem mannish now, only tall and collegiate and, under her work clothes, very much a woman.

"I definitely do not want to sleep alone," Anne said.

Pru smiled and then laughed as she noticed Portia's twisted shape, trying to get out of her harness. "Well, let her loose. She's going to have to get used to the place sometime."

Anne put down the groceries then undid the harness. Portia immediately shied away from them and began to sniff the floor carefully.

"She'll probably find a mouse and then I'll be embarrassed," Johnson said.

"Portia's too polite for that," Anne said. "She doesn't speak to strange mice."

"I hope she doesn't feel like a stranger," Pru said meaningfully. "I want her to be at home."

"Thank you," Anne said, letting their eyes meet.   Now Anne was trapped by Johnson's eyes and found it almost impossible to remember Esther's glance. She didn't want to think of Esther. She unbuttoned her jacket and threw it on the bed.

"Is the kitchen ready for me?" she asked.

"All shipshape," Johnson laughed, catching her jacket and swatting her with it. "Get in and cook, woman!"

"Watch out who you call a woman!" Anne jokingly rebelled.

Anne went into the kitchen. It was the first time she had entered it and was pleasantly surprised. Johnson had a completely modern set of cabinets and appliances. "You've put a lot of work in here," she said.

"One room at a time," Johnson nodded wearily. "If I had more money for materials, this whole house could be redone."

"Perhaps I can contribute," Anne impulsively volunteered. It made her feel good to say that. She wanted to become an active participant.

Pru smiled. "Much appreciated." Now she paused and remembered to entertain. "Would you like some music?"

"Classical, please," Anne assented, putting the groceries on the kitchen counter. She began sorting the ingredients: she had bought steak and frozen vegetables -- she had never had patience to cook either for herself or her family and dinner would be simple and quick to prepare. Still, for Pru she was making a special effort. She had bought sour cream and a cheese mix to dress the squash, parsley and olive oil for the boiled potatoes; a can of Campbell's Cream of Mushroom with added cream, finely chopped garlic and onions would do for the first course and dessert would come out of an instant chocolate-pudding package, garnished by Anne's own meringue. Anne surprised herself. It was a good menu for a first-time cook. And how domestic! How normal! How Straight!

But the fit was right. At home with her parents she had always been a misfit. And as for Mark, she never cooked for him -- they ate out instead. But cooking with and for Pru was different -- felt right!

Anne waited until everything else was mixed and on the stove then lit the broiler. "How do you like your steak?" she called out to Johnson who was now keeping Portia company on the couch.

"Steak!" Pru exclaimed. "Wow! Rare, please."

Anne was glad she had surprised her. "Okay, set the table," she called out.

"Already set," Johnson said.

"Soup's on, then," Anne said, coming in with the hot pan. She poured the soup into two cups, then went back to take one last look at the vegetables now done and warming on the stove.

She decided to put the steak immediately on the broiler, and readied raw garlic on the steak platter (a shot of *Grand Marnier* or whatever else Johnson might have in her liquor cabinet would also add to the gravy), then hurried to join Pru at the gaily decorated card table.

"It's only canned," she apologized for the soup which didn't quite look right with the extra onions. "Duh, is there another kind?" Johnson smiled dumbly. She dipped her spoon into it and tasted. It was still too hot to eat. "It's not canned," she said.

Anne smiled modestly. Pru was surely being polite.

They both ate hungrily then, looking forward to the main course.

Anne finished her soup quickly so that she might turn the steak and salt it while it was still blood-rare. Quickly marinating it on both sides, she put it on the broiler one more time just long enough to sear it, then brought it in on the serving plate and went back for the vegetables. The brandied-garlic aroma was mouth-watering.

This time Johnson was silent, expressing pleasure in her eyes. She took the carving knife and fork and cut the biggest piece for Anne, then a small piece for herself.

"Half and half," Anne said, putting part of her steak on Johnson's plate.

Pru accepted it silently and they ate.

"You're not eating your squash," Anne noticed.

"Is that what it is?" Johnson asked guiltily. "What's that on top of it?"

"Sour cream and melted cheese mix," Anne said. "Don't you like squash?"

"I've never had it this way," Johnson said. She eyed the dish suspiciously and took a sample.

Anne held her breath.

"Delicious," Johnson said meekly, and began eating the rest of it slowly. "Slovenian?"

Anne fibbed. "One of Mom's recipes." She smiled. Johnson didn't really like it. She was just being polite. "Want your dessert now?" she asked.

Johnson nodded, relieved, letting Anne take away the half-finished squash.

"Let's have it on the couch," Pru said. "I'm too full to sit up."

Anne went into the kitchen and came back with the chocolate pudding on a tray. She laid it next to the couch on a small coffee table and sat, waiting for Pru to join her, but she was already reclining way on her side of the couch. Portia dominated most of the space between them, now cleaning her paws.

Two creatures of comfort, Anne thought. She reached around Portia and took Johnson's hand.

Pru's hand responded, holding hers fondly. "How about some coffee first?"

Anne took the cue and went back into the kitchen.

"How was your day?" Johnson asked from the living room.

"Rotten," Anne said. She remembered Esther and knew she should tell Pru about it. "I had it out with Esther," she said cautiously, "about Carl. What is going on with them? Where is she always rushing off to?" she added impatiently.

"To her aunt, at Julliard," Johnson answered slowly, as if unsure she should reveal too much about Esther or Carl, "to practice. She's studying to be a concert pianist." Then she decided it was all right to tell Anne. "Don't be too hard on Carl," she added, "You don't know the whole story."

"Piano lessons?"

The revelation startled Anne. It had not occurred to her that Esther had a very different kind of secret life than she had supposed. But now that made sense, explained Esther's constant distraction. And her passionate sexuality.

But it also widened the gap even more between them. A grand piano was a much harder rival to compete with than another woman. And Anne was not inclined to play second fiddle.

"Just what is the whole story about Carl," Anne asked, returning to the living room and sitting on the edge of the couch.

Johnson sighed. It was not a pleasant story to recall, obviously traumatic. Back in 1944, Johnson's alcoholic foster parents drove her out of the house. For her, it was either the streets or back into an institution. On the streets and with nowhere to go, she spotted a Recruitment Office and decided to try lying about her age, "and before I knew it, they located my mother and got her consent, and I was in the Navy," Johnson said.

By 1950, she and Helen were both stationed in Korea. Helen wasn't in the Military -- she worked for the Red Cross -- while Pru, having topped all the I.Q. scores, by then had been assigned to Intelligence. Carl was her C.O.

"Then came McCarthyism, and there was a purge of all the Gays in the military," Pru continued painfully. "Carl signed my discharge papers before they got around to polygraphing me. He did that for a lot of us before they caught up with him. They had nothing on him but put him through a squeeze to name names. When he refused, they made an example of him. The admiral, his own father, turned him in, then shot himself."

"What a horror!" Anne said, suddenly reorganizing all of her misconceptions. She took hold of Johnson's hand again. "How terrible for Carl, for all of you!"

Johnson gripped her hand tighter for a moment then again let go. "Let's not talk anymore about that," she said. "Let's talk about you and Esther."

"There's nothing to talk about," Anne said. "There are too many barriers there. I don't see us being anything more than just friends."

Johnson smiled wisely. "Let's just see how things go."

It was excellent advice, if Anne could follow it. But this indecision had to stop soon. She couldn't bear belonging to two women at once.

(And then there was also Beth to think about, and Beth's letter, still unopened in her pocket.) And Pru, reclining on the couch, far more womanly than Esther and more wholesome than Beth, was now very much the focus of her physical attention.

Then, as if Pru sensed Anne needed to hear more, she added, "I'm not ready to think of someone else yet either."

Anne took special note of that. So that was it! Pru was not going to be so easy to get. Helen had hurt her too much. She wasn't ready to love again.

"I hate Helen for hurting you," Anne said.

Johnson laughed. "She couldn't help herself. She was never really happy with me."

"I think being happy with you is probably the easiest thing in the world," Anne said.

Johnson smiled and tugged warmly at her hand. "Are you spending Sunday with Esther?"

"No," Anne said. "I may meet her briefly on Sunday morning, though. And I guess afterwards she'll run off to her piano again."

"That leaves us nearly the whole holiday weekend, doesn't it?" Johnson smiled. She sat up, more attentively. "Or do you plan to spend it at Paradise?"

"Does that mean you want me around all that time?" Anne asked, heartened.

It hadn't occurred to her that Pru had no family to visit over Easter. She felt overjoyed now, and almost wanted to cry. She hugged Johnson instead, pressed her head into her soft, womanly bosom. "Pru, you're family! That's what you are!"

Johnson laughed, hugging Anne fondly. "Nonsense. I'm just shrewd. I'm dying to find out what you're going to serve for Easter Dinner!"

Anne let herself be held, feeling wonderfully safe in Johnson's warm embrace. She didn't want to let go. But Pru began to unwind her gently, saying, "Come on, let's not burn the coffee pot again."

They walked, still tightly holding hands, into the kitchen and Anne shut the burner then turned, her face intimately close to Pru.

"I want us to make love tonight," Anne said, "I mean really make love tonight. I want to fully know you."

Pru instantly responded, brought her lips down in an oh, so gentle kiss. "I should have held you the minute you came in the door tonight," she whispered breathlessly. "Why the hell did I wait so long!"

"Why the hell did you!" Anne echoed.

They clung to each other, trembling, each possessed with a need to grip and hug the other, their lips barely touching.

"I love you," now Anne blurted spontaneously, crying and trembling. "I know it's too soon for me to say that, but I can't help it! I need to say it! I love you!"

"Say it, even if you don't mean it," Pru echoed, but with sad restraint. (Anne could sense Helen still there between them, and Pru fighting to break free.) "I want to say it too," Pru whispered. "I need to say it. I love you! At least I think I do! I'm almost sure I do!"

Anne pressed her face into Johnson's shoulder, crying unashamedly, feeling ever so safe in her arms.

"Steady," Pru smiled, wiping Anne's cheek.

Now it was Anne who pressed her own lips to Pru in a passionate kiss and Pru's whole body responded, held Anne in a crushing embrace.

"Is it terrible of me to be moving so fast?" Anne gasped between kisses. "Can you forgive my being so easy?"

"Let's both take a shower," Pru said.

They broke away from each other reluctantly and walked back arm in arm to the living room, once there carefully removing each other's clothes -- Anne tracing her hands over Pru's body -- a perfect body, statuesque but well-proportioned, both firm and soft in all the right places.

"I don't think you should ever wear clothes!" Anne said.

Pru laughed. "Do you want to share me with the rest of the world?"

"No," Anne answered definitely, "I do not."

And now it was Pru who traced her hands over Anne, slowly, sensuously, awakening every part of her. "Let's take that shower," she confirmed.

Agonizingly, they separated and walked holding hands into the bathroom, then into the tub, and under the warm water streaming down on them, each soaping the other, washing every private nook and cranny, coming to know it as intimately as their own -- but in a chaste way, truly serious about the business of getting properly washed. Then they embraced each other strongly again, breast pressed against dripping breast, mouth upon mouth as the water rinsed them, removed the bitter soap from their lips, their face, and every part of them.

Finally Pru shut the water and they toweled each other dry.

Now Anne turned, drew Pru's face down for another long passionate kiss and Pru's lips responded, competed with hers. their arms also entwined, in a tender struggle for dominance.

"I feel different from last night," Anne whispered, resisting Pru, competing with Pru. "It's as if I want to give you something more than I can possibly give you."

"What is it you need from me, Anne," Pru responded, demanded. "Say it!"

"I'm afraid to say it," Anne said. "I'm afraid you'll be angry at me for saying it." She was thinking of Esther, of Esther's reaction to Anne's physical intrusion. "I'm afraid of doing the wrong thing, of offending you, of violating you."

"How? How could you possibly do that," Pru countered. "What is it you want, Anne? Tell me."

Anne put her lips to Pru's ear and whispered it. "I want to put myself entirely inside you!"

Her words conquered Pru, ended the competition between them. Johnson's body melted into pure femininity. "You magnificent creature, come into me," she breathed seductively into Anne's ear, "Enter me. I want you inside me!"

They found their way out of the shower, out of the bathroom, back onto the day couch that quickly uncovered into a bed and Pru lay down invitingly, ever so womanly.

Anne wasted no time falling into her arms again, this time on top of her, letting herself go as she had with Beth, with Esther, but this time feeling herself received in an entirely new way, welcomed, made one with the woman beneath her, joined to her in a myriad of twisted shapes, clinging, throbbing in space, joined as one to the woman containing her, until she heard Pru's joy cry out her name from a distance so great and so near --

10.

Anne yawned and stretched, looking much like Portia, warm on the bed and comfortable, so comfortable. What a bright day outside! She knew she had forgotten something for a moment and then remembered. It too was an office day, but so what? Nothing could spoil her afterglow! In the middle of the night Pru had turned her over, had mysteriously filled her in a way that was not the same as the way Esther had filled her but more so -- filled her not as Esther but as distinctly Prudence -- protean, inventive, passionate, tender --

had filled her with a part of Pru that wasn't exactly a part of her -- that couldn't possibly have been a part of her -- nevertheless with something that felt exactly like Mark inside her -- still -- not like Mark inside her but welcomed, most welcomed as all of Prudence filling her, as all of Prudence ever so intimately, so knowingly, so tirelessly conjoining with her, leaving Anne exquisitely, ecstatically satisfied and complete! What had she used? It didn't matter! It was all of Prudence, a woman filling her -- a gentle, mysterious man-woman filling her, teaching her how to feel her own womanhood!

What an incredible feeling to finally come to know her own womanhood in the embrace of a man-woman filling her! Anne no longer felt tired or pressured this morning as she had always felt when Mark took her; here, now, Anne felt rested, so marvelously rested! She reached out for Pru but found she had already gotten up and gone somewhere. The smell of coffee -- wonderful, fresh-brewed victorious coffee! -- filled the room and Anne saw a place had already been made for her at the breakfast table. She got up and filled a cup and began to get dressed. She had overslept. She would have to call her office again and give some excuse for coming in late.

"Sleep well?" Pru now came up the stairs, a morning smile on her face. But it really was Johnson smiling -- Johnson still remembering Anne's joy.

"Where have you been?" Anne said.

"Changing the sign," Johnson said. "Closed for the Holiday." Again she smiled.

"I'm late for work," Anne said, hurrying to the bathroom to brush her teeth and hair.

"The hell with work," Johnson said. "You're spending the day with me."

"But yesterday -- " Anne said, starting to remind her of the efficient way in which she had been hurried off to the office yesterday.

"Yesterday was yesterday," Pru said, now becoming soft and womanly again. She stood, watching Anne now both as Johnson and as Pru.

She's right, Anne thought, *Yesterday was different. Yesterday we weren't in love.*

"What are we going to do today?" Anne asked her.

"How about picnicking in the park or riding the Staten Island Ferry," Johnson suggested.

"But your store -- " Anne said, trying to be practical and responsible. She might lose her job if she stayed out today, and Pru would certainly miss out on holiday business. It wouldn't do for both of them to stop earning money.

"It'll be all right," both Pru and Johnson smiled. "After all, aren't we entitled to a honeymoon?"

Anne laughed, pleasantly surprised. *What a lovely thought. How right it feels!* "I'll call my office," she agreed. She went toward the telephone.

"But don't tell them you're sick." Johnson called after her. "Tell them you're eloping, and you'll be back next week to give notice."

"But -- " Anne said.

"Or do you really want that dead-end job?"

"No, I don't want it," Anne said. "But I need it."

"If it's just a job you want, there are plenty of Help Wanted signs right outside. But," Pru added, "weren't you also thinking about going back to school?"   "Or painting, or modeling, or acting, or whatever," Anne said.

"Why not all those things, why not decide to be all that you can be," Johnson smiled. "Stay with me, Anne. We can make it together."

Anne laughed again, stupefied. "Isn't this all too soon?"

"Is it?" Pru met her eyes quietly, yet Anne felt the ecstasy they had shared before.

No, it was not too soon. It was long delayed. She did want a life with Pru. She could think of nothing better than a life with Pru.

Anne turned toward the telephone and dialed.

She heard Juliette's strained voice on the other end. "Anne, are you sick again?"

"No," Anne laughed. "I'm eloping. I'm sorry it's so sudden."

"Eloping! Why, my goodness -- with that nice young man?"

"No," Anne laughed again. It amused her to think that it was not with Mark. "It's no one you know," she said. "I'll be back Monday to give two weeks' notice."

"But wait -- " Juliette sputtered.

"I've waited too long," Anne said. "See you Monday."

She hung up and felt wonderfully free.

Now Pru brought her toast and more coffee.

"I've made sandwiches for us to take along," she said. "It'll probably be too brisk out, but we'll try anyway."

Anne gulped her coffee down and bit hurriedly into her toast, eager to rush out into the sunshine.

Pru brought their jackets. "Better also take a scarf and gloves," she said.

Anne dug into her pockets for her gloves. She felt an envelope there and suddenly remembered. It was Beth's letter.

A look of concern crossed her face.

"What's the matter," Pru asked.

"Nothing." Anne said. "Just a letter. From Beth."

Pru waited silently for her to open it.

Anne was afraid. She tore at the envelope slowly, and they sat on the bed to read it together.

It was a hurried note, perhaps written before their chance meeting at Cora's. It spoke about a man she had met. *Rick Hastings -- you know, the producer. I'm going to marry him, Anne.*

Anne stopped reading. Beth's escort at Cora's was called Rick. She shivered slightly at the memory. *I'm going to star in his show,* the letter continued. *It's hitting Broadway in November.*

So Beth had made good. Anne was happy about that.

But we can still see each other, Anne. The tone of the last paragraph was urgent, the handwriting, nervous. Anne wanted to put it down. She didn't want to read anymore. She crumbled the letter in her hands and bent over Pru. But she could not force tears.

"Poor Beth," she said. "Poor poor poor Beth!"

Johnson held her, their bulky jackets coming a little between them. "Let's go on that picnic," she said.

Anne smiled again, taking the letter up and folding it carefully. "I think I'm over Beth," she said.

"I'm going to hold you to that," Pru said.

They took the paper bags with their picnic lunches, and walked downstairs into the day. For early April, it was warm after all and they rejoiced. They walked in the sun to the corner then headed toward Sixth Avenue.

"I'm glad I'm not working today," Anne said, "even though I think you're being unrealistic about my quitting so soon."

"Terribly unrealistic," Pru replied, "but I've been terribly frugal. Time to splurge."

Anne laughed. "Johnson, don't tell me you're independently wealthy."

"Hell no, but given a little time and luck, who knows?" Pru laughed with her. "Mind just eating hamburgers five times a week?"

"How about meatloaf," Anne said.

"I love meatloaf," Johnson said.

Now they skipped hand in hand like two young girls in a happy step, breathing the crisp air, and caught the bus to South Ferry.

She's beautiful this morning, Anne thought as they huddled together in the near-empty bus. She wondered what she could call her hair - dark blonde? Wheat, perhaps? Like part of a Fall meadow. And the rest of her like a statue, but warm.

"Where are we heading?" Anne asked, watching the city blocks go quickly by.

"There's a beach in Staten Island I like to go to," Johnson said.

"A beach!" Anne laughed. "That's funny. Yesterday I wanted so much to go to a beach."

"I guess we think alike," Johnson said. "I didn't think anyone else would be crazy enough to go to the beach off season."

"I see nothing crazy about it," Anne answered. Then she grew serious and looked at Pru, who seemed to be shaking with nervous merriment.

She's very sensitive, Anne thought, *She can hardly believe she's happy. I can hardly believe I'm happy too!*

"I want to know all about you," Anne said to her.

"It won't be easy to get me to talk," Pru said.

"You'll talk," Anne said. She dug her fingers in Pru's jacket pocket and took hold of her hand there. Pru blushed and took Anne's hand out of her pocket and held it still until the bus made a stop.

"When did you get the shop?" Anne asked.

"Just after Korea," Pru answered. "Helen and I pooled our savings and bought the house. She still owns the main house, but I kept the boutique as my half."

"Then you still see her," Anne said.

"Not really. Not often. And not in the same way." A serious look formed on Pru's face now and she lapsed into a silent mood.

Helen has tortured her all year, Anne thought. *I think I hate her.* "I'm going to take you away from Helen," she said.

276

"I think you already have," Pru said quietly. She held Anne's hand tightly now in the empty bus and her eyes were happier again.

"Last stop," the driver called out to them and Pru rose, pulled Anne up and out the door with her. It was cold and windy by the docks.

"Let's run," Pru said.

They ran, holding hands, from the bus stop to the Ferry terminal and then up the steps to the turnstiles. Pru had nickels ready, dropped them in the slot and pushed Anne through first.

It was cold in the waiting hall. Johnson put her arm over Anne's shoulders, and took her to a corner.

"I didn't know it could be so cold," Anne laughed.

"Want to turn back?" Pru asked.

Anne shook her head.

They stayed in the corner waiting for the ferry to dock.

"I love you," Anne whispered loudly.

Again Pru blushed. "I'm glad I took you home with me the other night," she said.

Anne smiled. "Are you going to keep me or take me back to the store?"

"Keep you," Pru said. She was very close to Anne now. "Is that what you want?"

"Yes, I want," Anne said.

Pru's lips were very close to hers. Anne wanted to kiss them. She fixed her eyes on Pru. Pru stopped smiling and bit her lips. *She wants to kiss me too,* Anne thought.

They turned away from each other now, forcing themselves to concentrate on the docking ferry. The doors to the gangplank were opening and people were crowding to them.

"Let's go," Johnson said, taking Anne's hand again.

They followed the others through the entrance, up the gangplank, and found a place on deck, deciding to brave the cold wind for a while, and smell the salt air.

They watched the ferry shove off from the dock.

It was warmer in the rear than it would have been up front, facing the headwind, so they stood where they were, sheltered by the cabin behind them, watched the seagulls follow them from the shore, watched Manhattan get smaller until the end of the island seemed only a block of jagged rocks with gleaming windows reflecting the sun.

"They're quartz, not skyscrapers now," Anne said. She had never ridden the Staten Island Ferry before. What a ride for a nickel!

Everyone else had gone inside and they were the only ones left on deck. They could speak loudly to each other without being listened to. It was wonderful to be able to speak freely in the open air. It filled them with warmth and made the cold air unimportant.

"I'm so happy I'm afraid of it," Anne said.

"I am too," Pru said. "Are you really happy?"

"I think so," Anne said. "Only some things still bother me. I worry about your wanting me to quit my job, for instance. I don't want to be kept. What shall I do?"

Pru laughed. "I'll teach you to do paste-ups and mechanicals so you can earn your keep."

"I'm serious," Anne said. She took Pru's hand and looked at her. "I don't want a man-woman relationship. I'm afraid you think I do."

"No I do not," Pru said emphatically. "That's what I had with Helen. That's what broke us up. I turned her Straight. Then she no longer wanted me."

The revelation puzzled Anne. She didn't know such a thing could happen, but after last night -- could it also happen to Anne? Pru had taken her more completely than Mark ever could have! But had Pru merely awakened the real woman in her? Was this lesbian moment only a phase she would eventually grow out of? And what would happen to Pru if that was so? Impulsively Anne grasped at Pru's collar: "Could that really happen, even with me?"

"Perhaps, and perhaps not," Pru smiled distantly, resigned, then lifted her mood. "Now what else is troubling you? Esther?"

Anne nodded, now disturbed. "Yesterday both of you seemed to have an equal claim on me. But after last night, I feel differently. Last night -- was complete!" She looked at Pru urgently wanting to know. "What is it about you? What did you do to me?"

"We both made love," Pru answered. "The difference is that both of us *really* made love."

"But no, it was more than that," Anne persisted. "It was something I've only dared dream of -- something that I would also want to do to you!"

Anne's words hit their mark. Pru forgot where they were standing for a moment, held her, met Anne's eyes squarely in an ever-so womanly stare. "Yes. When you're ready -- I will also want that from you."

"I'm ready now," Anne insisted.

Now the wind was getting stronger, pressing them against each other for warmth, for shelter.

"We'd better go inside," Pru said.

Anne reluctantly agreed.

They huddled together toward the door to the cabin then entered against the wind and found a lonely bench on the side, far from the rest of the passengers. It was warm inside. It cleared their minds and took some of Anne's confusion away. They huddled close, close enough to talk in a whisper, but still it was not close enough. They sat silently, aching to continue their intimate conversation, sat silently until the ferry landed and they followed the crowd to shore where they caught another bus to South Beach.

There were too many passengers on the bus to talk freely. Both of them began to regret having gone out at all -- why hadn't they just stayed home and made love again -- and again -- and again! Anne felt so filled with Pru, and also with the need to fill Pru, to hear her joy again, to fill her fully and be smothered in her strong embrace. It boiled her blood to remember their joy. She looked at Pru. Her face was flushed with the same wanting. Again Anne gripped Pru's hand deep inside her pocket and this time Pru did not pull away.

The bus was going down a street with squat houses seemingly made of tinder wood. The smell of salt water and cold wind blew in whenever the bus doors opened.

"Are we almost there?" Anne asked.

"Two more stops," Johnson said.

"You must come here often," Anne said.

"A few Sundays last Fall," Pru said. "I come alone, or -- Not to swim -- just to sit."

"So, Johnson," Anne teased, "others have also come this way with you."

"A few," Pru smiled distantly. "But none like you."

They kept holding hands, staring at each other, heads both tucked deep inside their jacket collars, until the bus reached its last stop again and they got off.

A chill breeze hit their faces, but the sun was strong. There was still brown snow mixed with sand and seaweed here and the shore was barren except for the makeshift summer cabins and canvassed amusement rides. Everything was boarded up, every window and door -- everything except a dingy deli-grocery-pizzeria that seemed determined to stay open all year. And behind it, attached to it, also a tiny liquor store.

"We need to stop there," Pru said. "But not for pizza," she added.

They skipped toward it and entered. It was a filthy place, tables dirty and floor unswept and saturated with a smell of greasy sauce. The owner, a very fat man with hairy arms, hailed them from the counter. "Hey there, nice to see you back. What'll you have?" It was clear that their presence was making his day.

"Just charcoal and lighter fluid," Johnson said.

"No clams?" he offered.

"Local?"

"Yeah," he nodded.

"No thanks," she said.

"We'll just build a bonfire and sit on the beach," she explained to Anne.

The fat man, panting, limped to the rear and returned with a bag of charcoal and a small can of starter and put them on the counter.

"That'll be a dollar," he said, looking at both of them, letting his lurid imagination run wild.

"And a bottle of Chianti, a pound of chestnuts, and two paper cups," she added.

"Another two-fifty," he said, turning to fill the order.

Pru paid him and they turned to leave.

"Going to have another picnic, I see," he called after them. Pru ignored him and Anne decided she had best get used to such stares.

"Wrap up tight this time," Pru said to Anne.

Anne pulled the hood up on her jacket and steeled herself against the wind. Walking out together in their hooded jackets they seemed just like any Straight couple on the beach.

It was not as cold as they had supposed. The sun was higher now and the April breeze had turned milder. They trudged through damp sand toward a row of boarded cabins that would shield them from the eyes of strangers, Anne all the while gathering up dried wood washed on shore, until they found a relatively dry spot with a large chunk of driftwood to sit on. She dumped all the flotsam in a pile and Pru poured starter over the bag of charcoal and lit it then threw a few of the dry boards over it.

The bonfire flared quickly and stayed hot and they sat on the log looking out to the Bay and set just far enough away to let the sea breeze safely fan the warmth from the fire their way.

Now they could finally talk and not be overheard. But first, Johnson threw a few chestnuts into the fire and the aroma spread quickly in every direction. Then she took out her Swiss Army knife and uncorked the Chianti, filling both paper cups, and began to unpack what she had brought for their lunch: two overstuffed deli heros, one with mustard, the other with mayo, and offered Anne her pick.

"Mustard," Anne said.

"Figures," Pru smiled. "Only Californians take mayo."

Anne held her overstuffed sandwich in helpless indecision. It was too thick to bite into gracefully.

"It's best if you break it with your hands first," Pru said, showing her, then taking up her papercup to click a toast. "Here's to our honeymoon," she said.

Suddenly, those were the wrong words.

Anne hesitated. Was it too soon for that kind of toast? Were both of them moving much too quickly? Was the spell of the night before suddenly lifting? What if Anne was not really a lesbian? Anne did not want to hurt Pru. She took up her papercup and clicked. "Here's to a great weekend," she corrected.

Pru took the cue and nodded. They both toasted, then looked at each other, Pru's eyes quiet yet intense. "Anne, are you still in love with Beth?"

"I can't be certain of anything right now," Anne admitted. "What I do know now is that Beth and I never made love the way you and I made love last night. Not yet, at least. I do know that with Beth I was too paralyzed with happiness to realize I was only being caressed, that something more was expected of me. And I also don't know about my own self -- who I am, where I am going. What I do know is that I could never hurt Beth the way I'm afraid I might possibly hurt you."

"You could have Beth back now," Pru said. "You could go to her, take her back, and she'd stay with you -- just as Helen stayed with me. But is that really what you want? Forget about hurting me, Anne. Is that really what you wan't?"

"I don't now," Anne said. It was all very confusing -- she could have Beth now, but did Anne really want her?

"Anne -- Helen never made love to me the way you did last night," Pru said. "For nearly eight years, I was nothing more than a male substitute. When she turned me over, it wasn't with passion. She was faking it. I could always sense she was faking it. Is that the kind of relationship you want, with Beth?"

"I don't know," Anne said again. All this was much too new for her. If only there were a handbook she could consult that would explain all her conflicting feelings. But there was none, and now she was beginning to realize how myriad love relationships in both Gay and Straight worlds were -- not black and white, but many shades of gray.

"I need time to think, to resolve things with Beth," she finally told Pru. "I can't commit to anyone else until I do that."

"Understood," now Johnson said stoically. (It was Johnson now, not Pru talking; Johnson almost like Mark talking.) "I'm willing to wait," Johnson said. "But now about Esther. How do you feel about her?"

"That's a lot easier to decide," Anne said. "Between you and Esther there's no comparison. I'm not inclincd to be anyone's backstage wife, and I definitely do not want a male substitute!"

"Then at least I'm Number Two," Johnson said, smiling sadly, then clicked papercups again. "Well, now let's eat, drink and celebrate the moment!"

Anne nodded, taking another sip of Chianti.

What a beautiful person she truly is, now Anne thought, admiring Pru's openness, her quiet presence. There was something truly angelic about her -- neither male nor female but simply radiant, full of grace.

Now Anne remembered one more time what it felt like to be in her arms, to have filled her and then to have been filled by her -- like two women being both women together, and yet not exactly women but persons, persons neither male nor female touching each other as persons, caressing, reacting, embracing . . .

Johnson read the thoughts crossing Anne's face. "That's not sunburn on your cheeks, is it?"

"No," Anne answered, returning her intense stare.

"There's a safe hotel in Tottenville," Johnson suggested. "Let's pack up our lunch and finish it there."

They left the bonfire to burn itself out, throwing wet seaweed on it to soften the flames and prevent sparks from flying. They carefully fenced it off with a circle of driftwood to keep passersby from stepping on the coals then they walked hand in hand through the damp sand back to the bus stop and got on the waiting bus that would pass Tottenville on its way back to the 'Ferry.

They sat in quiet anticipation, waiting for the driver to return from his break -- for an endless moment, it seemed -- then he came back and got behind the wheel.

"It's only a short distance," Johnson said.

"You've been there with others before," Anne said, now hesitant. She was very aware now of Johnson's masculinity and it frightened her to find herself rendered so responsive. Mark could never have evoked such a strong feminine response from her! Feeling Johnson inside her was so much more complete, agonizingly pleasurable, completely satisfying as it should have felt with Mark but had never been achieved with Mark. Had Mark been the problem? Would a different kind of man -- someone more gentle, more sensitive -- someone more like Prudence leave Anne feeling as womanly, as complete?

The thought frightened her. Her own intense womanly response frightened her. Was Prudence turning her Straight? Would Anne eventually hurt Pru the way Helen had? Anne didn't want that! Panic took hold of her. Yes, it was too soon for both of them. They were definitely moving too fast.

"I'd rather we skip the hotel," Anne said. "Let's just eat on the ferry and go home."

Now she snuggled tightly against Pru, wanting her to know this wasn't a rejection. It was simply too soon!

Pru understood and let Anne take the lead in dictating the mood of the moment, becoming less assertive, more feminine. "I have to stop making you into Helen," she said. "It's not what I want!"

"Habits are hard to break," Anne agreed.

I really need to stop making her into Mark, she reminded herself. *It's only her height and her clothes that make her look masculine.*

"Call me Butch," she said spontaneously. "Maybe that will help."

Pru laughed. "No, that's too crass. How about Slugger? I like Slugger - it suits you."

11.

THEY walked from the bus back to Pru's house still holding hands in what was now a warm spring afternoon, far from the sea blast on the ferry. Their faces were flushed and windblown and their jackets too warm now and hanging off their shoulders, zipped open.

"I wonder what people think when we walk down the street holding hands," Anne said. She really no longer cared. She looked up at Pru's face and felt happy, clean and alive.

"Most don't notice," Pru smiled, "like we don't notice them." Her face was both very red and splotched with freckles now, and her hair was bleached by the sun and salt air.

Anne wanted to kiss her. "You really have a sunburn," she said instead.

"So do you," Pru laughed. It was summer for a moment and they were coming home from the beach. "We'll go home and wash up and then go out again," she said, "maybe to dinner."

"No," Anne contradicted seductively. "Let's shop, and eat in."

They stopped at the A&P then walked more quickly, skipping happily down the narrow half-block to Pru's. All the shops were open now and the street was crowded with tourists. Only Pru's store was closed -- a young couple trying the door. "We're closed today," Pru called, waving to them.

"But we came all the way from Brooklyn," the young woman pleaded, pointing to something in the window and turning on her feminine charm. The rather innocuous looking man with her seemed to be her husband.

Pru blushed and smiled and looked at Anne.

Anne winked a yes. Neither of them wanted to turn down a lady.

"All right, then," Pru said, unlocking the door. She let the couple in first then Anne came past her, taking both their jackets and hanging them in the back. She was glad Pru had opened the store. It brought the day back to normal as life with Pru should be from now on, if --

Pru had already made the sale and the man was writing out a check. But the couple wasn't finished. They wanted to chat.

"How about a cup of coffee," Anne offered, joining Pru.

"Fine," the man said, looking first at his watch and then at his wife for approval.

"There's a hot plate in back," Pru said to Anne. She seemed relieved by Anne's interruption, as if she felt uncomfortable just chatting.

Anne patted her shoulder reassuringly and went to the back.

The workshop was surprisingly tidy. There were tables and machinery, and cans with solvents, paint, etc., but the room was large and everything had a place. The far corner had a makeshift cooking area. A window with happy orange curtains showed Pru's narrow strip of garden still brown from winter except for climbing ivy on the walls. *I love it here,* Anne thought. She rolled up her sleeves and hastily started making coffee, putting water to boil and filling a filter for the drip cone. Pru must have been in the habit of serving refreshments -- everything was there, even cookies.

Anne put some on a dish and carried it out first.

The couple had been joined by two more, seated in canvas chairs, looking at lithos Pru was taking from a rack and setting on the floor for them to see -- her own work. They were collectors.

Anne put the cookie dish on a small table near another woman whose platinum hair reminded her of Beth. "Are you working here too?" she asked Anne, turning from the conversation.

Anne nodded, looking at Pru. "I was hired this morning."

"Oh?" the woman seemed pleasantly interested.

She's very nice, Anne thought, *not at all concerned about whether we're Gay.* She looked at the man with her and thought them well matched. They seemed happy. Anne wanted to be happy with Pru in the same way. Looking at Pru now, she knew it was possible.

Anne started back for the coffee and heard the hanging bells tinkle again and knew someone else had come in. *It's a good thing Pru opened up,* she thought. *It would have been a shame to lose so much business.* She hurried to the back to bring out the coffee and then returned and saw Jacques.

"Hi," he said. "I just came by to deliver your mail."

"Hi," Anne smiled uneasily. She put the coffee tray down on a table and grabbed her jacket from the hook, anxious to head him off before he started calling her Alice.

"I forgot to get something at the A&P," she said, grabbing his arm. "Walk me there."

"Sure," he said, opening the door again.

Anne called out to Pru. "We're going to the store."

Pru smiled knowingly. "Right. See you later."

"Bye, now," Anne smiled at the two couples and they nodded back.

She went outside with Jacques and walked to where they could talk freely.

"I tried to phone you at work," he said. "They said you were getting married. Alice, what a camp!" he laughed loudly and then stopped. "Esther's flipping out. She called me three times today. She wants you to call her."

Anne darkened. The thought of Esther had bothered her since this morning. She would have to speak to her about Sunday. She hated the thought of having to go back on her word about Sunday, hated the thought of having to hurt her.

"Shall I tell her where you are?" Jacques asked and waited.

Anne thought for a moment.

"Yes," she said finally, "I guess that would be a good idea. Tell her I can't make it on Sunday. And tell her to come by the shop, whenever. Tell her Johnson and I are a pair."

"Got it," he winked.

He's more composed today, Anne thought. "Are you happy with the apartment?"

He nodded brightly. "What a relief to get a place of my own! I called my Mom and Dad, not a whisper of resistance."

"I'm glad," Anne said. She remembered how Orthodox his parents were and how tense things were at home --practically every conversation ending with a lecture on fire and brimstone. She thought of her own family. Luckily they weren't religious but still it was hard on them.

"Has my Dad shown up?" she asked.

"Ouch, Alice, I almost forgot!" Jacques thumped his head. "He called last night and I spent an hour on the telephone with him. He's very upset."

"What did you tell him?"

(Anne was no longer afraid of her father, only concerned that her family was being made to suffer this way. She didn't want to hurt them.)

"I told him you were all right," Jacques said. "I spent an hour trying to convince him. He's been to the police trying to find you, but they laughed and said it was now a civil matter and to talk to your lawyer. He's licked, I think, Alice," he said.

"I'm sorry," Anne said.

She resolved to see them sometime during Christmas if by then they had calmed down. Perhaps then, or someday, they would learn to accept her.

Christmas! That was far enough away. She wondered if she would still be with Johnson by Christmas. Or would she be with Beth?

Now she walked quietly beside Jacques and opened her mail. Just more ads. No more letters from Beth.

Beth! Anne could not help thinking of what Pru had said: *"You could have Beth back now. You could take her back and she'd stay with you, as Helen stayed with me."*

That seemed unbelievable, and yet now Anne believed it was possible. It made her afraid. It left things unfinished in her mind. It left her feelings about Beth up in the air. She had given Beth up because there had seemed to be no hope of winning her, and she was afraid because Beth's last letter seemed to imply that there was. And this made her afraid. She could not ignore Beth's letter. She would have to face her again. Before she could feel free to let herself fall in love with Pru she would have to resolve things with Beth.

They entered the supermarket and Anne took a cart and pushed it to the meat department. She would buy a ham for Easter Sunday and learn to cook it herself.

"You're so quiet, Alice," Jacques said. "Is anything wrong?"

"No," Anne smiled uneasily. She was letting her thoughts show.

She picked a large smoked ham and put it in the cart then turned to get cans of pineapple and fresh yams and asparagus.

Jacques followed silently, perhaps hoping he might be asked to Sunday's feast.

"Can you cook?" she asked him.

"Can I cook?" he echoed. "Yes, Alice, I can cook!"

"Then you're invited," she said.

The store was crowded with people returning from work. They got at the end of a very long line for the cash register, Anne now fighting impatience to get back to Pru's. But an even stronger impulse was growing in her. She also needed to see Beth. Tonight!

Too much had happened too soon. Anne needed to talk about it with the only person Anne could really confide in completely. Anne needed to see Beth!

She looked at Jacques. He was thinking of something else, perhaps the apartment.

All at once Anne could not bear waiting on line. She wanted to run away, to run back to Pru, and also to Beth. She was split in two over Pru and Beth -- or was it Johnson and Beth? She didn't know what or which she wanted. All the categories were changing, melting into one, but which one? Who or what was Anne?

Impatiently she took out her wallet and put ten dollars in Jacques's hand. "Will you pay for these and take them back to the store?" she asked.

"Huh?" Jacques snapped back to the present and looked at her.

"Would you?" Anne asked again.

"Sure," he said, a little puzzled.

Now she borrowed a pen from him and started to write a note to Pru. But what could she say to her? That she was running away from her to see Beth? As she had run away from Esther, and from Mark, and her father? Would Pru ever forgive her for not telling her in person? She crumpled the paper.

"Never mind." She returned Jacques' pen. "I'll tell her myself."

"Alice, you're cracking up!" He shrugged in exasperation and gave back her ten dollars.

"I'm sorry," Anne said.

She felt embarrassed. Jacques was looking at her, wondering what was wrong. She forced herself to wait patiently for her turn on line.

They walked back, carrying all the groceries.

It had become dark and the lights of the shops guided them back to Pru's street. Johnson had closed the store and Anne saw a light on in the upstairs apartment. She rang the doorbell and waited, letting the fresh air and the quiet of the street soothe the impatience she had felt since the supermarket.

Pru ran downstairs and opened the door for them then took Anne's packages. Her sleeves were rolled up and her hands were full of soap. "Goodness," she said, "did you shop for the month?" She ran up the stairs with the packages and Anne and Jacques followed.

Anne was quiet. She could barely face Pru -- she was ashamed of what she had intended to do before.

Pru brought the bags into the kitchen and then took Jacques' bags and also brought them into the kitchen. "Sit down. I'll be through in a minute," she called to them, back to washing dishes.

It was warm and cozy upstairs. Anne took off her jacket and helped Jacques with his and then went to the closet. Portia, recognizing Jacques, drew him seductively to the sofa, rolling on her back and boxing with him.

"That was a fifty-dollar sale," Pru said, tinkling the silverware. "Are you a rabbit's foot, Anne?"

I love her, Anne thought, and felt worse.

"Jacques is staying for supper, right?" Pru said.

"Yes, Jacques, please stay," Anne turned to him. But she hoped he would say no. She wanted to be alone with Pru now. She wanted to tell Pru what she had intended to do. The compulsion to run to Beth had abated, but she did want to tell Pru about it.

"I'd love to," Jacques said happily. It was as if he wanted them as family.

Anne groaned silently and resolved to make the best of the evening. She was determined to be hospitable. She had no right to burden either of them with her inner conflict. "Get out of the kitchen, woman," she called to Pru. "I'm the cook around here."

Pru laughed, dried her hands and came back to the living room. "All yours." She went to the card table and put it up. "Pick out an album, Jacques," she said, "I'll be right over." Then Pru stood and caught Anne as she went toward the kitchen. "What's for dinner?"

"Hamburgers," Anne said, not looking at her. She tried to break away but Johnson's strong arms gently held her.

"What's wrong, Anne?" she asked in a voice too soft to catch Jacques' attention.

Anne forced herself to look at Pru. "I almost didn't come back here. I had an irresistible urge -- to see Beth," she said, and waited.

Pru smiled and fondly rubbed Anne's chin. "It couldn't have been so irresistible, since you're here." She kissed Anne's lips lightly. "Don't worry about it. We can talk later."

Pru's eyes were kind and a relief. Anne pressed her head on Pru's breast for a moment and enjoyed the warm protective feeling of Johnson's whole body against hers, then broke away and went to the kitchen.

She began emptying the grocery bags on the kitchen counter, putting everything in the refrigerator. She was fighting a headache. She felt utterly divided. She hated the thought of cooking for Jacques and Johnson but at the same time wanted to cook for Pru. She lit the broiler impatiently and decided to make meatloaf since Jacques was staying. It would be simple to prepare and then she could join them in the living room while it baked. But her head still throbbed. She opened the window and let the fresh air soothe her. Anne wished she could take a long walk around the block.

"Need any help?" Johnson called to her from the living room. She was sitting with Jacques on the sofa, appraising Jacques' choice for the phonograph.

"No thanks," Anne said. She took out an onion and started to chop it. She looked for parsley on the spice shelf. Pru apparently had little interest in condiments. She cursed herself for not having thought to buy it. But chopping up a carrot for a meatloaf filler might do instead. *I was thinking of Beth rather than concentrating on shopping,* she scolded herself. But scolding did not make her thoughts behave. She was upset. She did not want to cook. She wanted to go out. Yes, the urge was still there. She needed to flee this overly-domestic scene. Needed to find out who she really was. She wanted, needed to find Beth.

Now Johnson came into the kitchen to sniff in all the pots. "Smells wonderful," she said, looking much like a young man hungry for supper.

"It's miserable," Anne countered in a small moan.

Johnson laughed and came to pat her cheek. "No it's not. I'm sure it's not."

"Don't be so damn sure!" Anne snapped, turning her face away. She immediately regretted her outburst and mentally blamed it on the headache.

Prudence put the pot cover down and took hold of Anne's hands, pulled her close. "Is it your period?" she asked, concerned.

Anne hugged her tightly. "No, it's not that. I'm just in a mean mood, that's all."

Pru held her tightly in return and stroked her hair. "Let's just get through dinner, then we'll talk," she said.

Anne nodded and turned to put the meatloaf in the oven then took Pru's hand, that familiar hand which fit so well around her own, and they walked hand in hand out of the kitchen.

Jacques had kicked off his shoes and was sitting on the day couch with Portia on his lap, browsing books from Pru's collection. He seemed so very small and young on the sofa.

Johnson sat on the floor and Anne sat in front of her, using Pru's body as a backrest.

"So, Jacques," Pru said, "are you also in the arts?"

"I'm studying ballet," he said. "Alice and I went to the same dance class."

"That's how we met," Anne explained.

"Why do you call her Alice?" Pru asked, amused at his mannerisms.

"It's some sort of Gay expression," Anne answered for him, feeling she had to defend him a little.

"It's because she's in wonderland," Jacques said. "You know, meeting queens."

It made them both laugh.

"I never realized that was why you called me that," Anne said. "I don't mind the name so much now."

"Is his name really Jacques," Pru now nudged Anne, "or is that only his stage name?"

"It's Jacob," Jacques confessed, a bit ashamed. "My father's a Rabbi."

They were about to comment when the telephone rang. Jacques was nearest to it and impulsively reached for it. "Johnson residence," he said, then exclaimed, "Esther! How did you know I'd be here!" he was puzzled. "Who am I? Jacques, of course, who else? No, you didn't dial a wrong number."

"Oh, oh," Pru scratched her head, a bit red in her face. "I guess I'm being found out." She got up and went to the telephone. "I think it's for me, Jacques."

Anne watched her, amused and a bit nervous. Esther was calling Prudence and now she would know about Anne.

"Hello, Es," Pru said. "I'm here with Jacques and Anne. Yes -- Anne. She's staying with me."

Anne listened intently, trying to imagine how Esther was taking it on the other end.

"Alice, what a triangle!" Jacques said, guessing the situation.

"Hush," Anne said, trying to listen to the conversation.

"Wait a minute," Pru said. "I'll put her on."

She held out the receiver. Anne got up nervously and took the telephone. "Hello," she said sheepishly.

"Anne, why the hell didn't you say it was Prudence?" Esther exclaimed, her tone highly flustered.

"I'm sorry," Anne said. "I didn't know whether Pru wanted me to tell you."

"*Merdre!*" Esther said, exasperated. "Are we seeing each other Sunday?"

"I don't know," Anne said. Then she looked at Pru quietly waiting and grew more determined. "I don't think so, Esther. I'm sorry."

"*Eh Bien,*" Esther said. Her voice was hard now, stony. "Well, I guess I can't blame you. Prudence is a good catch -- I've been trying myself all this time." She paused for a moment, then said coldly, "Goodbye, Anne."

Anne heard her hang up. Her face began to flush and she felt bad. She had deeply embarrassed Esther. She hadn't meant to. She put the telephone down slowly and sat on the bed. Pru meanwhile was silently laughing. She came over and rubbed Anne's neck. "Don't worry," she reassured her, "by next week she'll have forgiven and forgotten both of us."

"How can you be so sure!" Anne snapped, now angry and upset.

"She's right, Alice," Jacques said. "I know Esther. Nothing really sticks to her."

Pru ignored him and looked directly at Anne. "I'm afraid I've been holding back some information," she said. "You see, that Sunday morning date she was breaking was with me," she confessed, still a little amused and embarrassed.

"Then she was calling you to call it off," Anne said.

"No, she did that yesterday afternoon," Pru countered. "She asked me to postpone it until Sunday night. I asked her to call me back to confirm it. That's why she was calling now. I didn't expect Jacques to answer the phone. I would simply have put her off again, waiting on you."

Pru hesitated again, awkwardly, because Jacques was also listening to all this.

Anne walked away from the telephone. If only she could believe Pru, but now she did not trust her. Now she suspected Pru of having set Esther up. And now the thought of Beth returned strongly and she wanted to leave. At least Beth had always been honest with her.

"I think the meatloaf is burning," Anne said coldly, and went into the kitchen.

She came back and served them silently at the table, making no excuse for the simplicity of the meal. A stony silence had fallen on all of them and Pru broke it only to comment meekly on Anne's good cooking.

She knows I'm angry at her, Anne thought, and decided to remain angry. It was convenient to remain angry at Pru. It gave Anne a good excuse to call Beth.

Anne looked at them while they ate. They both seemed like small children scolded before dinner. But Jacques was perhaps was the only one suffering. Anne's silence had made him insecure and he knew he was in the way. He was eating nervously, trying to hurry through the meal. Pru on the other hand was quiet, but eating with a wholesome appetite. When she had cleaned her plate and finished all the bread she looked up and stretched and said, "Shall I run out and get us ice cream?"

"I guess so," Anne shrugged, damning Pru's self-confidence.

But Jacques interrupted. "No thanks," he said. "I have to get back. I told Peter I'd be home." He shifted uneasily, obviously fabricating, but both of them were certain Jacques would probably actually find a Peter to take home with him that night.

"Do come over for Easter dinner, Jacques," Pru said cordially, extending her hand to him, "We, or I, would love to have you." She looked toward Anne significantly. "That is, if you're not dining at Beth's by then."

Anne whitened. How could Pru know! How could Pru have read her thoughts.

"Thanks," Jacques said tentatively, looking at one and then the other and then back again and shaking his head. "I'll get my coat," he said.

Pru went to help him at the closet. "Please do come again," she said warmly.

He nodded gratefully and then looked over at Anne. "Well, good night, Alice."

Pru walked him to the head of the stairs and watched him leave. "He's a good friend," she said when he had gone.

"He's a crazy mixed-up kid, just like me," Anne said dryly.

"I think he's probably jail-bait even for the likes of you, Slugger," Pru countered fondly.

"We all are at first, I suppose," Anne shifted uneasily, sitting on the bed. "How old were you?"

"I was sixteen and Helen was twenty," Pru answered. "That now makes me twenty-four, but I feel a lot older. How old is Beth?"

"I haven't the foggiest," Anne answered. "Nor do I care. Does it matter?"

Pru sat on the edge of the sofa now, reaching out to stroke Anne's hair. "Always the lure of the well-seasoned older woman. I know it well, Slugger. It held me captive too!"

Anne softened. "And do you regret it now?"

"No," Pru said in earnest. "I regret none of it. It was what I desperately needed at that time. But it's not what I need now. Now I need an equal, and you may indeed still be too young for me."

Pru's words now challenged Anne, revived her interest in the older woman who was sitting there so smugly, smiling and yet not smiling, wanting and yet not wanting to be close to her.

"How is it I can be too young for you, but not for Beth," Anne countered.

"Because Beth wants something entirely different from you, Butch," Pru fondly tapped her shoulder, "and if there's ever to be something between us, you really do need to have it out with her first."

Pru got up now and determinedly went to the telephone. "Here, Slugger," she held it out to Anne, "call her and get it over with. By tomorrow, I may not be in the same giving mood."

"And what about us?" Anne was panicked now, resisted taking the phone. The last thing she wanted was to lose Pru -- even if she wanted Beth, she also needed, wanted Pru.

Pru saw Anne's reaction and almost changed her mind, but then steeled herself for the inevitable. "There is no us -- " she blurted out stoically, "not until you've resolved this. Now call her!" Then she added more reassuringly, "If she tosses you out, I'll still be waiting. But not for long, mind you!"

Anne finally accepted the phone and dialed Beth's. She was probably not home yet, probably dining out with Rick and the gang. Probably all this was for nothing and Pru would change her mood and they would make up and give their relationship more of a chance. One more passionate night with Pru and who knows how Anne might feel by morning!

But Beth was still home and Anne heard her silken voice say hello, and

Anne, looking at Pru's stoic countenance, became now determined to follow through.

"Beth?" Anne said, a little hoarse, then cleared her throat. "Beth, I got your letter. I want to see you tonight. May I come over?"

She heard Beth's startled pause on the other end. "Yes. Yes, of course," she said. "Rick's here with me, but I'm sure he'll understand -- "

"I don't want to see Rick," Anne interrupted. The mere mention of Rick made her angry. "I mean I want to see you alone."

Beth paused again for a long moment and finally said, "All right. Just give me some time. Call me again in a half hour."

She hung up.

Anne put the phone down in a strange mood, both cold and feverish, torn, still torn in two directions. She still wanted a life with Pru -- a life that now seemed real, warm, positive -- everything she could ever have wanted. But Beth's lure was too enticing. She had a much longer history with Beth, and Beth was a real woman -- in every sense a real woman, more so than Pru, or --

But it was Johnson now who took Anne in her arms, folded her arms around Anne protectively -- Johnson's lips that found Anne's. It took away the Butch feeling, melted Anne into a woman.

"How is it possible for me to feel like two distinctly different persons inside me, one after the other," she asked Pru, still reeling, still clinging to Pru.

"Don't fight it, Slugger," Pru answered knowingly, "just sit back, and enjoy!"

"Tell me about you and Helen," she asked, now sitting, catching her breath. "How could she possibly have left you!"

"It's never the sex, kiddo, it's the company," Pru quipped. "The hen party eventually got stagnant, boring. For both of us. By the time we got back from Korea -- we were no longer a twosome. Helen brought Tony into the picture because she felt both of us needed a man. And she was right. We both needed that input, in more ways than one. And especially I needed to grow. My body was ready and I needed to find out exactly who and what I was -- "

"Were you in love with Tony?" Anne interrupted, startled by this revelation.

"Yes and no," Pru answered. "I loved them both; still do. But now we've all grown up, and grown apart."

"Then you're not really Gay," Anne concluded, now entirely turned around.

"I don't even know what that word means, do you?" Pru countered. "What I do know is that the way we made love last night was complete for me, " she said deeply in earnest, "as I hope it was and will be for you."

"Yes," Anne responded. "It was complete."

Again she felt the rush inside her. Now Pru was no longer Johnson in Anne's eyes. She too was a woman like Beth, and Anne was now feeling the kind of need Esther had described -- a passion to make Pru feel Anne in a way only a man could make her feel. Anne wanted to be a man-woman for Pru. But could she really do that? Could she really commit to something so complete as that? It was so much easier to think of what life would be like with Beth -- Beth, who would always have Rick to fall back on as part of the equation -- Beth, who was not a lesbian, who would never be hurt if Anne left her, if Anne outgrew her.

Again Anne reeled in utter confusion. Whatever the outcome, Beth was now waiting and she had to resolve all of it, had to see for herself how far she could go on her own, what kind of life she could choose.

Pru nodded, understanding. "It's Beth time, isn't it," she sighed. "Well then, what's keeping you?"

Anne still tarried. "You know I'm split right down the middle, and I need to get whole."

"I know," Pru said, resigned. "I've been there."

"I love you -- " Anne spurted.

"I know," Pru answered, echoing that feeling. "Now go. I'll be leaving the light on for you -- and a key under the mat."

"Thanks," Anne lumped, holding back tears. "See you soon."

She turned and left quickly -- quickly, lest she linger too long.

12.

ANNE decided to walk the short distance across town and up to Beth's. It was not far and she needed to walk, needed to think, needed to clear her head. The past two weeks had thrown her into an emotional marathon and now she felt as though she was finally reaching the finish line. Her whole life was ahead of her, and the decision she would make tonight might determine the path she would take in the months, perhaps years to come.

Did she really want to commit to Pru? Did she want to live nearly a Straight life with someone who could be both male and female for her, both husband and wife? And in that kind of wholesome, semi-normal marriage, to go back to school and become whatever, but to give up the theater, modeling, everything that went with that other kind of life -- and especially the parties, the sexual frenzy, the sleaze that seemed to be an inevitable part of the scene? Or did she really want to follow in Beth's footsteps, be with her, accept her unconditionally?

Did Anne really want to be with Beth? All of Beth's excesses - the same excesses Anne despised in Mark but seemed willing to forgive in Beth - Beth's smoking, her drinking, her sexual vulnerability - were essential parts of what defined Beth's entire stage presence, her star quality. They seemed to be an inseparable part of the scene that Anne would have to embrace and emulate if she wanted to follow in the same career. Did Anne have that same star quality in her or would she end up living only in Beth's image, hovering and protecting her from backstage, as strictly her *Good-time-Charley?*

The physical urge to be a man for Beth was still very strong and still thoroughly unresolved in her. Beth's image continued to dominate all her sexual fantasies. Anne needed to feel the way a man feels making love to a woman - the way Pru had felt making love to Anne - needed to resolve that fantasy once and for all -- a fantasy had only with Beth and not yet fully experienced with Pru.   Before Pru, Beth and only Beth could have called up that kind of feeling in her, but now --   Come what may, Anne had to resolve this now!

Determined, she called Beth again from a phone booth across the street from her apartment house to make sure the coast was clear and heard Beth's concerned voice say, "Yes, come up."

Anne had never been upstairs before. She had stood in front of the building on a number of occasions, marking it as the place where Beth lived, but she had never been upstairs. It was on University Place, just off Washington Square -- a four-story building with no doorman. Anne had barely rung the bell when Beth buzzed back. She took the elevator slowly to the top floor, all the while giddy with the sheer unreality of it all.

"Anne?" Beth stood waiting for her at the door. She was especially radiant tonight, her makeup precise, her platinum hair carefully groomed, almost forming a halo around her face. Anne paused to marvel at her.

"Come in," Beth said hurriedly, stepping back from the door to give Anne room. She was in a dressing gown, seeming ready to change for a very special night out on the town.

Anne entered and looked around. It was an ordinary apartment, obviously barely lived in, but filled with both waxed and real flowers and small mementos -- all of them dainty, like Beth.

"I got your letter -- a little late, I guess," Anne said. She let Beth take her jacket and waited for her to come back from the closet.

"What's this all about, Anne," Beth asked, concerned. "Is it Mark? Are you in trouble?"

"No, nothing like that," Anne said, suddenly feeling quite awkward. "It's just that -- so much has happened since -- but I feel I have to resolve this - this whatever it is - between us."

"My God, Anne," Beth said. "Is that all you came to say?" She was clearly harried and annoyed.   She went to the liquor cabinet for a glass of scotch. "It was very embarrassing to ask Rick to leave."

"Yes, it must have been embarrassing," Anne said. The thought of Rick coming between them, being a part of their relationship, was not something she could stomach. Irrational as she knew it to be, Anne felt the rage inside her grow again. Beth was destroying herself. And the last thing she needed right now was a drink. Anne went to the cabinet and took the scotch from Beth's hand then pulled her close.   "Has Rick touched you tonight?"

"What a strange thing to ask, Anne!" Beth turned away evasively. "We had just gotten in when you called. I sent him right out again. Just what is it you want, Anne?"

Anne forced Beth to look at her. "I need to know where I stand with you. What are we to each other? Do you really want me, or Rick, or what? Because if you intend to spend your life with Rick, I really need to know that now!"

"Whatever's gotten into you, Anne!" Beth pulled away from her. "Can't all this wait a few days?"

"No," Anne said. "It can't wait. I need to know now! Just where do I fit in -- what is it you really feel for me?"

"I love you, of course, Anne -- in my own way," Beth allowed, avoiding her eyes. "But nothing's that simple. You know me, Anne -- I'm not someone anyone can tie down for any length of time. My art, my career always has to come first. And yes, I do have feelings for Rick, but you know me! Right now, he's convenient."

"And what about us," Anne said. "Am I also just convenient?"

"No, of course not!" Beth returned, now in earnest. "You've always been very special to me, Anne. I would never have been intimate with you if that hadn't been so."

"But you want Rick as well as me?" Anne persisted.

"Rick is impotent!" Beth snapped impatiently. Then she softened, and Anne saw her vulnerability, saw how sexually strung up Beth really was and trying to hide it, trying not to show it. But Anne saw it. It was Beth who wanted Anne now, Beth who was made nervous at Anne's touch. "I want us to be together, Anne -- often -- " she said, trembling, "But not yet -- right now, things are still too awkward. Not tonight!"

Beth's words grated Anne. She was juggling again, always compromising. And her career did take precedent. If Anne wanted Beth she would have to resign herself to that. This then was the final test of truth -- did Anne want a life with Beth on Beth's terms, or on her own terms, with Pru?

"That answer's not good enough," Anne said, grabbing Beth's shoulders, drawing her near. "I want a lot more from you than that. I want to be able to make love to you the way a man makes love to you -- I want you to want me more than any man -- and I don't want to wait in the wings for you and pretend we're only friends."

299

"Please, Anne -- " Beth tried to break away.

Anne held her fast. But gripping Beth did not feel the same as it had felt before -- despite her own words Anne was now only dully drawn to her, now acting only with cool and calculated passion. Desire and intensity had given way to an unreal feeling, making Anne aware of her own body in a whole new way, as strong and tall and very hard.

And Beth felt it too -- felt the man-woman grabbing her and stopped resisting, gave in, melted and clung to Anne, let herself be completely taken. Her body, ripe and needing in its womanhood, met Anne's, willing and impatient.

"You're very different tonight," she marveled, breathlessly. "How can I possibly turn you down this way -- please don't stop!"

"I won't," Anne said.

Anne lifted Beth up gently, surprised at her own strength. She carried her to the sofa then sat on the edge, watching her, waiting. But strangely now -- coldly, deliberately, half of her apart from the scene, as someone merely observing. For some reason, in that brief, full-bodied embrace, the man-woman feeling had vanished -- the hard-on, the fantasy no longer there -- all the lust for Beth -- simply gone! There was only Prudence in her place, the thought of Prudence, the longing for Prudence.

"Please don't stop," Beth repeated, drawing Anne up beside her, embracing her, kissing her -- Beth's puckered breasts, Beth's impatient legs, Beth's whole body heaving and open to receive her. But Anne had nothing there to give. Nothing real --

Nevertheless, Anne brought her hand to quiet Beth, but dutifully, distantly, still without passion. It wasn't as it had been before -- touching Beth did not seem wonderful anymore. And it wasn't as it had been with Pru. She had forgotten herself with Pru, and here she was apart from herself, almost contemptuous of Beth's lust. Yes, it was like the contempt some men must feel, invading a woman. Anne was invading Beth, filling Beth, sensuously, competently, though in masculine anger.

But shame soon overtook the anger. Anne tried to think of how it had been with Pru -- how magically complete it had been with Pru. She succeeded for a moment but then Beth's voice brought her back.

Beth had forgotten Anne -- her body lost in agonizing want. But not for Anne. Anne was only there by accident, by convenience. Beth was receiving a man inside her, was receiving Anne as a man inside her. And

Anne was again split in two -- half of her angry at being made nothing but a surrogate -- and the other half, with an erection she was now loathe to lose. Beth needed her there and Anne still loved and desired Beth -- though not in the way Beth would have wanted to be loved -- still, Anne couldn't leave Beth hanging. She had to complete what she had started.

Pru, where are you, Anne screamed inside her head. Only Beth's ecstatic grip around her -- and her tortured voice answered -- pleaded -- "More butch -- "

Beth's radio had stopped playing music and now filled the air with crackling static, making the soft-lit room seem to flicker in the light of a fireplace. Anne turned her head around and saw there really was a fireplace, although a gas-powered one. She got up wearily and went to the radio to turn it off. The immediate silence cleared her mind.

She went back and stood over Beth still lying on the sofa. Beth had turned her head and closed her eyes, not really sleeping but nearly so.

Anne wanted to leave Beth now, perhaps in the same way that Esther had left her three days ago. Anne wanted to leave without a word. But she did not. She owed Beth something.

She knelt down again and kissed Beth's hand. "I'm going now, " she said, and waited for Beth to speak.

Beth turned her head slowly and looked at Anne. Magnificence had returned to her face, the tension gone and the worry. Her shining hair was slightly mussed but still clinging around her head in goddess lines. How could Anne not admire her!

"Don't go," Beth said. "We still have time."

"I have to go," Anne said.

She felt nothing saying that. It was easy to leave Beth now. She hadn't changed at all. She was still expecting Rick to return, perhaps at any moment. Beth wanted Rick now as well as Anne. Anne could not be angry but something in her had died. She stood.

"Please don't go," Beth repeated. "Not yet."

"I can't stay," Anne agonized. She turned and paced the floor. It was difficult still to deny Beth. "And I don't think I can ever come back," she blurted.

Beth looked at her, puzzled. "Why?" she asked in a soft voice. "Did I

301

do something wrong?"

"No," Anne said. She knew that Beth had done nothing that was wrong, not for Beth.

"Yes, I must have," Beth now reflected. "I just let you see the whore in me, and that was wrong. You're still too new, too green to have been shown that."

"No, I'm not -- not anymore, Beth, not anymore," Anne returned. "And it wasn't you. You did absolutely nothing wrong! It's just that I can't be a man for you in the way that you need me to be, and I have no intention of ever sharing our bed with Rick."

Anne bit her lip. It was a hard thing to say to Beth, because there were other feelings still there -- true love, friendship -- always! She softened the blow: "We want very different things. You said it yourself -- you're not a lesbian, Beth."

Beth did a double-take on that, now embarrassed, stripped naked. But she quickly recovered, stood, nervously tying the straps to her dressing gown. "That's a whole lot of crap, Anne," she said. "You're not a lesbian either. There's no real difference between us. In time, you'll see that."

"I already see it," Anne said. "I've learned a lot about myself this past week. I've learned there's no hard and fast line between male and female, Gay and Straight. I've learned that I can be anything I want to be."

"Then you must know you haven't even begun to experience everything that our bodies and minds are capable of." Now Beth went to Anne, reached out to embrace her, kiss her, her whole body trembling, still needing to hold and be held. "I'm simply more attuned, at a very different hormonal stage than you," Beth whispered to her. "What you did to me tonight -- was complete for me. As complete as anything I could ever hope to expect from any man!"

Anne avoided Beth's searching lips but still hugged her close, in a fond embrace. "I know, but that doesn't change anything," she said almost coldly, thinking first of how it had been with Esther, then of how it had been with Pru. "For me, being with a woman is more than enough. But for you, it wouldn't be."

Again she kissed Beth, tenderly, but not with passion. "We really are two very different people, and at very different stages in our lives," she told her.

"All the more reason for you to stay," Beth urged, still clinging to her but feebly now, no longer believing in her own words. "There's so much that each of us can do for the other -- "

"If I were a man, yes - " Anne admitted. "But as a woman -- can't you see how impossible that would be? One look, one mistake, one hint of gossip and the tabloids would have at both of us with a vengeance! I can't be with you, Beth. Even if I could change, or you could change -- even if either of us could make the other into everything we wanted -- "

Anne stopped. She found it easier to be close again to Beth now, to embrace and shower her with kisses. But not as a lover -- as a friend or as the daughter her mother could never approach.

"Your talent, your career really must come first," she now reminded her, giving Beth strength. "Everything and everyone else has to take a back seat. I see it. I accept it. And I can't live that kind of life with you, always hiding, pretending. That's why I can't stay!"

"I suppose," Beth reflected, pulling herself together, sobering at her words. "As I said, my life is much to complicated. Eventually, there would be a bloody mess. But I'm running out of time, Anne, you must know that -- " she added, her eyes showing the strain. "If I don't make it this year, I never will!"

"You'll make it -- I know you will!" Anne promised her. "You have everything it takes to make it. Don't let me, or Rick, or anyone stand in your way!"

"Now who's giving the pep talk," Beth returned. She found Anne's lips again, pressed her warm body to her. "What an exceptional student you've turned out to be," she said. "Are you sure you want to leave me so soon?"

"I do love you, Beth," Anne said. "And I'll always be grateful to you, for everything!"

"Then why leave now," Beth insisted. "Can't you wait in the wings for me? For just a little while?"

"I can't!" Anne ached, torn but still resigned. "I have to!" She kissed Beth goodbye again, tenderly. "Don't ever stop loving me, Beth," she said, tears now welling in her eyes. "Don't ever stop loving me -- because although I have to leave, I never want to stop loving you!"

"Where are you going," Beth asked, not letting go of her hand. Her eyes too were moist.

"There's someone else!" Anne now managed to say, gently undoing her grasp. "Please forgive me!" Her words were not meant to hurt, but they splashed like ice-water on Beth's face.   The cut was final. Startled, Beth suddenly let go. But she quickly recovered, accepted the inevitable. "Of course," she said. "How blind of me not to have seen it! How stupid of me to have hoped -- "

Anne turned away from Beth and looked for her jacket, now anxious to leave, to find Pru.

Beth went to the closet and got it for her, held it out to her shakily, then went to the liquor cabinet for her scotch. Like the trooper she was, she had already made light of it, had pulled herself together for a good-luck toast to the happy couple.

"I'll send you two tickets for opening night," she said, tipping her glass. "Bring her with you, whoever she is -- and be sure to come backstage after the show. We'll all have a ball!"

Anne let Beth's be the last line and turned toward the door.   Dashing out, she brushed past Rick in the hallway without a word, silent tears now streaming down her cheeks. But she felt no anger or jealousy brushing past him now. They were walking in different worlds.

It had rained and now the street was shiny and full of the hissing of cars on wet pavement -- a clean sound, like the Spring air.

Anne walked, hearing the squish of her sneakers, and felt not alone on the empty street. Paradise was in one direction, and Pru's in the opposite, across the Square.

Pru had said she would leave the light on. But Anne didn't feel quite ready yet to slink back, her tail between her legs, admitting to Pru that she had been right all along. One drink at Paradise, she decided. One drink and just someone to talk to. Someone, anyone to take the edge off what had just happened tonight. She needed to come down, to clear her head of Beth, to think of Pru. She felt much like a caterpillar whose pod had just cracked open, but whose wings had not yet fully unfolded. She wanted to return to Pru -- ready for flight, for a passionate mating under a full moon -- but not yet.

Paradise on a Wednesday night was temptingly crowded. Anne had not expected it to be that full.   Too many women and now, none of them appealing! She almost changed her mind, almost decided not to go in. But she wasn't ready to return to Pru's -- she did need to take the edge off.

Just one drink, she decided.

She entered and easily got past Manny who immediately recognized her and let her through.

There were women everywhere, a college and office crowd, but it was hard to see who they were because of the low lights and the smoke. How sickening the smoke was, and how uninteresting all the young butches standing there, drinks in hand, all of them with their faces turned toward the door, nervously eyeing every new entry, all of them anxious to score.

Anne brushed passed them, remotely spotting Esther dancing in back, and Skippy or someone just like her, passed out at the bar.

It was both wild and dull in Paradise. Then Anne glimpsed a tall woman sitting by herself, dressed in Surplus fatigues -- way at the back of the bar, behind a pillar, a cup of coffee in front of her. Despite the dim light and the smoke Anne knew it was Pru. Her heart quickened, and she pushed through the crowd, bravely mounting the empty stool beside her.

"Prudence," Anne said, both apprehensive yet surprised and relieved to see her sitting alone -- not even drunk, just sitting. "How did you know where to find me?"

Pru looked up sleepily and smiled a confident smile. "Been there too, Slugger," she said.

Now Anne felt foolish. What should she do, apologize or simply stand her ground? But the bartender came, anxious to take her order. Anne started to say a double scotch then stopped herself. "Orange juice," she said to her, "and make it a tall one."

"That must have been some workout you just had, Slugger," Prudence quipped, sadly amused.

"Hardly at all," Anne returned, still shaking the tension out of her. "Actually, I came in here for a stiff drink, then I remembered how much I hate the smell of alcohol on anyone's breath."

"One more thing we have in common," Pru noted.

"Do you suppose we might just start over?" now Anne ventured sheepishly.

Prudence yawned and stretched tall, sliding off her stool.

"No, I don't think so, Slugger, not tonight," she sighed. "I'm too tired and this place is getting on my nerves."

"Mine too," Anne said.

Now her orange juice arrived and Anne gulped it down like an athlete ready for more.

"What next, then," Anne braved, also standing, pressing close against Pru, slightly afraid of the answer.

"Don't know, Slugger, don't know," Johnson said, butting heads with Anne fondly. "Don't know where either of us is going from here."

So that was it? No going back to what had been before?

No, Anne could not, *would not* let it end there.

"I really do love you, Prudence!" she blurted, now squarely meeting her eyes.

Those were the right words.

They brought back the magic, the real bond between them.

"W-well then - I guess it's settled," Pru stammered, stoic but clearly relieved. "Then - how about the two of us - simply - take each other home?"

Artemis Smith 1954

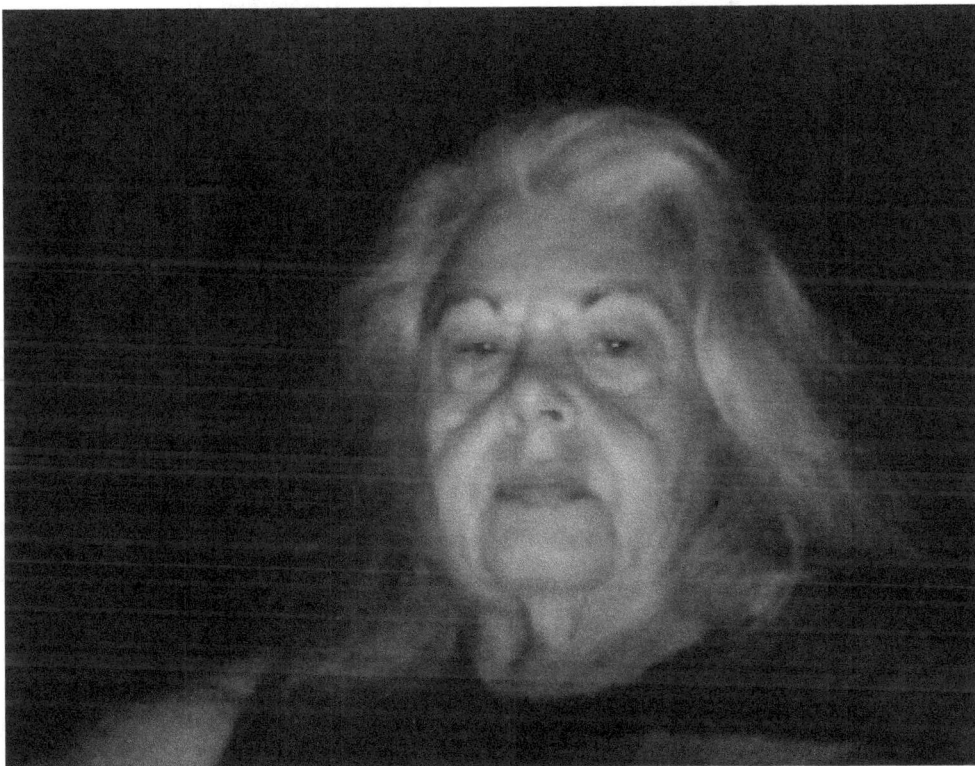

ArtemisSmith **2010**

Coming to E-Books and Bookstores in 2011:

ArtemisSmith's
GrandmaMoseX
the Final Testament before the Apocalipse

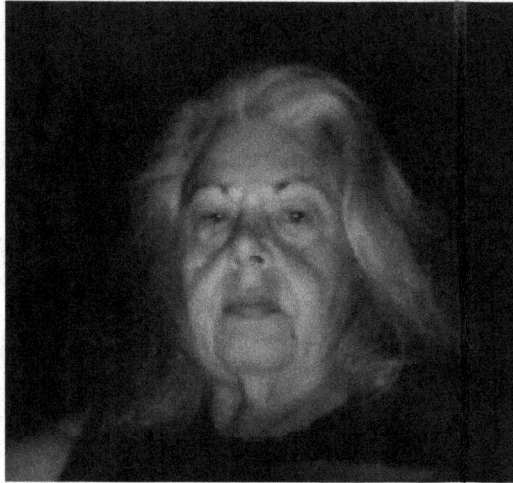

"No, Maggots, I am not frowning. I just need a facelift."

the
avant garde workshop
sag harbor . new york . usa ™

308

ArtemisSmith's

THE SKEETS TRILOGY

the e-book edition

ISBN 9781878998224

the
savant garde workshop

SAG HARBOR, NEW YORK, USA

"Memoirs, previously undisclosed insider facts, cameos comprising an eye-witness account of the formative years of the 1950-60's civil rights coalition movements by the author of the pulp fiction best sellers ***Odd Girl, The Third Sex,*** and ***This Bed We Made.*** An indispensable addition to every **Women's Studies, GLBT** and **20th Century Cultural Archive**. The trend-setting activist novel in the Appendix has been cited since 1959 by nearly all the name reviewers of the genre and is a recognized classic in demand by modern researchers." **Alana L. Collos**

ATTENTION LIBRARIANS
A Monograph of THE SAVANT GARDE INSTITUTE

Pre-Order ISBN: 978-1-878998-00-2 **LCCN:** 2010916162 **directly from** morpurgo@msn.com

Acquire a *VALUABLE* numbered and author-thumbprinted limited edition of this volume for your reference and rare manuscript collections *PLUS* a lucrative 2000 librarian copying Permissions Package for either institutional photocopying or academic E-Book resale: $1,999.99*

Discounted academic/library package includes:

1. One thumbprinted numbered 8.5x11 310 pp. photocopied color edition for your rare manuscripts collection, either unbound or bound as shown, or case-bound at no extra charge. Specify preference upon ordering.

2. PDF File Download with 2000 Permissions to reproduce for academic or library resale.

* Discounted price for copies numbered 101 to 1000.

www.ingramcontent.com/pod-product-compliance
Lightning Source LLC
Chambersburg PA
CBHW081145270326
41930CB00014B/3042